CHRISTIAN SCIENCE

THE OXFORD MARK TWAIN
Shelley Fisher Fishkin, Editor

The Prince and the Pauper
Introduction: Judith Martin
Afterword: Everett Emerson

Life on the Mississippi
Introduction: Willie Morris
Afterword: Lawrence Howe

Adventures of Huckleberry Finn
Introduction: Toni Morrison
Afterword: Victor A. Doyno

A Connecticut Yankee in King Arthur's Court
Introduction: Kurt Vonnegut, Jr.
Afterword: Louis J. Budd

Merry Tales
Introduction: Anne Bernays
Afterword: Forrest G. Robinson

The American Claimant
Introduction: Bobbie Ann Mason
Afterword: Peter Messent

The £1,000,000 Bank-Note and Other New Stories
Introduction: Malcolm Bradbury
Afterword: James D. Wilson

Tom Sawyer Abroad
Introduction: Nat Hentoff
Afterword: M. Thomas Inge

The Tragedy of Pudd'nhead Wilson and the Comedy
Those Extraordinary Twins
Introduction: Sherley Anne Williams
Afterword: David Lionel Smith

Christian Science

Mark Twain

FOREWORD

SHELLEY FISHER FISHKIN

INTRODUCTION

GARRY WILLS

AFTERWORD

HAMLIN HILL

New York   Oxford

OXFORD UNIVERSITY PRESS

1996

OXFORD UNIVERSITY PRESS

Oxford   New York

Athens, Auckland, Bangkok, Bogotá, Bombay

Buenos Aires, Calcutta, Cape Town, Dar es Salaam

Delhi, Florence, Hong Kong, Istanbul, Karachi

Kuala Lumpur, Madras, Madrid, Melbourne

Mexico City, Nairobi, Paris, Singapore

Taipei, Tokyo, Toronto

and associated companies in

Berlin, Ibadan

Published by

Oxford University Press, Inc.

198 Madison Avenue, New York,

New York 10016

Library of Congress

Cataloging-in-Publication Data

Twain, Mark, 1835–1910.

Christian Science / Mark Twain; with an

introduction by Garry Wills and an afterword by

Hamlin Hill.

p. cm. — (The Oxford Mark Twain)

A facsimile reprint of the 1st ed. of Twain's work

including the original illustrations.

Includes bibliographical references.

1. Christian Science—Controversial literature.

I. Title. II. Series.

BX6995.T84 1996

289.5—dc20

96—14731

CIP

ISBN 0-19-510155-3 (trade ed.)

ISBN 0-19-511424-8 (lib. ed.)

ISBN 0-19-511345-4 (lib. ed. set)

ISBN 0-19-509088-8 (trade ed. set)

9 8 7 6 5 4 3 2 1

Printed in the United States of America

on acid-free paper

FRONTISPIECE

Samuel L. Clemens is seen here in his New York

City apartment (21 Fifth Avenue) in 1907, the year

he published *Christian Science*. (The Mark Twain

House, Hartford, Connecticut)

CONTENTS

EDITOR'S NOTE

The Oxford Mark Twain consists of twenty-nine volumes of facsimiles of the first American editions of Mark Twain's works, with an editor's foreword, new introductions, afterwords, notes on the texts, and essays on the illustrations in volumes with artwork. The facsimiles have been reproduced from the originals unaltered, except that blank pages in the front and back of the books have been omitted, and any seriously damaged or missing pages have been replaced by pages from other first editions (as indicated in the notes on the texts).

In the foreword, introduction, afterword, and essays on the illustrations, the titles of Mark Twain's works have been capitalized according to modern conventions, as have the names of characters (except where otherwise indicated). In the case of discrepancies between the title of a short story, essay, or sketch as it appears in the original table of contents and as it appears on its own title page, the title page has been followed. The parenthetical numbers in the introduction, afterwords, and illustration essays are page references to the facsimiles.

FOREWORD

Shelley Fisher Fishkin

Samuel Clemens entered the world and left it with Halley's Comet, little dreaming that generations hence Halley's Comet would be less famous than Mark Twain. He has been called the American Cervantes, our Homer, our Tolstoy, our Shakespeare, our Rabelais. Ernest Hemingway maintained that "all modern American literature comes from one book by Mark Twain called *Huckleberry Finn*." President Franklin Delano Roosevelt got the phrase "New Deal" from *A Connecticut Yankee in King Arthur's Court*. *The Gilded Age* gave an entire era its name. "The future historian of America," wrote George Bernard Shaw to Samuel Clemens, "will find your works as indispensable to him as a French historian finds the political tracts of Voltaire."[1]

There is a Mark Twain Bank in St. Louis, a Mark Twain Diner in Jackson Heights, New York, a Mark Twain Smoke Shop in Lakeland, Florida. There are Mark Twain Elementary Schools in Albuquerque, Dayton, Seattle, and Sioux Falls. Mark Twain's image peers at us from advertisements for Bass Ale (his drink of choice was Scotch), for a gas company in Tennessee, a hotel in the nation's capital, a cemetery in California.

Ubiquitous though his name and image may be, Mark Twain is in no danger of becoming a petrified icon. On the contrary: Mark Twain lives. *Huckleberry Finn* is "the most taught novel, most taught long work, and most taught piece of American literature" in American schools from junior high to the graduate level.[2] Hundreds of Twain impersonators appear in theaters, trade shows, and shopping centers in every region of the country.[3] Scholars publish hundreds of articles as well as books about Twain every year, and he is the subject of daily exchanges on the Internet. A journalist somewhere in the world finds a reason to quote Twain just about every day. Television series such as *Bonanza, Star Trek: The Next Generation*, and *Cheers* broadcast episodes that feature Mark Twain as a character. Hollywood screenwriters regularly produce movies inspired by his works, and writers of mysteries and science fiction continue to weave him into their plots.[4]

A century after the American Revolution sent shock waves throughout Europe, it took Mark Twain to explain to Europeans and to his countrymen alike what that revolution had wrought. He probed the significance of this new land and its new citizens, and identified what it was in the Old World that America abolished and rejected. The founding fathers had thought through the political dimensions of making a new society; Mark Twain took on the challenge of interpreting the social and cultural life of the United States for those outside its borders as well as for those who were living the changes he discerned.

Americans may have constructed a new society in the eighteenth century, but they articulated what they had done in voices that were largely inter- changeable with those of Englishmen until well into the nineteenth century. Mark Twain became the voice of the new land, the leading translator of what and who the "American" was — and, to a large extent, is. Frances Trollope's *Domestic Manners of the Americans,* a best-seller in England, Hector St. John de Crèvecoeur's *Letters from an American Farmer,* and Tocqueville's *Democ- racy in America* all tried to explain America to Europeans. But Twain did more than that: he allowed European readers to *experience* this strange "new world." And he gave his countrymen the tools to do two things they had not quite had the confidence to do before. He helped them stand before the cul- tural icons of the Old World unembarrassed, unashamed of America's lack of palaces and shrines, proud of its brash practicality and bold inventiveness, unafraid to reject European models of "civilization" as tainted or corrupt. And he also helped them recognize their own insularity, boorishness, arrogance, or ignorance, and laugh at it — the first step toward transcending it and becom- ing more "civilized," in the best European sense of the word.

Twain often strikes us as more a creature of our time than of his. He appreciated the importance and the complexity of mass tourism and public relations, fields that would come into their own in the twentieth century but were only fledgling enterprises in the nineteenth. He explored the liberating potential of humor and the dynamics of friendship, parenting, and marriage. He narrowed the gap between "popular" and "high" culture, and he meditated on the enigmas of personal and national identity. Indeed, it would be difficult to find an issue on the horizon today that Twain did not touch on somewhere in his work. Heredity versus environment? Animal rights? The boundaries of gender? The place of black voices in the cultural heritage of the United States? Twain was there.

With startling prescience and characteristic grace and wit, he zeroed in on many of the key challenges — political, social, and technological — that would face his country and the world for the next hundred years: the challenge of race relations in a society founded on both chattel slavery and ideals of equality, and the intractable problem of racism in American life; the potential of new technologies to transform our lives in ways that can be both exhilarating and terrifying — as well as unpredictable; the problem of imperialism and the difficulties entailed in getting rid of it. But he never lost sight of the most basic challenge of all: each man or woman's struggle for integrity in the face of the seductions of power, status, and material things.

Mark Twain's unerring sense of the right word and not its second cousin taught people to pay attention when he spoke, in person or in print. He said things that were smart and things that were wise, and he said them incomparably well. He defined the rhythms of our prose and the contours of our moral map. He saw our best and our worst, our extravagant promise and our stunning failures, our comic foibles and our tragic flaws. Throughout the world he is viewed as the most distinctively American of American authors — and as one of the most universal. He is assigned in classrooms in Naples, Riyadh, Belfast, and Beijing, and has been a major influence on twentieth-century writers from Argentina to Nigeria to Japan. The Oxford Mark Twain celebrates the versatility and vitality of this remarkable writer.

The Oxford Mark Twain reproduces the first American editions of Mark Twain's books published during his lifetime.[5] By encountering Twain's works in their original format — typography, layout, order of contents, and illustrations — readers today can come a few steps closer to the literary artifacts that entranced and excited readers when the books first appeared. Twain approved of and to a greater or lesser degree supervised the publication of all of this material.[6] The Mark Twain House in Hartford, Connecticut, generously loaned us its originals.[7] When more than one copy of a first American edition was available, Robert H. Hirst, general editor of the Mark Twain Project, in cooperation with Marianne Curling, curator of the Mark Twain House (and Jeffrey Kaimowitz, head of Rare Books for the Watkinson Library of Trinity College, Hartford, where the Mark Twain House collection is kept), guided our decision about which one to use.[8] As a set, the volumes also contain more than eighty essays commissioned especially for The Oxford Mark Twain, in which distinguished contributors reassess Twain's achievement as a writer and his place in the cultural conversation that he did so much to shape.

Each volume of The Oxford Mark Twain is introduced by a leading American, Canadian, or British writer who responds to Twain — often in a very personal way — as a fellow writer. Novelists, journalists, humorists, columnists, fabulists, poets, playwrights — these writers tell us what Twain taught them and what in his work continues to speak to them. Reading Twain's books, both famous and obscure, they reflect on the genesis of his art and the characteristics of his style, the themes he illuminated, and the aesthetic strategies he pioneered. Individually and collectively their contributions testify to the place Mark Twain holds in the hearts of readers of all kinds and temperaments.

Scholars whose work has shaped our view of Twain in the academy today have written afterwords to each volume, with suggestions for further reading. Their essays give us a sense of what was going on in Twain's life when he wrote the book at hand, and of how that book fits into his career. They explore how each book reflects and refracts contemporary events, and they show Twain responding to literary and social currents of the day, variously accepting, amplifying, modifying, and challenging prevailing paradigms. Sometimes they argue that works previously dismissed as quirky or eccentric departures actually address themes at the heart of Twain's work from the start. And as they bring new perspectives to Twain's composition strategies in familiar texts, several scholars see experiments in form where others saw only form-lessness, method where prior critics saw only madness. In addition to eluci-dating the work's historical and cultural context, the afterwords provide an overview of responses to each book from its first appearance to the present.

Most of Mark Twain's books involved more than Mark Twain's words: unique illustrations. The parodic visual send-ups of "high culture" that Twain himself drew for *A Tramp Abroad*, the sketch of financial manipulator Jay Gould as a greedy and sadistic "Slave Driver" in *A Connecticut Yankee in King Arthur's Court*, and the memorable drawings of Eve in *Eve's Diary* all helped Twain's books to be sold, read, discussed, and preserved. In their es-says for each volume that contains artwork, Beverly R. David and Ray Sapirstein highlight the significance of the sketches, engravings, and pho-tographs in the first American editions of Mark Twain's works, and tell us what is known about the public response to them.

The Oxford Mark Twain invites us to read some relatively neglected works by Twain in the company of some of the most engaging literary figures of our time. Roy Blount Jr., for example, riffs in a deliciously Twain-like manner on "An Item Which the Editor Himself Could Not Understand," which may well rank as one of the least-known pieces Twain ever published. Bobbie Ann Mason celebrates the "mad energy" of Twain's most obscure comic novel, *The American Claimant*, in which the humor "hurtles beyond tall tale into simon-pure absurdity."[9] Garry Wills finds that *Christian Science* "gets us very close to the heart of American culture." Lee Smith reads "Political Economy" as a sharp and funny essay on language. Walter Mosley sees "The Stolen White Elephant," a story "reduced to a series of ridiculous telegrams related by an untrustworthy narrator caught up in an adventure that is as impossible as it is ludicrous," as a stunningly compact and economical satire of a world we still recognize as our own. Anne Bernays returns to "The Private History of a Campaign That Failed" and finds "an antiwar manifesto that is also confession, dramatic monologue, a plea for understanding and absolution, and a romp that gradually turns into atrocity even as we watch." After revisiting Captain Stormfield's heaven, Frederik Pohl finds that there "is no imaginable place more pleasant to spend eternity." Indeed, Pohl writes, "one would almost be willing to die to enter it."

While less familiar works receive fresh attention in The Oxford Mark Twain, new light is cast on the best-known works as well. Judith Martin ("Miss Manners") points out that it is by reading a court etiquette book that Twain's pauper learns how to behave as a proper prince. As important as etiquette may be in the palace, Martin notes, it is even more important in the slums.

> That etiquette is a sorer point with the ruffians in the street than with the proud dignitaries of the prince's court may surprise some readers. As in our own streets, etiquette is always a more volatile subject among those who cannot count on being treated with respect than among those who have the power to command deference.

And taking a fresh look at *Adventures of Huckleberry Finn,* Toni Morrison writes,

> much of the novel's genius lies in its quiescence, the silences that pervade it and give it a porous quality that is by turns brooding and soothing. It lies in . . . the subdued images in which the repetition of a simple word, such as "lonesome," tolls like an evening bell; the moments when nothing is said, when scenes and incidents swell the heart unbearably precisely because unarticulated, and force an act of imagination almost against the will.

Engaging Mark Twain as one writer to another, several contributors to The Oxford Mark Twain offer new insights into the processes by which his books came to be. Russell Banks, for example, reads *A Tramp Abroad* as "an important revision of Twain's incomplete first draft of *Huckleberry Finn,* a second draft, if you will, which in turn made possible the third and final draft." Erica Jong suggests that *1601,* a freewheeling parody of Elizabethan manners and mores, written during the same summer Twain began *Huckleberry Finn*, served as "a warm-up for his creative process" and "primed the pump for other sorts of freedom of expression." And Justin Kaplan suggests that "one of the transcendent figures standing behind and shaping" *Joan of Arc* was Ulysses S. Grant, whose memoirs Twain had recently published, and who, like Joan, had risen unpredictably "from humble and obscure origins" to become a "military genius" endowed with "the gift of command, a natural eloquence, and an equally natural reserve."

As a number of contributors note, Twain was a man ahead of his times. *The Gilded Age* was the first "Washington novel," Ward Just tells us, because "Twain was the first to see the possibilities that had eluded so many others." Commenting on *The Tragedy of Pudd'nhead Wilson*, Sherley Anne Williams observes that "Twain's argument about the power of environment in shaping character runs directly counter to prevailing sentiment where the negro was concerned." Twain's fictional technology, wildly fanciful by the standards of his day, predicts developments we take for granted in ours. DNA cloning, fax machines, and photocopiers are all prefigured, Bobbie Ann Mason tells us, in *The American Claimant*. Cynthia Ozick points out that the "telelectrophonoscope" we meet in "From the 'London Times' of 1904" is suspiciously like what we know as "television." And Malcolm Bradbury suggests that in the "phrenophones" of "Mental Telegraphy" "the Internet was born."

Twain turns out to have been remarkably prescient about political affairs as well. Kurt Vonnegut sees in *A Connecticut Yankee* a chilling foreshadowing (or perhaps a projection from the Civil War) of "all the high-tech atrocities which followed, and which follow still." Cynthia Ozick suggests that "The Man That Corrupted Hadleyburg," along with some of the other pieces collected under that title — many of them written when Twain lived in a Vienna ruled by Karl Lueger, a demagogue Adolf Hitler would later idolize — shoot up moral flares that shed an eerie light on the insidious corruption, prejudice, and hatred that reached bitter fruition under the Third Reich. And Twain's portrait in this book of "the dissolving Austria-Hungary of the 1890s," in Ozick's view, presages not only the Sarajevo that would erupt in 1914 but also "the disintegrated components of the former Yugoslavia" and "the *fin-de-siècle* Sarajevo of our own moment."

Despite their admiration for Twain's ambitious reach and scope, contributors to The Oxford Mark Twain also recognize his limitations. Mordecai Richler, for example, thinks that "the early pages of *Innocents Abroad* suffer from being a tad broad, proffering more burlesque than inspired satire," perhaps because Twain was "trying too hard for knee-slappers." Charles Johnson notes that the Young Man in Twain's philosophical dialogue about free will and determinism (*What Is Man?*) "caves in far too soon," failing to challenge what through late-twentieth-century eyes looks like "pseudoscience" and suspect essentialism in the Old Man's arguments.

Some contributors revisit their first encounters with Twain's works, recalling what surprised or intrigued them. When David Bradley came across "Fenimore Cooper's Literary Offences" in his college library, he "did not at first realize that Twain was being his usual ironic self with all this business about the 'nineteen rules governing literary art in the domain of romantic fiction,' but by the time I figured out there was no such list outside Twain's own head, I had decided that the rules made *sense.* . . . It seemed to me they were a pretty good blueprint for writing — Negro writing included." Sherley Anne Williams remembers that part of what attracted her to *Pudd'nhead Wilson* when she first read it thirty years ago was "that Twain, writing at the end of the nineteenth century, could imagine negroes as characters, albeit white ones, who actually thought for and of themselves, whose actions were the product of their thinking rather than the spontaneous ephemera of physical instincts that stereotype assigned to blacks." Frederik Pohl recalls his first reading of *Huckleberry Finn* as "a watershed event" in his life, the first book he read as a child in which "bad people" ceased to exercise a monopoly on doing "bad things." In *Huckleberry Finn* "some seriously bad things — things like the possession and mistreatment of black slaves, like stealing and lying, even like killing other people in duels — were quite often done by people who not only thought of themselves as exemplarily moral but, by any other standards I knew how to apply, actually *were* admirable citizens." The world that

Tom and Huck lived in, Pohl writes, "was filled with complexities and contradictions," and resembled "the world I appeared to be living in myself."

Other contributors explore their more recent encounters with Twain, explaining why they have revised their initial responses to his work. For Toni Morrison, parts of *Huckleberry Finn* that she "once took to be deliberate evasions, stumbles even, or a writer's impatience with his or her material," now strike her "as otherwise: as entrances, crevices, gaps, seductive invitations flashing the possibility of meaning. Unarticulated eddies that encourage diving into the novel's undertow — the real place where writer captures reader." One such "eddy" is the imprisonment of Jim on the Phelps farm. Instead of dismissing this portion of the book as authorial bungling, as she once did, Morrison now reads it as Twain's commentary on the 1880s, a period that "saw the collapse of civil rights for blacks," a time when "the nation, as well as Tom Sawyer, was deferring Jim's freedom in agonizing play." Morrison believes that Americans in the 1880s were attempting "to bury the combustible issues Twain raised in his novel," and that those who try to kick Huck Finn out of school in the 1990s are doing the same: "The cyclical attempts to remove the novel from classrooms extend Jim's captivity on into each generation of readers."

Although imitation-Hemingway and imitation-Faulkner writing contests draw hundreds of entries annually, no one has ever tried to mount a faux-Twain competition. Why? Perhaps because Mark Twain's voice is too much a part of who we are and how we speak even today. Roy Blount Jr. suggests that it is impossible, "at least for an American writer, to parody Mark Twain. It would be like doing an impression of your father or mother: he or she is already there in your voice."

Twain's style is examined and celebrated in The Oxford Mark Twain by fellow writers who themselves have struggled with the nuances of words, the structure of sentences, the subtleties of point of view, and the trickiness of opening lines. Bobbie Ann Mason observes, for example, that "Twain loved the sound of words and he knew how to string them by sound, like different shades of one color: 'The earl's barbaric eye,' 'the Usurping Earl,' 'a double-dyed humbug.'" Twain "relied on the punch of plain words" to show writers how to move beyond the "wordy romantic rubbish" so prevalent in nineteenth-century fiction, Mason says; he "was one of the first writers in America to deflower literary language." Lee Smith believes that "American writers have benefited as much from the way Mark Twain opened up the possibilities of first-person narration as we have from his use of vernacular language." (She feels that "the ghost of Mark Twain was hovering someplace in the background" when she decided to write her novel *Oral History* from the standpoint of multiple first-person narrators.) Frederick Busch maintains that "A Dog's Tale" "boasts one of the great opening sentences" of all time: "My father was a St. Bernard, my mother was a collie, but I am a Presbyterian." And Ursula Le Guin marvels at the ingenuity of the following sentence that she encounters in *Extracts from Adam's Diary*.

> . . . This made her sorry for the creatures which live in there, which she calls fish, for she continues to fasten names on to things that don't need them and don't come when they are called by them, which is a matter of no consequence to her, as she is such a numskull anyway; so she got a lot of them out and brought them in last night and put them in my bed to keep warm, but I have noticed them now and then all day, and I don't see that they are any happier there than they were before, only quieter.[10]

Le Guin responds,

> Now, that is a pure Mark-Twain-tour-de-force sentence, covering an immense amount of territory in an effortless, aimless ramble that seems to be heading nowhere in particular and ends up with breathtaking accuracy at the gold mine. Any sensible child would find that funny, perhaps not following all its divagations but delighted by the swing of it, by the word "numskull," by the idea of putting fish in the bed; and as that child grew older and reread it, its reward would only grow; and if that grown-up child had to write an essay on the piece and therefore earnestly studied and pored over this sentence, she would end up in unmitigated admiration of its vocabulary, syntax, pacing, sense, and rhythm, above all the beautiful

timing of the last two words; and she would, and she does, still find it funny.

The fish surface again in a passage that Gore Vidal calls to our attention, from *Following the Equator*: "'The Whites always mean well when they take human fish out of the ocean and try to make them dry and warm and happy and comfortable in a chicken coop,' which is how, through civilization, they did away with many of the original inhabitants. Lack of empathy is a principal theme in Twain's meditations on race and empire."

Indeed, empathy — and its lack — is a principal theme in virtually all of Twain's work, as contributors frequently note. Nat Hentoff quotes the following thoughts from Huck in *Tom Sawyer Abroad*:

> I see a bird setting on a dead limb of a high tree, singing with its head tilted back and its mouth open, and before I thought I fired, and his song stopped and he fell straight down from the limb, all limp like a rag, and I run and picked him up and he was dead, and his body was warm in my hand, and his head rolled about this way and that, like his neck was broke, and there was a little white skin over his eyes, and one little drop of blood on the side of his head; and laws! I could n't see nothing more for the tears; and I hain't never murdered no creature since that war n't doing me no harm, and I ain't going to.[11]

"The Humane Society," Hentoff writes, "has yet to say anything as powerful — and lasting."

Readers of The Oxford Mark Twain will have the pleasure of revisiting Twain's Mississippi landmarks alongside Willie Morris, whose own lower Mississippi Valley boyhood gives him a special sense of connection to Twain. Morris knows firsthand the mosquitoes described in *Life on the Mississippi* — so colossal that "two of them could whip a dog" and "four of them could hold a man down"; in Morris's own hometown they were so large during the flood season that "local wags said they wore wristwatches." Morris's Yazoo City and Twain's Hannibal shared a "rough-hewn democracy . . . complicated by all the visible textures of caste and class, . . . harmless boyhood fun and mischief right along with . . . rank hypocrisies, churchgoing sanctimonies, racial hatred, entrenched and unrepentant greed."

For the West of Mark Twain's *Roughing It*, readers will have George Plimpton as their guide. "What a group these newspapermen were!" Plimpton writes about Twain and his friends Dan De Quille and Joe Goodman in Virginia City, Nevada. "Their roisterous carryings-on bring to mind the kind of frat-house enthusiasm one associates with college humor magazines like the *Harvard Lampoon*." Malcolm Bradbury examines Twain as "a living example of what made the American so different from the European." And Hal Holbrook, who has interpreted Mark Twain on stage for some forty years, describes how Twain "played" during the civil rights movement, during the Vietnam War, during the Gulf War, and in Prague on the eve of the demise of Communism.

Why do we continue to read Mark Twain? What draws us to him? His wit? His compassion? His humor? His bravura? His humility? His understanding of who and what we are in those parts of our being that we rarely open to view? Our sense that he knows we can do better than we do? Our sense that he knows we can't? E. L. Doctorow tells us that children are attracted to *Tom Sawyer* because in this book "the young reader confirms his own hope that no matter how troubled his relations with his elders may be, beneath all their disapproval is their underlying love for him, constant and steadfast." Readers in general, Arthur Miller writes, value Twain's "insights into America's always uncertain moral life and its shifting but everlasting hypocrisies"; we appreciate the fact that he "is not using his alienation from the public illusions of his hour in order to reject the country implicitly as though he could live without it, but manifestly in order to correct it." Perhaps we keep reading Mark Twain because, in Miller's words, he "wrote much more like a father than a son. He doesn't seem to be sitting in class taunting the teacher but standing at the head of it challenging his students to acknowledge their own humanity, that is, their immemorial attraction to the untrue."

Mark Twain entered the public eye at a time when many of his countrymen considered "American culture" an oxymoron; he died four years before a world conflagration that would lead many to question whether the contradiction in terms was not "European civilization" instead. In between he worked in journalism, printing, steamboating, mining, lecturing, publishing, and editing, in virtually every region of the country. He tried his hand at humorous sketches, social satire, historical novels, children's books, poetry, drama, science fiction, mysteries, romance, philosophy, travelogue, memoir, polemic, and several genres no one had ever seen before or has ever seen since. He invented a self-pasting scrapbook, a history game, a vest strap, and a gizmo for keeping bed sheets tucked in; he invested in machines and processes designed to revolutionize typesetting and engraving, and in a food supplement called "Plasmon." Along the way he cheerfully impersonated himself and prior versions of himself for doting publics on five continents while playing out a charming rags-to-riches story followed by a devastating riches-to-rags story followed by yet another great American comeback. He had a long-running real-life engagement in a sumptuous comedy of manners, and then in a real-life tragedy not of his own design: during the last fourteen years of his life almost everyone he ever loved was taken from him by disease and death.

Mark Twain has indelibly shaped our views of who and what the United States is as a nation and of who and what we might become. He understood the nostalgia for a "simpler" past that increased as that past receded — and he saw through the nostalgia to a past that was just as complex as the present. He recognized better than we did ourselves our potential for greatness and our potential for disaster. His fictions brilliantly illuminated the world in which he lived, changing it — and us — in the process. He knew that our feet often danced to tunes that had somehow remained beyond our hearing; with perfect pitch he played them back to us.

My mother read *Tom Sawyer* to me as a bedtime story when I was eleven. I thought Huck and Tom could be a lot of fun, but I dismissed Becky Thatcher as a bore. When I was twelve I invested a nickel at a local garage sale in a book that contained short pieces by Mark Twain. That was where I met Twain's Eve. Now, *that's* more like it, I decided, pleased to meet a female character I could identify *with* instead of against. Eve had spunk. Even if she got a lot wrong, you had to give her credit for trying. "The Man That Corrupted

Hadleyburg" left me giddy with satisfaction: none of my adolescent reveries of getting even with my enemies were half as neat as the plot of the man who got back at that town. "How I Edited an Agricultural Paper" set me off in uncontrollable giggles.

People sometimes told me that I looked like Huck Finn. "It's the freckles," they'd explain — not explaining anything at all. I didn't read *Huckleberry Finn* until junior year in high school in my English class. It was the fall of 1965. I was living in a small town in Connecticut. I expected a sequel to *Tom Sawyer*. So when the teacher handed out the books and announced our assignment, my jaw dropped: "Write a paper on how Mark Twain used irony to attack racism in *Huckleberry Finn*."

The year before, the bodies of three young men who had gone to Mississippi to help blacks register to vote — James Chaney, Andrew Goodman, and Michael Schwerner — had been found in a shallow grave; a group of white segregationists (the county sheriff among them) had been arrested in connection with the murders. America's inner cities were simmering with pent-up rage that began to explode in the summer of 1965, when riots in Watts left thirty-four people dead. None of this made any sense to me. I was confused, angry, certain that there was something missing from the news stories I read each day: the why. Then I met Pap Finn. And the Phelpses.

Pap Finn, Huck tells us, "had been drunk over in town" and "was just all mud." He erupts into a drunken tirade about "a free nigger . . . from Ohio — a mulatter, most as white as a white man," with "the whitest shirt on you ever see, too, and the shiniest hat; and there ain't a man in town that's got as fine clothes as what he had."

> . . . they said he was a p'fessor in a college, and could talk all kinds of languages, and knowed everything. And that ain't the wust. They said he could *vote*, when he was at home. Well, that let me out. Thinks I, what is the country a-coming to? It was 'lection day, and I was just about to go and vote, myself, if I warn't too drunk to get there; but when they told me there was a State in this country where they'd let that nigger vote, I drawed out. I says I'll never vote agin. Them's the very words I said. . . . And to see the

cool way of that nigger — why, he wouldn't a give me the road if I hadn't shoved him out o' the way.[12]

Later on in the novel, when the runaway slave Jim gives up his freedom to nurse a wounded Tom Sawyer, a white doctor testifies to the stunning altruism of his actions. The Phelpses and their neighbors, all fine, upstanding, well-meaning, churchgoing folk,

> agreed that Jim had acted very well, and was deserving to have some notice took of it, and reward. So every one of them promised, right out and hearty, that they wouldn't curse him no more.
>
> Then they come out and locked him up. I hoped they was going to say he could have one or two of the chains took off, because they was rotten heavy, or could have meat and greens with his bread and water, but they didn't think of it.[13]

Why did the behavior of these people tell me more about why Watts burned than anything I had read in the daily paper? And why did a drunk Pap Finn railing against a black college professor from Ohio whose vote was as good as his own tell me more about white anxiety over black political power than anything I had seen on the evening news?

Mark Twain knew that there was nothing, absolutely *nothing*, a black man could do — including selflessly sacrificing his freedom, the only thing of value he had — that would make white society see beyond the color of his skin. And Mark Twain knew that depicting racists with chilling accuracy would expose the viciousness of their world view like nothing else could. It was an insight echoed some eighty years after Mark Twain penned Pap Finn's rantings about the black professor, when Malcolm X famously asked, "Do you know what white racists call black Ph.D.'s?" and answered, "'*Nigger!*'"[14]

Mark Twain taught me things I needed to know. He taught me to understand the raw racism that lay behind what I saw on the evening news. He taught me that the most well-meaning people can be hurtful and myopic. He taught me to recognize the supreme irony of a country founded in freedom that continued to deny freedom to so many of its citizens. Every time I hear of another effort to kick Huck Finn out of school somewhere, I recall everything that Mark Twain taught *this* high school junior, and I find myself jumping into the fray.[15] I remember the black high school student who called CNN during the phone-in portion of a 1985 debate between Dr. John Wallace, a black educator spearheading efforts to ban the book, and myself. She accused Dr. Wallace of insulting her and all black high school students by suggesting they weren't smart enough to understand Mark Twain's irony. And I recall the black cameraman on the *CBS Morning News* who came up to me after he finished shooting another debate between Dr. Wallace and myself. He said he had never read the book by Mark Twain that we had been arguing about — but now he really wanted to. One thing that puzzled him, though, was why a white woman was defending it and a black man was attacking it, because as far as he could see from what we'd been saying, the book made whites look pretty bad.

As I came to understand *Huckleberry Finn* and *Pudd'nhead Wilson* as commentaries on the era now known as the nadir of American race relations, those books pointed me toward the world recorded in nineteenth-century black newspapers and periodicals and in fiction by Mark Twain's black contemporaries. My investigation of the role black voices and traditions played in shaping Mark Twain's art helped make me aware of their role in shaping all of American culture.[16] My research underlined for me the importance of changing the stories we tell about who we are to reflect the realities of what we've been.[17]

Ever since our encounter in high school English, Mark Twain has shown me the potential of American literature and American history to illuminate each other. Rarely have I found a contradiction or complexity we grapple with as a nation that Mark Twain had not puzzled over as well. He insisted on taking America seriously. And he insisted on *not* taking America seriously: "I think that there is but a single specialty with us, only one thing that can be called by the wide name 'American,'" he once wrote. "That is the national devotion to ice-water."[18]

Mark Twain threw back at us our dreams and our denial of those dreams, our greed, our goodness, our ambition, and our laziness, all rattling around together in that vast echo chamber of our talk — that sharp, spunky American talk that Mark Twain figured out how to write down without robbing it of its energy and immediacy. Talk shaped by voices that the official arbiters of "culture" deemed of no importance — voices of children, voices of slaves, voices of servants, voices of ordinary people. Mark Twain listened. And he made us listen. To the stories he told us, and to the truths they conveyed. He still has a lot to say that we need to hear.

Mark Twain lives — in our libraries, classrooms, homes, theaters, movie houses, streets, and most of all in our speech. His optimism energizes us, his despair sobers us, and his willingness to keep wrestling with the hilarious and horrendous complexities of it all keeps us coming back for more. As the twenty-first century approaches, may he continue to goad us, chasten us, delight us, berate us, and cause us to erupt in unrestrained laughter in unexpected places.

NOTES

1. Ernest Hemingway, *Green Hills of Africa* (New York: Charles Scribner's Sons, 1935), 22. George Bernard Shaw to Samuel L. Clemens, July 3, 1907, quoted in Albert Bigelow Paine, *Mark Twain: A Biography* (New York: Harper and Brothers, 1912), 3:1398.

2. Allen Carey-Webb, "Racism and *Huckleberry Finn*: Censorship, Dialogue and Change," *English Journal* 82, no. 7 (November 1993):22.

3. See Louis J. Budd, "Impersonators," in J. R. LeMaster and James D. Wilson, eds., *The Mark Twain Encyclopedia* (New York: Garland Publishing Company, 1993), 389–91.

4. See Shelley Fisher Fishkin, "Ripples and Reverberations," part 3 of *Lighting Out for the Territory: Reflections on Mark Twain and American Culture* (New York: Oxford University Press, 1996).

5. There are two exceptions. Twain published chapters from his autobiography in the *North American Review* in 1906 and 1907, but this material was not published in book form in Twain's lifetime; our volume reproduces the material as it appeared in the *North American Review*. The other exception is our final volume, *Mark Twain's Speeches*, which appeared two months after Twain's death in 1910.

An unauthorized handful of copies of *1601* was privately printed by an Alexander Gunn of Cleveland at the instigation of Twain's friend John Hay in 1880. The first American edition authorized by Mark Twain, however, was printed at the United States Military Academy at West Point in 1882; that is the edition reproduced here.

XXVIII : SHELLEY FISHER FISHKIN

It should further be noted that four volumes — *The Stolen White Elephant and Other Detective Stories, Following the Equator and Anti-imperialist Essays, The Diaries of Adam and Eve, and 1601, and Is Shakespeare Dead?* — bind together material originally published separately. In each case the first American edition of the material is the version that has been reproduced, always in its entirety. Because Twain constantly recycled and repackaged previously published works in his collections of short pieces, a certain amount of duplication is unavoidable. We have selected volumes with an eye toward keeping this duplication to a minimum.

Even the twenty-nine-volume Oxford Mark Twain has had to leave much out. No edition of Twain can ever claim to be "complete," for the man was too prolix, and the file drawers of both ephemera and as yet unpublished texts are deep.

6. With the possible exception of *Mark Twain's Speeches*. Some scholars suspect Twain knew about this book and may have helped shape it, although no hard evidence to that effect has yet surfaced. Twain's involvement in the production process varied greatly from book to book. For a fuller sense of authorial intention, scholars will continue to rely on the superb definitive editions of Twain's works produced by the Mark Twain Project at the University of California at Berkeley as they become available. Dense with annotation documenting textual emendation and related issues, these editions add immeasurably to our understanding of Mark Twain and the genesis of his works.

7. Except for a few titles that were not in its collection. The American Antiquarian Society in Worcester, Massachusetts, provided the first edition of *King Leopold's Soliloquy*; the Elmer Holmes Bobst Library of New York University furnished the 1906–7 volumes of the *North American Review* in which *Chapters from My Autobiography* first appeared; the Harry Ransom Humanities Research Center at the University of Texas at Austin made their copy of the West Point edition of *1601* available; and the Mark Twain Project provided the first edition of *Extract from Captain Stormfield's Visit to Heaven*.

8. The specific copy photographed for Oxford's facsimile edition is indicated in a note on the text at the end of each volume.

9. All quotations from contemporary writers in this essay are taken from their introductions to the volumes of The Oxford Mark Twain, and the quotations from Mark Twain's works are taken from the texts reproduced in The Oxford Mark Twain.

10. *The Diaries of Adam and Eve*, The Oxford Mark Twain [hereafter OMT] (New York: Oxford University Press, 1996), p. 33.

11. *Tom Sawyer Abroad*, OMT, p. 74.

12. *Adventures of Huckleberry Finn*, OMT, p. 49–50.

13. Ibid., p. 358.

14. Malcolm X, *The Autobiography of Malcolm X*, with the assistance of Alex Haley (New York: Grove Press, 1965), p. 284.

15. I do not mean to minimize the challenge of teaching this difficult novel, a challenge for which all teachers may not feel themselves prepared. Elsewhere I have developed some concrete strategies for approaching the book in the classroom, including teaching it in the context of the history of American race relations and alongside books by black writers. See Shelley Fisher Fishkin, "Teaching *Huckleberry Finn*," in James S. Leonard, ed., *Making Mark Twain Work in the Classroom* (Durham: Duke University Press, forthcoming). See also Shelley Fisher Fishkin, *Was Huck Black? Mark Twain and African-American Voices* (New York: Oxford University Press, 1993), pp. 106–8, and a curriculum kit in preparation at the Mark Twain House in Hartford, containing teaching suggestions from myself, David Bradley, Jocelyn Chadwick-Joshua, James Miller, and David E. E. Sloane.

16. See Fishkin, *Was Huck Black?* See also Fishkin, "Interrogating 'Whiteness,' Complicating 'Blackness': Remapping American Culture," in Henry Wonham, ed., *Criticism and the Color Line: Desegregating American Literary Studies* (New Brunswick: Rutgers UP, 1996, pp. 251–90 and in shortened form in *American Quarterly* 47, no. 3 (September 1995):428–66.

17. I explore the roots of my interest in Mark Twain and race at greater length in an essay entitled "Changing the Story," in Jeffrey Rubin-Dorsky and Shelley Fisher Fishkin, eds., *People of the Book: Thirty Scholars Reflect on Their Jewish Identity* (Madison: U of Wisconsin Press, 1996), pp. 47–63.

18. "What Paul Bourget Thinks of Us," *How to Tell a Story and Other Essays*, OMT, p. 197.

INTRODUCTION Twain and Eddy
Garry Wills

When Andrew Carnegie said that America is a Christian nation, Mark Twain answered, "Why, Carnegie, so is hell ... but we don't brag of this."[1] Twain, as a close student of America, was continually fascinated (to use as neutral a term as will fit his horrified gaze) with American religion. He grew up among Campbellite revivalists — the kind of believers Huck Finn sees as "they sung, and shouted, and flung themselves down on the straw, just crazy and wild."[2]

Like most of those who went west in the middle of the nineteenth century, Twain in Utah had little sympathy with the Mormons. The best he could say of them was that after seeing some Mormon women, he considered anyone who married them in droves a person of self-mortifying charity.[3]

The use of religion in politics, especially as a justification for imperial expansion, brought out Twain's fierce hatred of hypocrisy. The crooked Senator Dilworthy of *The Gilded Age* piously claims that everything he has accomplished he owes to his Sunday school.[4] And Colonel Sellers, by a logic all his own, invokes religion against the education of blacks: education would only give the black man "wider scope to injure himself." Religion, by contrast, will "elevate his soul" in harmless ways: "that's just it; you can't make his soul too immortal, but I wouldn't touch *him*, himself."[5]

It was inevitable that Twain would turn an eye on so typically American a development as the "Christian Science" preached by Mary Baker Eddy (1821–1910). At first he was far from critical of Eddy's claims to effect "mind-cure" by use of the Bible. In fact, he recommended Christian Science for his daughter Susy's pulmonary troubles.[6] The nineteenth-century vogue for psychic manipulation of the body seemed plausible to him, and he experimented with it in his own case, with hypnotism as well as with health foods, osteopathy, and "natural" medicine.[7] Some critics of his *Christian Science* book later condemned his willingness to admit that cures did occur under Mrs. Eddy's regimen. Not surprisingly, a medical journal took offense: "He already says that Christian Science can abolish *four-fifths* of the disease that afflicts mankind! Clearly, Mark Twain is already four-fifths Eddyite."[8] But Twain was aware of the mind's ability to affect the body, to cause "psychosomatic" symptoms — and the converse seemed an inevitable corollary. What the mind can do, it can undo. The deplorable state of nineteenth-century medicine and its practitioners made Twain listen to what would today be called "holistic" curers and the believers in exercise and massage rather than medicines and surgery. If Mrs. Eddy had confined herself to disciplines like these he would have ranked her with his favored physicians of "natural cure" (men like Rudolph Virchow, the inventor of "Plasmon" powder).[9]

It was the theological superstructure Eddy raised over her "practice," and the ludicrous terminology she invented, that were his first targets. He gave her full credit for her organizational genius, making him suppose that Christian Science was "the Standard Oil of the future." As usual, he was more amused than angered by a folly that did not conquer or repress other people by force: "When we contemplate her (Eddy) and what she has achieved, it is blasphemy to longer deny to the Supreme Being the possession of a sense of humor."[10]

It was in this almost frivolous vein that Twain wrote his first attack on Christian Science while living in Vienna in 1898–99. It took the form of a burlesque tale followed by philosophical musings on the tale. He meant to publish the two parts together, but *Cosmopolitan* published only the tale (in October 1899). It was easy to treat this as a skit or spoof, and not a serious criticism. Twain describes a man who, returning from a health cure in the mountains, falls off a cliff and finds his bones projecting from him like the arms of a hat rack. After a course of treatment from a Christian Science practitioner, he calls in a veterinarian and pays the Christian Scientist with an imaginary check for an imaginary cure.

The musings went deeper, and apparently scared Twain's American publishers, Harper and Brothers. In the next volume of his collected stories, the tale and musings (the first eight chapters of *Christian Science* as we have it) were included in the German and British editions, but excluded from the American. The musings (chapters 5–8) eventually appeared in the *North American Review* for December 1902, by which time responses to his tale had prompted Twain to plan a book on Mrs. Eddy and her science. What became chapter 9 of the book ran in the *North American Review* in February 1903, and "Mrs. Eddy in Error" ran in the April issue.

Christian Scientists still make it hard to do research on their founder, who suppressed earlier editions of her writings. Twain had to advertise for copies in *Harper's Weekly*. Mrs. Eddy's writings would be the subject of the entire second half of his own book. Twain had spelled out, in his very first musings, what he was willing to grant Mrs. Eddy in the realm of curative powers.

> The power which a man's imagination has over his body to heal it or make it sick is a force which none of us is born without. The first man had it, the last one will possess it. If left to himself, a man is most likely to use only the mischievous half of the force — the half which invents imaginary ailments for him and cultivates them; and if he is one of these very wise people, he is quite likely to scoff at the beneficent half of the force and deny its existence. And so, to heal or help that man, *two* imaginations are required: his own and some outsider's. The outsider, B, must imagine that *his* incantations are the healing-power that is curing A, and A must imagine that this is so. I think it is not so, at all; but no matter, the cure is effected, and that is the main thing. The outsider's work is unquestionably valuable; so valuable that it may fairly be likened to the essential work performed by the engineer when he handles the throttle and turns on the steam; the actual power is lodged exclusively in the engine, but if the engine were left alone it would never start of itself. (84–85)

Christian Science takes this commonsense finding and creates a monopoly on it, by the development of a secretive and exclusive cult around the mobilization of such forces. Twain treats Mrs. Eddy's church as a typical nineteenth-century trust, like those erected by the railroad combines or "the gold ring." Mrs. Eddy had cornered the market on Mind, and was turning a good penny — the Jay Gould of the spirit: "I do not think that she has ever allowed a dollar that had no friends to get by her alive" (201).

The longer Twain dealt with the Scientists, the testier he got — the second half of his book, written in a rush in 1902, was so harsh that Harper's, after announcing publication in 1903, waited four years before risking it. By 1907, Christian Science had attracted enough other criticism for Twain's work not to stand alone.

It may seem odd that what irks Twain most is Mrs. Eddy's prose style. But Twain took language as the key to a person's thought. Self-deception, like the deception of others, shows up in the refusal of words to get themselves into a position where they can be tested, weighed, or challenged. What Twain gives us is the picture of a woman engaged in massive self-evasion, delusions so vague that it is doubtful even she can know what she is trying to say.

> Mrs. Eddy has one very curious and interesting peculiarity: whenever she notices that she is chortling along without saying anything, she pulls up with a sudden "God is over us all," or some other sounding irrelevancy, and for the moment it seems to light up the whole district; then, before you can recover from the shock, she goes flitting pleasantly and meaninglessly along again, and you hurry hopefully after her, thinking you are going to get something this time; but as soon as she has led you far enough away from her turkeylet she takes to a tree. (122)

(That long sentence is itself a model of the stop-and-go rhythms of a baffled hunt.) Twain labors at various passages, trying to make sense of them. Like this: "His spiritual noumenon and phenomenon silenced portraiture." Presumably, Eddy meant to say something like "His greatness could not be described." But the words do not *say* that; in fact, they do not say anything. As Twain concludes, of the sentence:

> I realize that noumenon is a daisy; and I will not deny that I shall use it whenever I am in a company which I think I can embarrass with it; but, at

the same time, I think it is out of place among friends in an autobiography. There, I think a person ought not to have anything up his sleeve. It undermines confidence. But my dissatisfaction with the quoted passage is not on account of noumenon; it is on account of the misuse of the word "silenced." You cannot silence portraiture with a noumenon; if portraiture should make a noise, a way could be found to silence it, but even then it could not be done with a noumenon. Not even with a brick, some authorities think. (121)

Twain spares us much attention to what he calls Mrs. Eddy's "alleged poems," but they back up his claim that she had no control over her own language. She celebrated the emancipation of slaves by the Thirteenth Amendment with stanzas including this one:

Joy in every belfry bell —
Joy for the captive! Sound it long!
Ye who have wept four-score can tell
The holy meaning of their dong.[11]

Twain is not simply having fun with Mrs. Eddy's style. It is important for his argument that he reveal what Eddy sounds like when she is herself — so that he can identify the passages in which she is "inspired." The *inspired* Eddy lapses into grammar. Whatever one thinks of its message, Eddy's "Bible," the church's official *Science and Health*, is written in prose that does mean *something*. Twain is confident that he can tell at a glance the difference between Eddy inspired and Eddy being herself: "It is evident that whenever, under the inspiration of the Deity, she turns out a book, she is always allowed to do some of the preface. I wonder why that is? It always mars the work. I think it is done in humorous malice" (131). To think that the author of *Science and Health* wrote Mrs. Eddy's lectures and autobiography is like thinking that Jonathan Edwards wrote the humorous sketches of Josh Billings.

So Mrs. Eddy relied on a holy ghostwriter. Was it the Holy Ghost? To say so would seem blasphemous, since the ghostwriter needs many tries to get things right. "An inspirer cannot inspire for Mrs. Eddy and keep his reputation" (250). It is now generally recognized that James Henry Wiggin, among others, tidied up Mrs. Eddy's grammar as *Science and Health* worked its laborious way through 382 improved editions in her lifetime.[12] In other places her "inspiration" took the form of direct plagiarism. How Twain would have liked to see the proof assembled that some passages of "Eddy" came straight out of Ruskin and Carlyle.[13]

It was Eddy's dishonesty—with herself and with her followers—that Twain traced in her language. The dishonesty served a quest for power that was shrewd enough to transcend Eddy's limitations, mental and stylistic. Though Twain claimed that he kept studying Eddy just to savor the absurdity of life, his urbanity slips, in places, and turns to denunciation of Eddy's absolutist church structure, which he compares to that of the Inquisition — and even to "satanic concentrations of irresponsible power" (211).

Christian Scientists have rightly claimed that they fell victim to Twain's darkening attitude toward all religions. It is true that he considers Eddy's verbal tangles a manifestation of all theologians' tendency to a "Spiral Twist."

> That is a technicality—that phrase. I got it off an uncle of mine. He had once studied in a theological cemetery, he said, and he called the Department of Biblical Exegesis the Spiral Twist "for short." He said it was always difficult to drive a straight text through an unaccommodating cork, but that if you twisted it it would go. He had kept bar in his less poetical days. (196–97)

Twain is less distantly amused by Eddy than he had been by the Campbellites or Mormons. His black later writings on Satan as the true author of religion had brought him to the stark conclusion of Lucretius:

> *Tantum religio potuit suadere malorum.*
> How suasive is religion to our bane.[14]

Thus Twain's relatively neglected book can be read at several levels, all rewarding — first, as a satire on Christian Science's wilder pretensions and its founder's deceptions; then, as an example of Twain's regard for language as the indicator of mental and moral conditions; and finally, as part of a biographical descent into the nihilism of his last days. On all these counts *Christian Science* gets us very close to the heart of American culture. Like most of his books, it is episodic and rambling. But part of its incoherence comes from the fact that he was punching fiercely in what he felt, increasingly, was a lost cause.

Great was truth, he concluded — but it would *not* prevail.

NOTES

1. *Mark Twain in Eruption*, edited by Bernard DeVoto (Capricorn Books, 1968), pp. 50–51.

2. Mark Twain, *Mississippi Writings*, edited by Guy Cardwell (Library of America, 1982), p. 753.

3. Mark Twain, *Roughing It* (Penguin Books, 1985), p. 138.

4. Mark Twain and Charles Dudley Warner, *The Gilded Age* (Signet Books, 1969), p. 369.

5. Ibid., pp. 152–53.

6. Justin Kaplan, *Mr. Clemens and Mark Twain* (Pocket Books, 1968), p. 384.

7. Ibid., pp. 385 (hypnotism), 417–18 (osteopathy), and 400 (séances).

8. *Philadelphia Medical Journal* 11 (January 3, 1903), p. 5.

9. Kaplan, op. cit., p. 417.

10. Quoted in ibid., p. 435.

11. Quoted in Ernest Sutherland Bates and John V. Dittemore, *Mary Baker Eddy: The Truth and the Tradition* (Knopf, 1932), p. 104.

12. Sidney Ahlstrom, *Notable American Women 1607–1956* (Harvard University Press, 1971), pp. 556–57.

13. Edwin F. Dakin, *Mrs. Eddy* (Charles Scribner's Sons, 1930), pp. 531–38.

14. Lucretius, *de rerum natura*, book 1, line 101.

[1906]

CHRISTIAN SCIENCE

WITH NOTES CONTAINING
CORRECTIONS TO DATE

BY

MARK TWAIN

ILLUSTRATED

NEW YORK AND LONDON
HARPER & BROTHERS PUBLISHERS
1907

ILLUSTRATIONS

PREFACE

BOOK I. of this volume occupies a quarter or a third of the volume, and consists of matter written about four years ago, but not hitherto published in book form. It contained errors of judgment and of fact. I have now corrected these to the best of my ability and later knowledge.

Book II. was written at the beginning of 1903, and has not until now appeared in any form. In it my purpose has been to present a character-portrait of Mrs. Eddy, drawn from her own acts and words solely, not from hearsay and rumor; and to explain the nature and scope of her Monarchy, as revealed in the Laws by which she governs it, and which she wrote herself.

MARK TWAIN.

NEW YORK, *January, 1907.*

BOOK I

CHRISTIAN SCIENCE

*"It is the first time since the dawn-days of Creation that
a Voice has gone crashing through space with such
placid and complacent confidence and command."*

CHAPTER I

THIS last summer, when I was on my way
back to Vienna from the Appetite-Cure in the
mountains, I fell over a cliff in the twilight
and broke some arms and legs and one thing
or another, and by good luck was found by
some peasants who had lost an ass, and they
carried me to the nearest habitation, which
was one of those large, low, thatch - roofed
farm-houses, with apartments in the garret for
the family, and a cunning little porch under
the deep gable decorated with boxes of bright-
colored flowers and cats; on the ground - floor
a large and light sitting-room, separated from

the milch‑cattle apartment by a partition; and in the front yard rose stately and fine the wealth and pride of the house, the manure‑pile. That sentence is Germanic, and shows that I am acquiring that sort of mastery of the art and spirit of the language which enables a man to travel all day in one sentence without changing cars.

There was a village a mile away, and a horse‑doctor lived there, but there was no surgeon. It seemed a bad outlook; mine was distinctly a surgery case. Then it was remembered that a lady from Boston was summering in that village, and she was a Christian Science doctor and could cure anything. So she was sent for. It was night by this time, and she could not conveniently come, but sent word that it was no matter, there was no hurry, she would give me "absent treatment" now, and come in the morning; meantime she begged me to make myself tranquil and comfortable and re‑member that there was nothing the matter with me. I thought there must be some mistake.

"Did you tell her I walked off a cliff seventy‑five feet high?"

"Yes."

"And struck a bowlder at the bottom and bounced?"

"Yes."

"And struck another one and bounced again?"

"Yes."

"And struck another one and bounced yet again?"

"Yes."

"And broke the bowlders?"

"Yes."

"That accounts for it; she is thinking of the bowlders. Why didn't you tell her I got hurt, too?"

"I did. I told her what you told me to tell her: that you were now but an incoherent series of compound fractures extending from your scalp-lock to your heels, and that the comminuted projections caused you to look like a hat-rack."

"And it was after this that she wished me to remember that there was nothing the matter with me?"

"Those were her words."

"I do not understand it. I believe she has not diagnosed the case with sufficient care. Did she look like a person who was theorizing, or did she look like one who has fallen off precipices herself and brings to the aid of abstract science the confirmations of personal experience?"

"*Bitte?*"

It was too large a contract for the *Stubenmadchen's* vocabulary; she couldn't call the hand. I allowed the subject to rest there, and asked for something to eat and smoke, and something hot to drink, and a basket to pile my legs in; but I could not have any of these things.

"Why?"

"She said you would need nothing at all."

"But I am hungry and thirsty, and in desperate pain."

"She said you would have these delusions, but must pay no attention to them. She wants you to particularly remember that there are no such things as hunger and thirst and pain."

"She does, does she?"

"It is what she said."

"Does she seem to be in full and functionable possession of her intellectual plant, such as it is?"

"*Bitte ?*"

"Do they let her run at large, or do they tie her up?"

"Tie her up?"

"There, good-night, run along; you are a good girl, but your mental *Geschirr* is not arranged for light and airy conversation. Leave me to my delusions."

CHAPTER II

It was a night of anguish, of course—at least, I supposed it was, for it had all the symptoms of it—but it passed at last, and the Christian Scientist came, and I was glad. She was middle-aged, and large and bony, and erect, and had an austere face and a resolute jaw and a Roman beak and was a widow in the third degree, and her name was Fuller. I was eager to get to business and find relief, but she was distressingly deliberate. She unpinned and unhooked and uncoupled her upholsteries one by one, abolished the wrinkles with a flirt of her hand, and hung the articles up; peeled off her gloves and disposed of them, got a book out of her hand-bag, then drew a chair to the bedside, descended into it without hurry, and I hung out my tongue. She said, with pity but without passion:

"Return it to its receptacle. We deal with the mind only, not with its dumb servants."

I could not offer my pulse, because the connection was broken; but she detected the apology before I could word it, and indicated by a negative tilt of her head that the pulse was another dumb servant that she had no use for. Then I thought I would tell her my symptoms and how I felt, so that she would understand the case; but that was another inconsequence, she did not need to know those things; moreover, my remark about how I felt was an abuse of language, a misapplication of terms.

"One does not *feel*," she explained; "there is no such thing as feeling: therefore, to speak of a non-existent thing as existent is a contradiction. Matter has no existence; nothing exists but mind; the mind cannot feel pain, it can only imagine it."

"But if it hurts, just the same—"

"It doesn't. A thing which is unreal cannot exercise the functions of reality. Pain is unreal; hence, pain cannot hurt."

In making a sweeping gesture to indicate the act of shooing the illusion of pain out of the mind, she raked her hand on a pin in her dress, said "Ouch!" and went tranquilly on with her talk. "You should never allow yourself to speak of how you feel, nor permit others to ask you how you are feeling; you should never concede that you are ill, nor permit others to talk about disease or pain or death or similar non-existences in your presence. Such talk only encourages the mind to continue its empty imaginings." Just at that point the *Stuben-mādchen* trod on the cat's tail, and the cat let fly a frenzy of cat-profanity. I asked, with caution:

"Is a cat's opinion about pain valuable?"

" A cat has no opinion; opinions proceed from mind only; the lower animals, being eternally perishable, have not been granted mind; without mind, opinion is impossible."

"She merely *imagined* she felt a pain—the cat?"

" She cannot imagine a pain, for imagining is an effect of mind; without mind, there is no imagination. A cat has no imagination."

"Then she had a *real* pain?"

"I have already told you there is no such *thing* as real pain."

"It is strange and interesting. I do wonder

what was the matter with the cat. Because,
there being no such thing as a real pain, and
she not being able to imagine an imaginary one,
it would seem that God in His pity has com-
pensated the cat with some kind of a mysterious emotion usable when her tail is trodden on
which, for the moment, joins cat and Christian
in one common brotherhood of—"

She broke in with an irritated—

"Peace! The cat feels nothing, the Christian feels nothing. Your empty and foolish
imaginings are profanation and blasphemy, and
can do you an injury. It is wiser and better
and holier to recognize and confess that there
is no such thing as disease or pain or death."

"I am full of imaginary tortures," I said,
"but I do not think I could be any more uncomfortable if they were real ones. What must
I do to get rid of them?"

"There is no occasion to get rid of them,
since they do not exist. They are illusions
propagated by matter, and matter has no existence; there is no such thing as matter."

"It sounds right and clear, but yet it seems
in a degree elusive; it seems to slip through,

just when you think you are getting a grip on it."

"Explain."

"Well, for instance: if there is no such thing as matter, how can matter propagate things?"

In her compassion she almost smiled. She would have smiled if there were any such thing as a smile.

"It is quite simple," she said; "the fundamental propositions of Christian Science explain it, and they are summarized in the four following self-evident propositions: 1. God is All in all. 2. God is good. Good is Mind. 3. God, Spirit, being all, nothing is matter. 4. Life, God, omnipotent Good, deny death, evil, sin, disease. There—now you see."

It seemed nebulous; it did not seem to say anything about the difficulty in hand--how non-existent matter can propagate illusions. I said, with some hesitancy:

"Does—does it explain?"

"*Doesn't* it? Even if read backward it will do it."

With a budding hope, I asked her to do it backward.

"Very well. Disease sin evil death deny Good omnipotent God life matter is nothing all being Spirit God Mind is Good good is God all in All is God. There—do you understand now?"

"It—it—well, it is plainer than it was before; still—"

"Well?"

"Could you try it some more ways?"

"As many as you like; it always means the same. Interchanged in any way you please it cannot be made to mean anything different from what it means when put in any other way. Because it is perfect. You can jumble it all up, and it makes no difference: it always comes out the way it was before. It was a marvellous mind that produced it. As a mental *tour de force* it is without a mate, it defies alike the simple, the concrete, and the occult."

"It seems to be a corker."

I blushed for the word, but it was out before I could stop it.

"A what?"

"A—wonderful structure—combination, so to speak, of profound thoughts—unthinkable ones—un—"

"It is true. Read backward, or forward, or perpendicularly, or at any given angle, these four propositions will always be found to agree in statement and proof."

"Ah—proof. Now we are coming at it. The *statements* agree; they agree with—with—anyway, they agree; I noticed that; but what is it they prove—I mean, in particular?"

"Why, nothing could be clearer. They prove: 1. GOD—Principle, Life, Truth, Love, Soul, Spirit, Mind. Do you get that?"

"I—well, I seem to. Go on, please."

"2. MAN—God's universal idea, individual, perfect, eternal. Is it clear?"

"It—I think so. Continue."

"3. IDEA—An image in Mind; the immediate object of understanding. There it is—the whole sublime Arcana of Christian Science in a nutshell. Do you find a weak place in it anywhere?"

"Well—no; it seems strong."

"Very well. There is more. Those three constitute the Scientific Definition of Immortal Mind. Next, we have the Scientific Definition of Mortal Mind. Thus. FIRST DEGREE:

Depravity. 1. Physical — Passions and appetites, fear, depraved will, pride, envy, deceit, hatred, revenge, sin, disease, death."

"Phantasms, madam—unrealities, as I understand it."

"Every one. Second Degree: *Evil Disappearing.* 1. Moral—Honesty, affection, compassion, hope, faith, meekness, temperance. Is it clear?"

"Crystal."

"Third Degree: *Spiritual Salvation.* 1. Spiritual—Faith, wisdom, power, purity, understanding, health, love. You see how searchingly and co-ordinately interdependent and anthropomorphous it all is. In this Third Degree, as we know by the revelations of Christian Science, mortal mind disappears."

"Not earlier?"

"No, not until the teaching and preparation for the Third Degree are completed."

"It is not until then that one is enabled to take hold of Christian Science effectively, and with the right sense of sympathy and kinship, as I understand you. That is to say, it could not succeed during the processes of the Second

Degree, because there would still be remains of mind left; and therefore—but I interrupted you. You were about to further explain the good results proceeding from the erosions and disintegrations effected by the Third Degree. It is very interesting; go on, please."

"Yes, as I was saying, in this Third Degree mortal mind disappears. Science so reverses the evidence before the corporeal human senses as to make this scriptural testimony true in our hearts, 'the last shall be first and the first shall be last,' that God and His idea may be to us— what divinity really is, and must of necessity be—all-inclusive."

"It is beautiful. And with what exhaustive exactness your choice and arrangement of words confirm and establish what you have claimed for the powers and functions of the Third Degree. The Second could probably produce only temporary absence of mind; it is reserved to the Third to make it permanent. A sentence framed under the auspices of the Second could have a kind of meaning—a sort of deceptive semblance of it—whereas it is only under the magic of the Third that that defect would disappear. Also, without doubt, it is the Third Degree that contributes another remarkable specialty to Christian Science—viz., ease and flow and lavishness of words, and rhythm and swing and smoothness. There must be a special reason for this?"

"Yes—God - all, all - God, good God, non-Matter, Matteration, Spirit, Bones, Truth."

"That explains it."

"There is nothing in Christian Science that is not explicable; for God is one, Time is one, Individuality is one, and may be one of a series, one of many, as an individual man, individual horse; whereas God is one, not one of a series, but one alone and without an equal."

"These are noble thoughts. They make one burn to know more. How does Christian Science explain the spiritual relation of systematic duality to incidental deflection?"

"Christian Science reverses the seeming relation of Soul and body—as astronomy reverses the human perception of the movement of the solar system—and makes body tributary to the Mind. As it is the earth which is in motion, while the sun is at rest, though in viewing the sun rise one finds it impossible to believe the sun not to be really rising, so the body is but the humble servant of the restful Mind, though it seems otherwise to finite sense; but we shall never understand this while we admit that soul is in body, or mind in matter, and that man is included in non-intelligence. Soul is God, unchangeable and eternal; and man coexists with and reflects Soul, for the All-in-all is the Altogether, and the Altogether embraces the All-one, Soul-Mind, Mind-Soul, Love, Spirit, Bones, Liver, one of a series, alone and without an equal."

"What is the origin of Christian Science? Is it a gift of God, or did it just happen?"

"In a sense, it is a gift of God. That is to say, its powers are from Him, but the credit of the discovery of the powers and what they are for is due to an American lady."

"Indeed? When did this occur?"

"In 1866. That is the immortal date when pain and disease and death disappeared from the earth to return no more forever. That is, the fancies for which those terms stand disappeared. The things themselves had never existed; therefore, as soon as it was perceived that there were no such things, they were easily banished. The history and nature of the great discovery are set down in the book here, and—"

"Did the lady write the book?"

"Yes, she wrote it all, herself. The title is *Science and Health, with Key to the Scriptures*—for she explains the Scriptures; they were not understood before. Not even by the twelve Disciples. She begins thus—I will read it to you."

But she had forgotten to bring her glasses.

"Well, it is no matter," she said. "I remember the words—indeed, all Christian Scientists know the book by heart; it is necessary in our practice. We should otherwise make mistakes and do harm. She begins thus: 'In the year 1866 I discovered the Science of Metaphysical Healing, and named it Christian Science.' And she says—quite beautifully, I think—'Through Christian Science, religion and medicine are inspired with a diviner nature and essence, fresh pinions are given to faith and understanding, and thoughts acquaint themselves intelligently with God.' Her very words."

"It is elegant. And it is a fine thought, too —marrying religion to medicine, instead of medicine to the undertaker in the old way; for religion and medicine properly belong together, they being the basis of all spiritual and physical health. What kind of medicine do you give for the ordinary diseases, such as—"

"We never give medicine in *any* circumstances whatever! We—"

"But, madam, it *says*—"

"I don't care what it says, and I don't wish to talk about it."

"I am sorry if I have offended, but you see the mention seemed in some way inconsistent, and—"

"There *are* no inconsistencies in Christian Science. The thing is impossible, for the Science is absolute. It cannot be otherwise, since it proceeds directly from the All-in-all and the Everything-in-Which, also Soul, Bones, Truth, one of a series, alone and without equal. It is Mathematics purified from material dross and made spiritual."

"I can see that, but—"

"It rests upon the immovable basis of an Apodictical Principle."

The word flattened itself against my mind in trying to get in, and disordered me a little, and before I could inquire into its pertinency, she was already throwing the needed light:

"This Apodictical Principle is the absolute Principle of Scientific Mind - healing, the sovereign Omnipotence which delivers the children of men from pain, disease, decay, and every ill that flesh is heir to."

"Surely not every ill, every decay?"

"Every one; there are no exceptions; there is no such thing as decay—it is an unreality, it has no existence."

"But without your glasses your failing eyesight does not permit you to—"

"My eyesight cannot fail; nothing can fail; the Mind is master, and the Mind permits no retrogression."

She was under the inspiration of the Third Degree, therefore there could be no profit in continuing this part of the subject. I shifted to other ground and inquired further concerning the Discoverer of the Science.

"Did the discovery come suddenly, like Klondike, or after long study and calculation, like America?"

"The comparisons are not respectful, since they refer to trivialities—but let it pass. I will answer in the Discoverer's own words: 'God had been graciously fitting me, during many years, for the reception of a final revelation of the absolute Principle of Scientific Mind-healing.'"

"Many years. How many?"

"Eighteen centuries!"

"All - God, God - good, good - God, Truth, Bones, Liver, one of a series, alone and without equal—it is amazing!"

"You may well say it, sir. Yet it is but the truth. This American lady, our revered and sacred Founder, is distinctly referred to, and her coming prophesied, in the twelfth chapter of the Apocalypse; she could not have been more plainly indicated by St. John without actually mentioning her name."

"How strange, how wonderful!"

"I will quote her own words, from her *Key to the Scriptures*: 'The twelfth chapter of the

Apocalypse *has a special suggestiveness in con-nection with this nineteenth century.'* There—do you note that? Think—note it well."

"But—what does it mean?"

"Listen, and you will know. I quote her inspired words again: 'In the opening of the Sixth Seal, typical of six thousand years since Adam, there is one distinctive feature *which has special reference to the present age.* Thus:

"'Revelation xii. 1. And there appeared a great wonder in heaven—a *woman* clothed with the sun, and the moon under her feet, and upon her head a crown of twelve stars.'

"That is our Head, our Chief, our Discoverer of Christian Science—nothing can be plainer, nothing surer. And note this:

"'Revelation xii. 6. And the woman fled into the wilderness, where she had a place prepared of God.'

"That is Boston. I recognize it, madam. These are sublime things, and impressive; I never understood these passages before; please go on with the—with the—proofs."

"Very well. Listen:

"'And I saw another mighty angel come down from heaven, clothed with a cloud; and a rainbow was upon his head, and his face was as it were the sun, and his feet as pillars of fire. And he held in his hand *a little book.*'

"A little book, merely a little book—could words be modester? Yet how stupendous its importance! Do you know what book that was?"

"Was it—"

"I hold it in my hand—Christian Science!"

"Love, Livers, Lights, Bones, Truth, Kidneys, one of a series, alone and without equal—it is beyond imagination for wonder!"

"Hear our Founder's eloquent words: 'Then will a voice from harmony cry, "Go and take the little book: take it and eat it up, and it shall make thy belly bitter; but it shall be in thy mouth sweet as honey." Mortal, obey the heavenly evangel. Take up Divine Science. Read

it from beginning to end. Study it, ponder it.
It will be, indeed, sweet at its first taste, when
it heals you; but murmur not over Truth, if you
find its digestion bitter.' You now know the
history of our dear and holy Science, sir, and
that its *origin* is not of this earth, but only its
discovery. I will leave the book with you and
will go, now; but give yourself no uneasiness—
I will give you absent treatment from now till I
go to bed."

CHAPTER III

UNDER the powerful influence of the near treatment and the absent treatment together, my bones were gradually retreating inward and disappearing from view. The good work took a brisk start, now, and went on swiftly. My body was diligently straining and stretching, this way and that, to accommodate the processes of restoration, and every minute or two I heard a dull click inside and knew that the two ends of a fracture had been successfully joined. This muffled clicking and gritting and grinding and rasping continued during the next three hours, and then stopped—the connections had all been made. All except dislocations; there were only seven of these: hips, shoulders, knees, neck; so that was soon over; one after another they slipped into their sockets with a sound like pulling a distant cork, and I jumped up as good as new, as to framework, and sent for the horse-doctor.

I was obliged to do this because I had a stomach-ache and a cold in the head, and I was not willing to trust these things any longer in the hands of a woman whom I did not know, and in whose ability to successfully treat mere disease I had lost all confidence. My position was justified by the fact that the cold and the ache had been in her charge from the first, along with the fractures, but had experienced not a shade of relief; and, indeed, the ache was even growing worse and worse, and more and more bitter, now, probably on account of the protracted abstention from food and drink.

The horse-doctor came, a pleasant man and full of hope and professional interest in the case. In the matter of smell he was pretty aromatic—in fact, quite horsy—and I tried to arrange with him for absent treatment, but it was not in his line, so, out of delicacy, I did not press it. He looked at my teeth and examined my hock, and said my age and general condition were favorable to energetic measures; therefore he would give me something to turn the stomach-ache into the botts and the cold in the head into the blind staggers; then he should

3

be on his own beat and would know what to do.
He made up a bucket of bran-mash, and said a
dipperful of it every two hours, alternated with
a drench with turpentine and axle-grease in it,
would either knock my ailments out of me in
twenty-four hours, or so interest me in other
ways as to make me forget they were on the
premises. He administered my first dose himself, then took his leave, saying I was free to
eat and drink anything I pleased and in any
quantity I liked. But I was not hungry any
more, and did not care for food.

I took up the Christian Science book and
read half of it, then took a dipperful of drench
and read the other half. The resulting experi-
ences were full of interest and adventure. All
through the rumblings and grindings and quak-
ings and effervescings accompanying the evolution of the ache into the botts and the cold into
the blind staggers I could note the generous
struggle for mastery going on between the mash
and the drench and the literature; and often I
could tell which was ahead, and could easily dis-
tinguish the literature from the others when
the others were separate, though not when

they were mixed; for when a bran-mash and an eclectic drench are mixed together they look just like the Apodictical Principle out on a lark, and no one can tell it from that. The finish was reached at last, the evolutions were complete, and a fine success, but I think that this result could have been achieved with fewer materials. I believe the mash was necessary to the conversion of the stomach-ache into the botts, but I think one could develop the blind staggers out of the literature by itself; also, that blind staggers produced in this way would be of a better quality and more lasting than any produced by the artificial processes of the horse-doctor.

For of all the strange and frantic and incomprehensible and uninterpretable books which the imagination of man has created, surely this one is the prize sample. It is written with a limitless confidence and complacency, and with a dash and stir and earnestness which often compel the effects of eloquence, even when the words do not seem to have any traceable meaning. There are plenty of people who imagine they understand the book; I know this, for I have talked with them; but in all cases they were people who also imagined that there were no such things as pain, sickness, and death, and no realities in the world; nothing actually existent but Mind. It seems to me to modify the value of their testimony. When these people talk about Christian Science they do as Mrs. Fuller did: they do not use their own language, but the book's; they pour out the book's showy incoherences, and leave you to find out later that they were not originating, but merely quoting; they seem to know the volume by heart, and to revere it as they would a Bible—another Bible, perhaps I ought to say. Plainly the book was written under the mental desolations of the Third Degree, and I feel sure that none but the membership of that Degree can discover meanings in it. When you read it you seem to be listening to a lively and aggressive and oracular speech delivered in an unknown tongue, a speech whose spirit you get but not the particulars; or, to change the figure, you seem to be listening to a vigorous instrument which is making a noise which it thinks is a tune, but which, to persons not members of the band, is only the martial tooting of a trombone, and merely stirs the soul through the noise, but does not convey a meaning.

The book's serenities of self-satisfaction do almost seem to smack of a heavenly origin—they have no blood-kin in the earth. It is more than human to be so placidly certain about things, and so finely superior, and so airily content with one's performance. Without ever presenting anything which may rightfully be called by the strong name of Evidence, and sometimes without even *mentioning* a reason for a deduction at all, it thunders out the startling words, " I have *Proved* " so and so. It takes the Pope and all the great guns of his Church in battery assembled to authoritatively settle and establish the meaning of a sole and single unclarified passage of Scripture, and this at vast cost of time and study and reflection, but the author of this work is superior to all that: she finds the whole Bible in an unclarified condition, and at small expense of time and no expense of mental effort she clarifies it from lid to lid, reorganizes and improves the meanings, then authoritatively settles and establishes

them with formulas which you cannot tell from
"Let there be light!" and "Here you have it!"
It is the first time since the dawn-days of Creation that a Voice has gone crashing through
space with such placid and complacent confidence and command.[1]

[1] *January*, 1903. The first reading of any book whose
terminology is new and strange is nearly sure to leave the
reader in a bewildered and sarcastic state of mind. But
now that, during the past two months, I have, by diligence,
gained a fair acquaintanceship with *Science and Health*
technicalities, I no longer find the bulk of that work hard
to understand.—M. T.

P. S. The wisdom harvested from the foregoing
thoughts has already done me a service and saved me a
sorrow. Nearly a month ago there came to me from one
of the universities a tract by Dr. Edward Anthony Spitz-
ka on the "Encephalic Anatomy of the Races." I judged
that my opinion was desired by the university, and I was
greatly pleased with this attention and wrote and said I
would furnish it as soon as I could. That night I put my
plodding and disheartening Christian Science mining aside
and took hold of the matter. I wrote an eager chapter, and
was expecting to finish my opinion the next day, but was
called away for a week, and my mind was soon charged
with other interests. It was not until to-day, after the
lapse of nearly a month, that I happened upon my Encephalic chapter again. Meantime, the new wisdom had
come to me, and I read it with shame. I recognized that
I had entered upon that work in far from the right temper
—far from the respectful and judicial spirit which was its

due of reverence. I had begun upon it with the following paragraph for fuel:

"FISSURES OF THE PARIETAL AND OCCIPITAL LOBES (LATERAL SURFACE).—*The Postcentral Fissural Complex.*—In this hemicerebrum, the postcentral and subcentral are combined to form a continuous fissure, attaining a length of 8.5 cm. Dorsally, the fissure bifurcates, embracing the gyre indented by the caudal limb of the paracentral. The caudal limb of the postcentral is joined by a transparietal piece. In all, five additional rami spring from the combined fissure. A vadum separates it from the parietal; another from the central."

It humiliates me, now, to see how angry I got over that; and how scornful. I said that the style was disgraceful; that it was labored and tumultuous, and in places violent, that the treatment was involved and erratic, and almost, as a rule, bewildering; that to lack of simplicity was added a lack of vocabulary; that there was quite too much feeling shown; that if I had a dog that would get so excited and incoherent over a tranquil subject like Encephalic Anatomy I would not pay his tax; and at that point I got excited myself and spoke bitterly of these mongrel insanities, and said a person might as well try to understand *Science and Health.*

I know, now, where the trouble was, and am glad of the interruption that saved me from sending my verdict to the university. It makes me cold to think what those people might have thought of me.—M. T.

No one doubts—certainly not I—that the mind exercises a powerful influence over the body. From the beginning of time, the sorcerer, the interpreter of dreams, the fortune-teller, the charlatan, the quack, the wild medicine-man, the educated physician, the mesmerist, and the hypnotist have made use of the client's *imagination* to help them in their work. They have all recognized the potency and availability of that force. Physicians cure many patients with a bread pill; they know that where the disease is only a fancy, the patient's confidence in the doctor will make the bread pill effective.

Faith in the doctor. Perhaps that is the entire thing. It seems to look like it. In old times the King cured the king's evil by the touch of the royal hand. He frequently made extraordinary cures. Could his footman have done it? No—not in his own clothes. Disguised as the King, could he have done it? I think we may

not doubt it. I think we may feel sure that
it was not the King's touch that made the cure
in any instance, but the patient's faith in the
efficacy of a King's touch. Genuine and remarkable cures have been achieved through
contact with the relics of a saint. Is it not
likely that any other bones would have done as
well if the substitution had been concealed
from the patient? When I was a boy a farmer's wife who lived five miles from our village
had great fame as a faith-doctor—that was
what she called herself. Sufferers came to her
from all around, and she laid her hand upon
them and said, "Have faith—it is all that is
necessary," and they went away well of their
ailments. She was not a religious woman, and
pretended to no occult powers. She said that
the patient's faith in her did the work. Several times I saw her make immediate cures of
severe toothaches. My mother was the patient. In Austria there is a peasant who drives
a great trade in this sort of industry, and has
both the high and the low for patients. He
gets into prison every now and then for practising without a diploma, but his business is as

brisk as ever when he gets out, for his work is unquestionably successful and keeps his reputation high. In Bavaria there is a man who performed so many great cures that he had to retire from his profession of stage-carpentering in order to meet the demand of his constantly increasing body of customers. He goes on from year to year doing his miracles, and has become very rich. He pretends to no religious helps, no supernatural aids, but thinks there is something in his make-up which inspires the confidence of his patients, and that it is this confidence which does the work, and not some mysterious power issuing from himself.[1]

Within the last quarter of a century, in America, several sects of curers have appeared under various names and have done notable things in the way of healing ailments without

[1] *January*, 1903. I have personal and intimate knowledge of the "miraculous" cure of a case of paralysis which had kept the patient helpless in bed during two years, in spite of all that the best medical science of New York could do. The travelling "quack" (that is what they called him), came on two successive mornings and lifted the patient out of bed and said "Walk!" and the patient walked. That was the end of it. It was forty-one years ago. The patient has walked ever since.—M. T.

the use of medicines. There are the Mind Cure, the Faith Cure, the Prayer Cure, the Mental-Science Cure, and the Christian-Science Cure; and apparently they all do their miracles with the same old, powerful instrument — *the patient's imagination.* Differing names, but no difference in the process. But they do not give that instrument the credit; each sect claims that its way differs from the ways of the others.

They all achieve some cures, there is no question about it; and the Faith Cure and the Prayer Cure probably do no harm when they do no good, since they do not forbid the patient to help out the cure with medicines if he wants to; but the others bar medicines, and claim ability to cure every conceivable human ailment through the application of their mental forces alone. There would seem to be an element of danger here. It has the look of claiming too much, I think. Public confidence would probably be increased if less were claimed.[1]

[1] *February,* 1903. I find that Christian Science claims that the healing-force which it employs is radically differ-

The Christian Scientist was not able to cure my stomach-ache and my cold; but the horse-doctor did it. This convinces me that Christian Science claims too much. In my opinion it ought to let diseases alone and confine itself to surgery. There it would have everything its own way.

The horse-doctor charged me thirty kreutzers, and I paid him; in fact, I doubled it and gave him a shilling. Mrs. Fuller brought in an itemized bill for a crate of broken bones mended in two hundred and thirty-four places—one dollar per fracture.

"Nothing exists but Mind?"

"Nothing," she answered. "All else is substanceless, all else is imaginary."

I gave her an imaginary check, and now she is suing me for substantial dollars. It looks inconsistent.

Note.—The foregoing chapters appeared originally in the *Cosmopolitan Magazine*, about three years ago.—M. T.

ent from the force used by any other party in the healing business. I shall talk about this towards the end of this work.—M. T.

CHAPTER V

LET us consider that we are all partially insane. It will explain us to each other; it will
unriddle many riddles; it will make clear and
simple many things which are involved in
haunting and harassing difficulties and obscurities now.

Those of us who are not in the asylum, and
not demonstrably due there, are nevertheless,
no doubt, insane in one or two particulars. I
think we must admit this; but I think that we
are otherwise healthy - minded. I think that
when we all see one thing alike, it is evidence
that, as regards that one thing, our minds are
perfectly sound. Now there are really several
things which we do all see alike; things which
we all accept, and about which we do not dispute. For instance, we who are outside of the
asylum all agree that water seeks its level; that
the sun gives light and heat; that fire consumes;
that fog is damp; that six times six are thirty-

six, that two from ten leaves eight; that eight and seven are fifteen. These are, perhaps, the only things we are agreed about; but, although they are so few, they are of inestimable value, because they make an infallible standard of sanity. Whosoever accepts them him we know to be substantially sane; sufficiently sane; in the working essentials, sane. Whoever disputes a single one of them him we know to be wholly insane, and qualified for the asylum.

Very well, the man who disputes none of them we concede to be entitled to go at large. But that is concession enough. We cannot go any further than that; for we know that in all matters of mere *opinion* that same man is insane—just as insane as we are; just as insane as Shakespeare was. We know exactly where to put our finger upon his insanity: *it is where his opinion differs from ours*.

That is a simple rule, and easy to remember. When I, a thoughtful and unbiassed Presbyterian, examine the Koran, I know that beyond any question every Mohammedan is insane; not in all things, but in religious matters. When

a thoughtful and unbiassed Mohammedan examines the Westminster Catechism, he knows
that beyond any question I am spiritually insane. I cannot prove to him that he is insane, because you never can prove anything to
a lunatic—for that is a part of his insanity and
the evidence of it. He cannot prove to me
that I am insane, for my mind has the same defect that afflicts his. All Democrats are insane, but not one of them knows it; none but
the Republicans and Mugwumps know it. All
the Republicans are insane, but only the Democrats and Mugwumps can perceive it. The
rule is perfect: *in all matters of opinion our ad-
versaries are insane.* When I look around me,
I am often troubled to see how many people are
mad. To mention only a few:

The Atheist,	The Theosophists,
The Infidel,	The Swedenborgians,
The Agnostic,	The Shakers,
The Baptist,	The Millerites,
The Methodist,	The Mormons,
The Christian Scien- tist.	The Laurence Oliphant Harrisites.

The Catholic, and the 115 Christian sects, the Presbyterian excepted,

The 72 Mohammedan sects,

The Buddhist,

The Blavatsky-Buddhist,

The Nationalist,

The Confucian,

The Spiritualist,

The 2000 East Indian sects,

The Peculiar People,

The Grand Lama's people,

The Monarchists,

The Imperialists,

The Democrats,

The Republicans (but not the Mugwumps),

The Mind-Curists,

The Faith-Curists,

The Mental Scientists,

The Allopaths,

The Homœopaths,

The Electropaths,

The ———

But there's no end to the list; there are millions of them! And all insane; each in his own way; insane as to his pet fad or opinion, but otherwise sane and rational.

This should move us to be charitable towards one another's lunacies. I recognize that in his special belief the Christian Scientist is insane, because he does not believe as I do; but I hail him as my mate and fellow, because I am as insane as he—insane from his point of view, and his point of view is as authoritative as mine and worth as much. That is to say, worth a brass farthing. Upon a great religious or political question, the opinion of the dullest head in the world is worth the same as the opinion of the brightest head in the world—a brass farthing. How do we arrive at this? It is simple. The affirmative opinion of a stupid man is neutralized by the negative opinion of his stupid neighbor—no decision is reached; the affirmative opinion of the intellectual giant Gladstone is neutralized by the negative opinion of the intellectual giant Newman—no decision is reached. Opinions that prove nothing are, of course, without value—any but a dead person knows that much. This obliges us to admit the truth of the unpalatable proposition just mentioned above—that, in disputed matters political and religious, one man's opinion is worth no more than his peer's, and hence it follows that no man's opinion possesses any real value. It is a humbling thought, but there is no way to get around it: *all* opinions upon these great subjects are brass-farthing opinions.

4

It is a mere plain, simple fact—as clear and as certain as that eight and seven make fifteen. And by it we recognize that we are all insane, as concerns those matters. If we were sane, we should all see a political or religious doctrine alike; there would be no dispute: it would be a case of eight and seven—just as it is in heaven, where all are sane and none insane. There there is but one religion, one belief; the harmony is perfect; there is never a discordant note.

Under protection of these preliminaries, I suppose I may now repeat without offence that the Christian Scientist is insane. I mean him no discourtesy, and I am not charging—nor even imagining—that he is insaner than the rest of the human race. I think he is more picturesquely insane than some of us. At the same time, I am quite sure that in one important and splendid particular he is much saner than is the vast bulk of the race.

Why is he insane? I told you before: it is because his opinions are not ours. I know of no other reason, and I do not need any other; it is the only way we *have* of discovering insanity when it is not violent. It is merely the picturesqueness of his insanity that makes it more interesting than my kind or yours. For instance, consider his "little book"; the "little book" exposed in the sky eighteen centuries ago by the flaming angel of the Apocalypse, and handed down in our day to Mrs. Mary Baker G. Eddy, of New Hampshire, and translated by her, word for word, into English (with help of a polisher), and now published and distributed in hundreds of editions by her at a clear profit per volume, above cost, of seven hundred per cent.![1]—a profit which distinctly belongs to the angel of the Apocalypse, and let him collect it if he can; a "little book" which the C. S. very frequently calls by just that name, and always enclosed in quotation-marks to keep its high origin exultantly in mind; a "little book" which "explains" and reconstructs and new - paints and decorates the Bible, and puts a mansard

[1] *February*, 1903. This has been disputed by novices. It is not possible that the copy possessed by me could have cost above thirty-seven and a half cents. I have been a printer and book-maker myself. I shall go into some particulars concerning this matter in a later chapter.—M. T.

roof on it and a lightning-rod and all the other modern improvements; a "little book" which for the present affects to travel in yoke with the Bible and be friendly to it, and within half a century will hitch the Bible in the rear and thenceforth travel tandem, itself in the lead, in the coming great march of Christian Scientism through the Protestant dominions of the planet.

CHAPTER VI

" Hungry ones throng to hear the Bible read in connection with the text-book of Christian Science, *Science
and Health, with Key to the Scriptures,* by Mary Baker
G. Eddy. *These* are our only preachers. *They* are the
word of God."—*Christian Science Journal,* October,
1898.

Is that picturesque?   A lady has told me that
in a chapel of the Mosque in Boston there is a
picture or image of Mrs. Eddy, and that before
it burns a never-extinguished light.[1]   Is that
picturesque?   How long do you think it will be
before the Christian Scientist will be worshipping that picture or image and praying to it?
How long do you think it will be before it is
claimed that Mrs. Eddy is a Redeemer, a Christ,
and Christ's equal?[2]   Already her army of disciples speak of her reverently as " Our Mother."

[1] *February,* 1903.   There is a dispute about that picture.   I will render justice concerning it in the new half of
this book.—M. T.

[2] This suggestion has been scorned.   I will examine the
matter in the new half of the book.—M. T.

How long will it be before they place her on the steps of the Throne beside the Virgin—and, later, a step higher? First, Mary the Virgin and Mary the Matron; later, with a change of precedence, Mary the Matron and Mary the Virgin. Let the artist get ready with his canvas and his brushes; the new Renaissance is on its way, and there will be money in altar-canvases—a thousand times as much as the Popes and their Church ever spent on the Old Masters; for their riches were poverty as compared with what is going to pour into the treasure-chest of the Christian-Scientist Papacy by-and-by, let us not doubt it. We will examine the financial outlook presently and see what it promises. A favorite subject of the new Old Master will be the first verse of the twelfth chapter of Revelation—a verse which Mrs. Eddy says (in her Annex to the Scriptures) has "one distinctive feature which has special reference to the present age"—and to *her*, as is rather pointedly indicated:

"And there appeared a great wonder in heaven; a *woman* clothed with the sun, and the moon under her feet," etc.

The woman clothed with the sun will be a portrait of Mrs. Eddy.

Is it insanity to believe that Christian Scientism is destined to make the most formidable show that any new religion has made in the world since the birth and spread of Mohammedanism, and that within a century from now it may stand second to Rome only, in numbers and power in Christendom?

If this is a wild dream it will not be easy to prove it so just yet, I think. There seems argument that it may come true. The Christian-Science "boom," proper, is not yet five years old; yet already it has two hundred and fifty churches.[1]

It has its start, you see, and it is a phenomenally good one. Moreover, it is latterly spreading with a constantly accelerating swiftness. It has a better chance to grow and prosper and achieve permanency than any other existing "ism"; for it has *more to offer* than any other. The past teaches us that in order to succeed, a

[1] *February*, 1903. Through misinformation I doubled those figures when I wrote this chapter four years ago.— M. T.

movement like this must not be a mere philosophy, it must be a religion; also, that it must not claim entire originality, but content itself with passing for an improvement on an *existing* religion, and show its hand later, when strong and prosperous—like Mohammedanism.

Next, there must be money — and plenty of it.

Next, the power and authority and capital must be concentrated in the grip of a small and irresponsible clique, with nobody outside privileged to ask questions or find fault.

Next, as before remarked, it must bait its hook with some new and attractive advantages over the baits offered by its competitors.

A new movement equipped with some of these endowments—like spiritualism, for instance—may count upon a considerable success; a new movement equipped with the bulk of them—like Mohammedanism, for instance—may count upon a widely extended conquest. Mormonism had all the requisites but one—it had nothing new and nothing valuable to bait with. Spiritualism lacked the important detail of concentration of money and authority in the hands of an irresponsible clique.

The above equipment is excellent, admirable, powerful, but not perfect. There is yet another detail which is worth the whole of it put together—and more; a detail which has never been joined (in the *beginning* of a religious movement) to a supremely good working equipment since the world began, until now: *a new personage to worship.*[1] Christianity had the Saviour, but at first and for generations it lacked money and concentrated power. In Mrs. Eddy, Christian Science possesses the new personage for worship, and in addition—here in the very beginning—a working equipment that has not a flaw in it. In the beginning, Mohammedanism had no money; and it has never had anything to offer its client but heaven— nothing here below that was valuable. In addition to heaven hereafter, Christian Science has *present health and a cheerful spirit* to offer; and in comparison with this bribe all other this-

[1] *That* has been disputed by a Christian-Science friend. This surprises me. I will examine this detail in the new half of the book.—M. T.

world bribes are poor and cheap. You recognize that this estimate is admissible, do you not?

To whom does Bellamy's "Nationalism" appeal? Necessarily to the few: people who read and dream, and are compassionate, and troubled for the poor and the hard-driven. To whom does Spiritualism appeal? Necessarily to the few; its "boom" has lasted for half a century, and I believe it claims short of four millions of adherents in America. Who are attracted by Swedenborgianism and some of the other fine and delicate "isms"? The few again: educated people, sensitively organized, with superior mental endowments, who seek lofty planes of thought and find their contentment there. And who are attracted by Christian Science? There is no limit; its field is horizonless; its appeal is as universal as is the appeal of Christianity itself. It appeals to the rich, the poor, the high, the low, the cultured, the ignorant, the gifted, the stupid, the modest, the vain, the wise, the silly, the soldier, the civilian, the hero, the coward, the idler, the worker, the godly, the godless, the freeman, the slave, the adult, the child; *they who are ailing in body or mind, they who have friends that are ailing in body or mind.* To mass it in a phrase, its clientage is the Human Race. Will it march? I think so.

Remember its principal great offer: to *rid the Race of pain and disease.* Can it do so? In large measure, yes. How much of the pain and disease in the world is created by the imaginations of the sufferers, and then kept alive by those same imaginations? Four-fifths? Not anything short of that, I should think. Can Christian Science banish that four-fifths? I think so. Can any other (organized) force do it? None that I know of. Would this be a new world when that was accomplished? And a pleasanter one—for us well people, as well as for those fussy and fretting sick ones? Would it seem as if there was not as much gloomy weather as there used to be? I think so.

In the mean time, would the Scientist kill off a good many patients? I think so. More than get killed off now by the legalized methods? I will take up that question presently.

At present, I wish to ask you to examine some of the Scientist's performances, as registered in his magazine, *The Christian Science*

Journal—October number, 1898. First, a Baptist clergyman gives us this true picture of "the average orthodox Christian"—and he could have added that it is a true picture of the average (civilized) human being:

"He is a worried and fretted and fearful man; afraid of himself and his propensities, afraid of colds and fevers, afraid of treading on serpents or drinking deadly things."

Then he gives us this contrast:

"The average Christian Scientist has put all anxiety and fretting under his feet. He does have a victory over fear and care that is not achieved by the average orthodox Christian."

He has put all anxiety and fretting under his feet. What proportion of your earnings or income would you be willing to pay for that frame of mind, year in, year out? It really outvalues any price that can be put upon it. Where can you purchase it, at any outlay of any sort, in any Church or out of it, except the Scientist's?

Well, it is the anxiety and fretting about colds, and fevers, and draughts, and getting our feet wet, and about forbidden food eaten in terror of indigestion, that brings on the cold and the fever and the indigestion and the most of our other ailments; and so, if the Science can banish that anxiety from the world I think it can reduce the world's disease and pain about four-fifths.[1]

In this October number many of the redeemed testify and give thanks; and not coldly, but with passionate gratitude. As a rule they seem drunk with health, and with the surprise of it, the wonder of it, the unspeakable glory and splendor of it, after a long, sober spell spent in inventing imaginary diseases and concreting them with doctor-stuff. The first witness testifies that when "this most beautiful Truth first dawned on him" he had "nearly all the ills that flesh is heir to"; that those he did not

---

[1] *February*, 1903. In a letter to me, a distinguished New York physician finds fault with this notion. If four-fifths of our pains and diseases are not the result of unwholesome fears and imaginings, the Science has a smaller field than I was guessing; but I still think four-fifths is a sound guess.—M. T.

have he thought he had—and this made the tale about complete. What was the natural result? Why, he was a dump-pit "for all the doctors, druggists, and patent medicines of the country." Christian Science came to his help, and "the old sick conditions passed away," and along with them the "dismal forebodings" which he had been accustomed to employ in conjuring up ailments. And so he was a healthy and cheerful man, now, and astonished.

But I am not astonished, for from other sources I know what must have been his method of applying Christian Science. If I am in the right, he watchfully and diligently *diverted his mind from unhealthy channels and compelled it to travel in healthy ones.* Nothing contrivable by human invention could be more formidably effective than that, in banishing imaginary ailments and in closing the entrances against subsequent applicants of their breed. I think his method was to keep saying, "I am well! I am sound!—sound and well! well and sound! Perfectly sound, perfectly well! I have no pain; there's no such thing as pain! I have no disease; there's no such thing as disease! Nothing is real but Mind; all is Mind, All-Good-Good-Good, Life, Soul, Liver, Bones, one of a series, ante and pass the buck!"

I do not mean that that was exactly the formula used, but that it doubtless contains the spirit of it. The Scientist would attach value to the *exact* formula, no doubt, and to the religious spirit in which it was used. I should think that *any* formula that would divert the mind from unwholesome channels and force it into healthy ones would answer every purpose with some people, though not with all. I think it most likely that a very religious man would find the addition of the religious spirit a powerful reinforcement in his case.

The second witness testifies that the Science banished "an old organic trouble," which the doctor and the surgeon had been nursing with drugs and the knife for seven years.

He calls it his "claim." A surface-miner would think it was not *his* claim at all, but the property of the doctor and his pal the surgeon

—for he would be misled by that word, which is Christian-Science slang for "ailment." The Christian Scientist *has* no ailment; to him there is no such thing, and he will not use the hateful word. All that happens to him is that upon his attention an imaginary disturbance sometimes obtrudes itself which *claims* to be an ailment but isn't.

This witness offers testimony for a clergyman seventy years old who had preached forty years in a Christian church, and has now gone over to the new sect. He was "almost blind and deaf." He was treated by the C. S. method, and "when he heard the voice of Truth he saw spiritually." Saw spiritually? It is a little indefinite; they had better treat him again. Indefinite testimonies might properly be waste-basketed, since there is evidently no lack of definite ones procurable; but this C. S. magazine is poorly edited, and so mistakes of this kind must be expected.

The next witness is a soldier of the Civil War. When Christian Science found him, he had in stock the following claims:

Indigestion,	Atrophy of the muscles
Rheumatism,	of
Catarrh,	Arms, ⎫
Chalky deposits in	Shoulders, ⎭
Shoulder-joints, ⎫	Stiffness of all those
Arm-joints, ⎬	joints,
Hand-joints, ⎭	Excruciating pains
Insomnia,	most of the time.

These claims have a very substantial sound.
They came of exposure in the campaigns. The
doctors did all they could, but it was little.
Prayers were tried, but "I never realized any
physical relief from that source." After thirty
years of torture, he went to a Christian Scientist and took an hour's treatment and went
home painless. Two days later, he "began to
eat like a well man." Then "the claims vanished—some at once, others more gradually";
finally, "they have almost entirely disappeared." And—a thing which is of still greater
value—he is now "*contented and happy.*" That
is a detail which, as earlier remarked, is a Scien-
tist-Church specialty. And, indeed, one may
go further and assert with little or no exaggera-

tion that it is a Christian-Science monopoly. With thirty-one years' effort, the Methodist Church had not succeeded in furnishing it to this harassed soldier.

And so the tale goes on. Witness after witness bulletins his claims, declares their prompt abolishment, and gives Mrs. Eddy's Discovery the praise. Milk-leg is cured; nervous prostration is cured; consumption is cured; and St. Vitus's dance is made a pastime. Even without a fiddle. And now and then an interesting new addition to the Science slang appears on the page. We have "demonstrations over chilblains" and such things. It seems to be a curtailed way of saying "demonstrations of the power of Christian-Science Truth over the fiction which masquerades under the name of Chilblains." The children, as well as the adults, share in the blessings of the Science. "Through the study of the 'little book' they are learning how to be healthful, peaceful, and wise." Sometimes they are cured of their little claims by the professional healer, and sometimes more advanced children say over the formula and cure themselves.

A little Far-Western girl of nine, equipped
with an adult vocabulary, states her age and
says, "I thought I would write a demonstration
to you." She had a claim, derived from getting
flung over a pony's head and landed on a rock-
pile. She saved herself from disaster by re-
membering to say "God is All" while she was
in the air. I couldn't have done it. I shouldn't
even have thought of it. I should have been
too excited. Nothing but Christian Science
could have enabled that child to do that calm
and thoughtful and judicious thing in those circumstances. She came down on her head, and
by all the rules she should have broken it; but
the intervention of the formula prevented that,
so the only claim resulting was a blackened eye.
Monday morning it was still swollen and shut.
At school "it hurt pretty badly—that is, it
seemed to." So "I was excused, and went
down to the basement and said, 'Now I am
depending on mamma instead of God, and I
will depend on God instead of mamma.'" No
doubt this would have answered; but, to make
sure, she added Mrs. Eddy to the team and re-
cited "the Scientific Statement of Being,"

which is one of the principal incantations, I judge. Then "I felt my eye opening." Why, dear, it would have opened an oyster. I think it is one of the touchingest things in child-history, that pious little rat down cellar pumping away at the Scientific Statement of Being.

There is a page about another good child— little Gordon. Little Gordon "came into the world without the assistance of surgery or anæsthetics." He was a "demonstration." A painless one; therefore, his coming evoked "joy and thankfulness to God and the Discoverer of Christian Science." It is a noticeable feature of this literature—the so frequent linking together of the Two Beings in an equal bond; also of Their Two Bibles. When little Gordon was two years old, "he was playing horse on the bed, where I had left my 'little book.' I noticed him stop in his play, take the book carefully in his little hands, kiss it softly, then look about for the highest place of safety his arms could reach, and put it there." This pious act filled the mother "with such a train of thought as I had never experienced before. I thought of the sweet mother of long ago who kept things in her heart," etc. It is a bold comparison; however, unconscious profanations are about as common in the mouths of the lay membership of the new Church as are frank and open ones in the mouths of its consecrated chiefs.

Some days later, the family library—Christian-Science books—was lying in a deep-seated window. This was another chance for the holy child to show off. He left his play and went there and pushed all the books to one side, except the Annex. "*It* he took in both hands, slowly raised it to his lips, then removed it carefully, and seated himself in the window." It had seemed to the mother too wonderful to be true, that first time; but now she was convinced that "neither imagination nor accident had anything to do with it." Later, little Gordon let the author of his being see him do it. After that he did it frequently; probably every time anybody was looking. I would rather have that child than a chromo. If this tale has any object, it is to intimate that the inspired book was supernaturally able to convey a sense of its sacred and awful character to this innocent little creature, without the intervention of outside aids. The magazine is not edited with high-priced discretion. The editor has a "claim," and he ought to get it treated.

Among other witnesses there is one who had a "jumping toothache," which several times tempted her to "believe that there was sensation in matter, but each time it was overcome by the power of Truth." She would not allow the dentist to use cocaine, but sat there and let him punch and drill and split and crush the tooth, and tear and slash its ulcerations, and pull out the nerve, and dig out fragments of bone; and she wouldn't once confess that it hurt. And to this day she thinks it didn't, and I have not a doubt that she is nine-tenths right, and that her Christian-Science faith did her better service than she could have gotten out of cocaine.

There is an account of a boy who got broken all up into small bits by an accident, but said over the Scientific Statement of Being, or some of the other incantations, and got well and sound without having suffered any real pain and without the intrusion of a surgeon.

Also, there is an account of the restoration to perfect health, in a single night, of a fatally injured *horse*, by the application of Christian Science. I can stand a good deal, but I recognize that the ice is getting thin, here. That horse had as many as fifty claims; how could *he* demonstrate over them? Could he do the All-Good, Good-Good, Good-Gracious, Liver, Bones, Truth, All down but Nine, Set them up on the Other Alley? Could he intone the Scientific Statement of Being? Now, could he? Wouldn't it give him a relapse? Let us draw the line at horses. Horses and furniture.

There is plenty of other testimonies in the magazine, but these quoted samples will answer. They show the kind of trade the Science is driving. Now we come back to the question, Does the Science kill a patient here and there and now and then? We must concede it. Does it compensate for this? I am persuaded that it can make a plausible showing in that direction. For instance: when it lays its hand upon a soldier who has suffered thirty years of helpless torture and makes him whole in body and mind, what is the actual sum of that achievement? This, I think: that it has restored to life a subject who had essentially died ten deaths a year for thirty years, and each of them a long and painful one. But for its interference that man in the three years which have since elapsed, would have essentially died thirty times more. There are thousands of young people in the land who are now ready to enter upon a life - long death similar to that man's. Every time the Science captures one of these and secures to him life-long immunity from imagination-manufactured disease, it may plausibly claim that in his person it has saved three hundred lives. Meantime, it will kill a man every now and then. But no matter, it will still be ahead on the credit side.

NOTE.—I have received several letters (two from educated and ostensibly intelligent persons), which contained, in substance, this protest: "I don't object to men and women chancing their lives with these people, but it is a burning shame that the law should allow them to trust their helpless little children in their deadly hands." Isn't it touching? Isn't it deep? Isn't it modest? It is as if the person said: "I know that to a parent his child is the core of his heart, the apple of his eye, a possession so dear, so precious that he will trust its life in no hands but those which he believes, with all his soul, to be the very best and the very safest, but it is a burning shame that the law does not require him to come to *me* to ask what kind of healer I will allow him to call." The public is merely a multiplied "me."—M. T.

CHAPTER VII[1]

"We consciously declare that *Science and Health, with Key to the Scriptures*, was foretold, *as well as its author*, Mary Baker Eddy, in Revelation x. She is the 'mighty angel,' or God's highest thought to this age (verse 1), giving us the spiritual interpretation of the Bible in the 'little book *open*' (verse 2). Thus we prove that Christian Science is the second coming of Christ—Truth—Spirit."— *Lecture by Dr. George Tomkins, D.D. C.S.*

THERE you have it in plain speech. She is the mighty angel; she is the divinely and officially sent bearer of God's highest thought. For the present, she *brings* the Second Advent. We must expect that before she has been in her grave fifty years she will be regarded by her following as having been *herself* the Second Advent. She is already worshipped, and we must expect this feeling to spread, territorially, and also to deepen in intensity.[2]

[1] Written in Europe in 1899, but not hitherto published in book form.—M. T.

[2] After *raising a dead child to life*, the disciple who did it writes an account of her performance to Mrs. Eddy, and

Particularly after her death; for then, as any one can foresee, Eddy-Worship will be taught in the Sunday-schools and pulpits of the cult. Already whatever she puts her trade-mark on, though it be only a memorial-spoon, is holy and is eagerly and gratefully bought by the disciple, and becomes a fetich in his house. I say bought, for the Boston Christian-Science Trust gives nothing away; everything it has is for sale. And the terms are cash; and not only cash, but cash in advance. Its god is Mrs. Eddy first, then the Dollar. Not a spiritual Dollar, but a real one. From end to end of the Christian-Science literature not a single (material) thing in the world is conceded to be real, except the Dollar. But all through and through its advertisements that reality is eagerly and persistently recognized.

The Dollar is hunted down in all sorts of ways; the Christian-Science Mother-Church and

closes it thus: "My prayer daily is to be more spiritual. that I may do more as you would have me do, . . . and may we all love you more, and so live it that the world may know that the Christ is come."—*Printed in the Concord, N. H., Independent Statesman, March* 9, 1899. If this is not worship. it is a good imitation of it.—M. T.

Bargain - Counter in Boston peddles all kinds
of spiritual wares to the faithful, and always
on the one condition — *cash*, cash in advance.
The Angel of the Apocalypse could not go there
and get a copy of his own pirated book on credit. Many, many precious Christian - Science
things are to be had there—for cash: Bible Lessons; Church Manual; C. S. Hymnal; History
of the building of the Mother-Church; lot of
Sermons; Communion Hymn, "Saw Ye My
Saviour," by Mrs. Eddy, half a dollar a copy,
"words used by special permission of Mrs.
Eddy." Also we have Mrs. Eddy's and the
Angel's little Bible-Annex in eight styles of
binding at eight kinds of war-prices; among
these a sweet thing in "levant, divinity circuit,
leather lined to edge, round corners, gold edge,
silk sewed, each, *prepaid*, $6," and if you take a
million you get them a shilling cheaper—that
is to say, "prepaid, $5.75." Also we have Mrs.
Eddy's *Miscellaneous Writings*, at 'andsome
big prices, the divinity-circuit style heading the
extortions, shilling discount where you take an
edition. Next comes *Christ and Christmas*, by
the fertile Mrs. Eddy—a *poem*—would God I

could see it!—price $3, cash in advance. Then
follow five more books by Mrs. Eddy, at high-
wayman's rates, some of them in "leatherette
covers," some of them in "pebbled cloth," with
divinity-circuit, compensation-balance, twin-
screw, and the other modern improvements;
and at the same bargain-counter can be had
The Christian Science Journal.

Christian-Science literary discharges are a
monopoly of the Mother-Church Headquarters
Factory in Boston; none genuine without the
trade-mark of the Trust. You must apply
there and not elsewhere.[1]

The Trust has still other sources of income.
Mrs. Eddy is president (and proprietor) of the
Trust's Metaphysical College in Boston, where
the student of C. S. healing learns the game by
a three weeks' course, and pays *one hundred
dollars* for it.[2]   And I have a case among my

[1] *February,* 1903. I applied last month, but they returned my money, and wouldn't play. We are not on
speaking terms now.—M. T.

[2] An error. For one hundred, read *three* hundred. That
was for twelve brief lessons. But this cheapness only
lasted until the end of 1888—fourteen years ago. [I am
making this note in December, 1902]. Mrs. Eddy—over

From a stereograph, copyright, 1906, by H. C. White Co., N. Y.

THE FIRST CHURCH OF CHRIST, SCIENTIST, BOSTON, MASS.,
KNOWN AS THE MOTHER-CHURCH

statistics where the student had a three weeks'
course and paid *three* hundred for it.

The Trust does love the Dollar, when it isn't
a spiritual one.

In order to force the sale of Mrs. Eddy's
Bible-Annex, no healer, Metaphysical-College-
bred or other, is allowed to practise the game
unless he possesses a copy of that book.   That
means a large and constantly augmenting income for the Trust.   No C. S. family would
consider itself loyal or pious or pain-proof without an Annex or two in the house.   That means
an income for the Trust, in the near future, of
millions; not thousands—millions a year.

No member, young or old, of a branch Christian - Scientist church can acquire and retain
membership in the Mother - Church unless he
pay "capitation tax" (of "not less than a dollar," say the By-Laws) to the Boston Trust
every year.   That means an income for the
Trust, in the near future, of—let us venture to
say—millions more per year.

her own signature—then made a change; the new terms
were three hundred dollars for *seven* lessons. See *Christian Science Journal* for December, 1888.—M. T.

It is a reasonably safe guess that in America in 1920 there will be ten million[1] Christian Scientists, and three millions in Great Britain; that these figures will be trebled in 1930; that in America in 1920 the Christian Scientists will be a political force, in 1930 politically formidable, and in 1940 the governing power in the Republic—to remain that, permanently. And I think it a reasonable guess that the Trust (which is already in our day pretty brusque in its ways) will then be the most insolent and unscrupulous and tyrannical politico-religious master that has dominated a people since the palmy days of the Inquisition. And a stronger master than the strongest of bygone times, because this one will have a financial strength not dreamed of by any predecessor; as effective a concentration of irresponsible power as any predecessor has had;[2] in the railway, the telegraph, and the subsidized newspaper, better

[1] Written in 1899. It is intended to include men, women, and children. Although the calculation was based upon inflated statistics, I believe to-day that it is not far out.—M. T.

[2] It can be put stronger than that and still be true.—M. T.

facilities for watching and managing his empire than any predecessor has had; and, after a generation or two, he will probably divide Christendom with the Catholic Church.

The Roman Church has a perfect organization, and it has an effective centralization of power—but not of its cash. Its multitude of Bishops are rich, but their riches remain in large measure in their own hands. They collect from two hundred millions of people, but they keep the bulk of the result at home. The Boston Pope of by-and-by will draw his dollar-a-head capitation-tax from three hundred millions of the human race,[1] and the Annex and the rest of his book - shop stock will fetch in as much more; and his Metaphysical Colleges, the annual pilgrimage to Mrs. Eddy's tomb, from all over the world—admission, the Christian - Science Dollar (payable in advance)— purchases of consecrated glass beads, candles,

[1] In that day by force; it is voluntary now. In the new half of this book the reader will perceive that all imaginable compulsions are possible under the Mother-Church's body of Laws. To-day more is expected than the one dollar. This is indicated in the wording of the By-Law. Much more comes, from many members.—M. T.

memorial spoons, aureoled chromo‑portraits and bogus autographs of Mrs. Eddy; cash offerings at her shrine—no crutches of cured cripples received, and no imitations of miraculously restored broken legs and necks allowed to be hung up except when made out of the Holy Metal and proved by fire-assay; cash for miracles worked at the tomb: these money-sources, with a thousand to be yet invented and ambushed upon the devotee, will bring the annual increment well up above a billion. And nobody but the Trust will have the handling of it. In that day, the Trust will monopolize the manufacture and sale of the Old and New Testaments as well as the Annex, and raise their price to Annex rates, and compel the devotee to buy (for even to-day a healer has to have the Annex *and* the Scriptures or he is not allowed to work the game), and that will bring several hundred million dollars more. In those days, the Trust will have an income approaching five million dollars a day, and no expenses to be taken out of it; no taxes to pay, and *no charities to support.* That last detail should not be lightly passed over by the reader ; it is well entitled to attention.

No charities to support. No, nor even to contribute to. One searches in vain the Trust's advertisements and the utterances of its organs for any suggestion that it spends a penny on orphans, widows, discharged prisoners, hospitals, ragged schools, night missions, city missions, libraries, old people's homes, or any other object that appeals to a human being's purse through his heart.[1]

I have hunted, hunted, and hunted, by correspondence and otherwise, and have not yet got upon the track of a farthing that the Trust has spent upon any worthy object. Nothing makes a Scientist so uncomfortable as to ask him if he knows of a case where Christian Science has spent money on a benevolence, either among its own adherents or elsewhere. He is obliged to say " No." And then one discovers that the person questioned has been

[1] In two years (1898-99) the membership of the Established Church in England gave voluntary contributions amounting to seventy-three millions of dollars to the Church's benevolent enterprises. Churches that give have nothing to hide.—M. T.

6

asked the question many times before, and that it is getting to be a sore subject with him. Why a sore subject? Because he has written his chiefs and asked with high confidence for an answer that will confound these questioners—and the chiefs did not reply. He has written again, and then again—not with confidence, but humbly, now—and has begged for defensive ammunition in the voice of supplication. A reply does at last come—to this effect: "We must have faith in Our Mother, and rest content in the conviction that whatever She[1] does with the money it is in accordance with orders from Heaven, for She does no act of any kind without first 'demonstrating over' it."

That settles it—as far as the disciple is concerned. His mind is satisfied with that answer; he gets down his Annex and does an incantation or two, and that mesmerizes his spirit and puts *that* to sleep—brings it peace. Peace and comfort and joy, until some inquirer punctures the old sore again.

Through friends in America I asked some

[1] I may be introducing the capital S a little early—still, it is on its way.—M. T.

questions, and in some cases got definite and informing answers; in other cases the answers were not definite and not valuable. To the question, "Does any of the money go to charities?" the answer from an authoritative source was: "No, *not in the sense usually conveyed by this word.*" (The italics are mine.) That answer is cautious. But definite, I think—utterly and unassailably definite — although quite Christian-Scientifically foggy in its phrasing. Christian-Science testimony is generally foggy, generally diffuse, generally garrulous. The writer was aware that the first word in his phrase answered the question which I was asking, but he could not help adding nine dark words. Meaningless ones, unless explained by him. It is quite likely, as intimated by him, that Christian Science has invented a new class of objects to apply the word "charity" to, but without an explanation we cannot know what they are. We quite easily and naturally and confidently guess that they are in all cases objects which will return five hundred per cent. on the Trust's investment in them, but guessing is not knowledge; it is merely, in this case, a sort of nine-tenths certainty deducible from what we think we know of the Trust's trade principles and its sly and furtive and shifty ways.[1]

Sly? Deep? Judicious? The Trust understands its business. The Trust does not give itself away. It defeats all the attempts of us impertinents to get at its trade secrets. To this day, after all our diligence, we have not been able to get it to confess what it does with the money. It does not even let its own disciples find out. All it says is, that the matter has been "demonstrated over." Now and then a lay Scientist says, with a grateful exultation, that Mrs. Eddy is enormously rich, but he stops there; as to whether any of the money goes to other charities or not, he is obliged to admit that he does not know. However, the Trust is composed of human beings; and this justifies the conjecture that if it had a charity

[1] *February,* 1903. A letter has come to me, this month, from a lady who says that while she was living in Boston, a few years ago, she visited the Mother-Church and offices and had speech with Judge Septimius J. Hanna, the "first reader," who "stated positively that the Church, as a body, does no philanthropic work whatever."—M. T.

on its list which it was proud of, we should soon
hear of it.

"Without money and without price." Those
used to be the terms. Mrs. Eddy's Annex can-
cels them. The motto of Christian Science is,
"The laborer is worthy of his hire." And now
that it has been "demonstrated over," we find
its spiritual meaning to be, "Do anything and
everything your hand may find to do; and
charge cash for it, and collect the money in advance." The Scientist has on his tongue's end
a cut-and-dried, Boston-supplied set of rather
lean arguments, whose function is to show that
it is a Heaven-commanded *duty* to do this, and
that the croupiers of the game have no choice
but to obey.[1]

[1] *February*, 1903. If I seem to be charging any one outside of the Trust with an exaggerated appetite for money,
I have not meant to do it. The exactions of the ordinary
C. S. "healer" are not exorbitant. If I have prejudices
against the Trust—and I do feel that I have—they do
not extend to the lay membership. "The laborer is
worthy of his hire." And is entitled to receive it, too,
and charge his own price (when he is laboring in a lawful
calling). The great surgeon charges a thousand dollars,
and no one is justified in objecting to it. The great
preacher and teacher in religion receives a large salary,
and is entitled to it; Henry Ward Beecher's was twenty

The Trust seems to be a reincarnation. Exodus xxxii. 4.

thousand dollars. Mrs. Eddy's Metaphysical College was chartered by the State, and she had a legal right to charge amazing prices, and she did it. She allows only a few persons to *teach* Christian Science. The calling of these teachers is not illegal. Mrs. Eddy appoints the sum their students must pay, and it is a round one; but that is no matter, since they need not come unless they want to.

But when we come to the C. S. "healer," the *practitioner*, that is another thing. He exists by the hundred; his services are prized by his C. S. patient, they are preferred above all other human help, and are thankfully paid for. As I have just remarked, his prices are not large. But there is hardly a State wherein he can lawfully practise his profession. In the name of religion, of morals, and of Christ—represented on the earth by Mrs. Eddy —he enters upon his trade a commissioned law-breaker.

A law-breaker. It is curious, but if the Second Advent should happen now, Jesus could not heal the sick in the State of New York. He could not do it lawfully; therefore He could not do it morally; therefore He could not do it at all.—M. T.

March 12, 1903. While I am reading the final proofs of this book, the following letter has come to me. It is not marked private, therefore I suppose I may without impropriety insert it here, if I suppress the signature:

"DEAR SIR,—In the *North American Review* for January is the statement, in effect, that Christian Scientists give nothing to charities. It has had wide reading and is doubtless credited. To produce a true impression, it seems as if other facts should have been stated in connection.

I have no reverence for the Trust, but I am
not lacking in reverence for the sincerities of

"With regret for adding anything to the burden of
letters from strangers, I am impelled to write what I
know from a limited acquaintance in the sect. I am not
connected with it myself.

"The charity freely given by individual practitioners,
so far as I know it, is at least equal to that of regular
physicians. Charges are made with much more than
equal consideration of the means of the patient. Of
course druggists' bills and the enormous expenses involved in the employment of a trained nurse, exist in
small degree or not at all.

"As to organized charities: It is hard to find one where
the most intelligent laborers in it feel that they are reaching the root of an evil. They are putting a few plasters
on a body of disease. Complaint is made, too, that the
machinery, by which of necessity systematic charity must
be administered, prevents the personal friendliness and
sympathy which should pervade it throughout.

"Christian Science claims to be able to abolish the need
for charity. The results of drunkenness make great demands upon the charitable. But the principle of Christian Science takes away the desire for strong drink. If
sexual propensities were dominated, not only by reason,
but by Christian love for both the living and the unborn
—Christian Science is emphatic on this subject—many
existing charitable societies would have no reason to be.
So far as Christian Science prevents disease, the need for
hospitals is lessened. Not only illness, but poverty, is a
subject for the practice of Christian Science. If this evil
were prevented there would be no occasion to alleviate
its results.

the lay membership of the new Church. There
is every evidence that the lay members are
entirely sincere in their faith, and I think sincerity is always entitled to honor and respect,
let the inspiration of the sincerity be what it
may. Zeal and sincerity can carry a new religion further than any other missionary except
fire and sword, and I believe that the new religion will conquer the half of Christendom in a
hundred years. I am not intending this as a
compliment to the human race; I am merely
stating an opinion. And yet I think that perhaps it *is* a compliment to the race. I keep in
mind that saying of an orthodox preacher—
quoted further back. He conceded that this
new Christianity frees its possessor's life from
*frets, fears, vexations, bitterness, and all sorts of
imagination-propagated maladies and pains, and
fills his world with sunshine and his heart with*

"The faith, hope, and love which the few Christian
Scientists I have known have lived and radiated, made
conditions needing organized charity vanish before them.

"With renewed apology for intrusion upon one whose
own 'Uncle Silas' was 'loved back' to sanity,

"I am, etc., etc.

"WOBURN, MASS.,
"*March* 10, 1903."

gladness. If Christian Science, with this stupendous equipment—and final salvation added —cannot win half the Christian globe, I must be badly mistaken in the make-up of the human race.

I think the Trust will be handed down like the other Papacy, and will always know how to handle its limitless cash. It will press the button; the zeal, the energy, the sincerity, the enthusiasm of its countless vassals will do the rest.

THE power which a man's imagination has over his body to heal it or make it sick is a force which none of us is born without. The first man had it, the last one will possess it. If left to himself, a man is most likely to use only the mischievous half of the force—the half which invents imaginary ailments for him and cultivates them; and if he is one of these very wise people, he is quite likely to scoff at the beneficent half of the force and deny its existence. And so, to heal or help that man, *two* imaginations are required: his own and some outsider's. The outsider, B, must imagine that *his* incantations are the healing-power that is curing A, and A must imagine that this is so. I think it is not so, at all; but no matter, the cure is effected, and that is the main thing. The outsider's work is unquestionably valuable; so valuable that it may fairly be likened to the essential work performed by the engineer when he handles the throttle and turns on the steam; the actual power is lodged exclusively in the engine, but if the engine were left alone it would never start of itself. Whether the engineer be named Jim, or Bob, or Tom, it is all one—his services are necessary, and he is entitled to such wage as he can get you to pay. Whether he be named Christian Scientist, or Mental Scientist, or Mind Curist, or King's-Evil Expert, or Hypnotist, it is all one; he is merely the Engineer; he simply turns on the same old steam and the engine does the whole work.

The Christian-Scientist engineer drives exactly the same trade as the other engineers, yet he out-prospers the whole of them put together.[1]

Is it because he has captured the takingest name? I think that that is only a small part of it. I think that the secret of his high prosperity lies elsewhere.

The Christian Scientist has *organized* the business. Now that was certainly a gigantic idea. Electricity, in limitless volume, has ex-

[1] *February*, 1903. As I have already remarked in a foot-note, the Scientist claims that he uses a force not used by any of the others.—M. T.

isted in the air and the rocks and the earth and everywhere since time began—and was going to waste all the while. In our time we have *organized* that scattered and wandering force and set it to work, and backed the business with capital, and concentrated it in few and competent hands, and the results are as we see.

The Christian Scientist has taken a force which has been lying idle in every member of the human race since time began, and has organized it, and backed the business with capital, and concentrated it at Boston headquarters in the hands of a small and very competent Trust, and there are results.

Therein lies the promise that this monopoly is going to extend its commerce wide in the earth. I think that if the business were conducted in the loose and disconnected fashion customary with such things, it would achieve but little more than the modest prosperity usually secured by unorganized great moral and commercial ventures; but I believe that so long as this one remains compactly organized and closely concentrated in a Trust, the spread of its dominion will continue.

CHAPTER IX

FOUR years ago I wrote the preceding chapters.[1] I was assured by the wise that Christian Science was a fleeting craze and would soon perish. This prompt and all-competent stripe of prophet is always to be had in the market at ground-floor rates. He does not stop to load, or consider, or take aim, but lets fly just as he stands. Facts are nothing to him, he has no use for such things; he works wholly by inspiration. And so, when he is asked why he considers a new movement a passing fad and quickly perishable, he finds himself unprepared with a reason and is more or less embarrassed. For a moment. Only for a moment. Then he waylays the first spectre of a reason that goes flitting through the desert places of his mind, and is at once serene again and ready for conflict. Serene and confident. Yet he should not be so, since he has

[1] That is to say, in 1898.

had no chance to examine his catch, and cannot know whether it is going to help his contention or damage it.

The impromptu reason furnished by the early prophets of whom I have spoken was this:

"There is nothing *to* Christian Science; there is nothing about it that appeals to the intellect; its market will be restricted to the unintelligent, the mentally inferior, the people who do not think."

They called that a reason why the cult would not flourish and endure. It seems the equivalent of saying:

"There is no money in tinware; there is nothing about it that appeals to the rich; its market will be restricted to the poor."

It is like bringing forward the best reason in the world why Christian Science should flourish and live, and then blandly offering it as a reason why it should sicken and die.

That reason was furnished me by the complacent and unfrightened prophets four years ago, and it has been furnished me again to-day. If conversions to new religions or to old ones

were in any considerable degree achieved
through the intellect, the aforesaid reason
would be sound and sufficient, no doubt; the
inquirer into Christian Science might go away
unconvinced and unconverted. But we all
know that conversions are seldom made in that
way; that such a thing as a serious and pains-
taking and fairly competent inquiry into the
claims of a religion or of a political dogma is a
rare occurrence; and that the vast mass of men
and women are far from being capable of making such an examination. They are not capable, for the reason that their minds, howsoever good they may be, are not trained for such
examinations. The mind not trained for that
work is no more competent to do it than are
lawyers and farmers competent to make successful clothes without learning the tailor's
trade. There are seventy-five million men and
women among us who do not know how to cut
out and make a dress-suit, and they would not
think of trying; yet they all think they can
competently think out a political or religious
scheme without any apprenticeship to the business, and many of them believe they have act-

ually worked that miracle. But, indeed, the truth is, almost all the men and women of our nation or of any other get their religion and their politics where they get their astronomy —entirely at second hand. Being untrained, they are no more able to intelligently examine a dogma or a policy than they are to calculate an eclipse.

Men are usually competent thinkers along the lines of their specialized training only. Within these limits alone are their opinions and judgments valuable; outside of these limits they grope and are lost—usually without knowing it. In a church assemblage of five hundred persons, there will be a man or two whose trained minds can seize upon each detail of a great manufacturing scheme and recognize its value or its lack of value promptly; and can pass the details in intelligent review, section by section, and finally as a whole, and then deliver a verdict upon the scheme which cannot be flippantly set aside nor easily answered. And there will be one or two other men there who can do the same thing with a great and complicated educational project; and one or two others who can do the like with a large scheme for applying electricity in a new and unheard-of way; and one or two others who can do it with a showy scheme for revolutionizing the scientific world's accepted notions regarding geology. And so on, and so on. But the manufacturing experts will not be competent to examine the educational scheme intelligently, and their opinion about it would not be valuable; neither of these two groups will be able to understand and pass upon the electrical scheme; none of these three batches of experts will be able to understand and pass upon the geological revolution; and probably not one man in the entire lot will be competent to examine, capably, the intricacies of a political or religious scheme, new or old, and deliver a judgment upon it which any one need regard as precious.

There you have the top crust. There will be four hundred and seventy-five men and women present who can draw upon their training and deliver incontrovertible judgments concerning cheese, and leather, and cattle, and hardware, and soap, and tar, and candles, and patent medicines, and dreams, and apparitions, and

garden truck, and cats, and baby food, and
warts, and hymns, and time-tables, and freight-
rates, and summer resorts, and whiskey, and
law, and surgery, and dentistry, and black-
smithing, and shoemaking, and dancing, and
Huyler's candy, and mathematics, and dog
fights, and obstetrics, and music, and sausages,
and dry goods, and molasses, and railroad
stocks, and horses, and literature, and labor
unions, and vegetables, and morals, and lamb's
fries, and etiquette, and agriculture. And not
ten among the five hundred—let their minds
be ever so good and bright—will be competent,
by grace of the requisite specialized mental
training, to take hold of a complex abstraction
of any kind and make head or tail of it.

The whole five hundred are thinkers, and
they are all capable thinkers—but only within
the narrow limits of their specialized trainings.
Four hundred and ninety of them cannot competently examine either a religious plan or a
political one. A scattering few of them do examine both—that is, they think they do. With
results as precious as when I examine the nebular theory and explain it to myself.

If the four hundred and ninety got their religion through their minds, and by weighed and measured detail, Christian Science would not be a scary apparition. But they don't; they get a little of it through their minds, more of it through their feelings, and the overwhelming bulk of it through their environment.

Environment is the chief thing to be considered when one is proposing to predict the future of Christian Science. It is not the ability to reason that makes the Presbyterian, or the Baptist, or the Methodist, or the Catholic, or the Mohammedan, or the Buddhist, or the Mormon; it is *environment*. If religions were got by reasoning, we should have the extraordinary spectacle of an American family with a Presbyterian in it, and a Baptist, a Methodist, a Catholic, a Mohammedan, a Buddhist, and a Mormon. A Presbyterian family does not produce Catholic families or other religious brands, it produces its own kind; and not by intellectual processes, but by association. And so also with Mohammedanism, the cult which in our day is spreading with the sweep of a world-conflagration through the Orient, that native home of profound thought and of subtle intellectual fence, that fertile womb whence has sprung every great religion that exists. Including our own; for with all our brains we cannot invent a religion and market it.

The language of my quoted prophets recurs to us now, and we wonder to think how small a space in the world the mighty Mohammedan Church would be occupying now, if a successful trade in its line of goods had been conditioned upon an exhibit that would "appeal to the intellect" instead of to "the unintelligent, the mentally inferior, the people who do not think."

The Christian Science Church, like the Mohammedan Church, makes no embarrassing appeal to the intellect, has no occasion to do it, and can get along quite well without it.

Provided. Provided what? That it can secure that thing which is worth two or three hundred thousand times more than an "appeal to the intellect"—an *environment.* Can it get that? Will it be a menace to regular Christianity if it gets that? Is it time for regular Christianity to get alarmed? Or shall regular

Christianity smile a smile and turn over and take another nap? Won't it be wise and proper for regular Christianity to do the old way, the customary way, the historical way—lock the stable-door after the horse is gone? Just as Protestantism has smiled and nodded this long time (while the alert and diligent Catholic was slipping in and capturing the public schools), and is now beginning to hunt around for the key when it is too late?

Will Christian Science get a chance to show its wares? It has *already* secured that chance. Will it flourish and spread and prosper if it shall create for itself the one thing essential to those conditions—an environment? It has *already* created an environment. There are families of Christian Scientists in every community in America, and each family is a factory; each family turns out a Christian Science product at the customary intervals, and contributes it to the Cause in the only way in which contributions of recruits to Churches are ever made on a large scale—by the puissant forces of personal contact and association. Each family is an agency for the Cause, and makes converts among the neighbors, and starts some more factories.

Four years ago there were six Christian Scientists in a certain town that I am acquainted with; a year ago there were two hundred and fifty there; they have built a church, and its membership now numbers four hundred. This has all been quietly done; done without frenzied revivals, without uniforms, brass bands, street parades, corner oratory, or any of the other customary persuasions to a godly life. Christian Science, like Mohammedanism, is "restricted" to the "unintelligent, the people who do not think." There lies the danger. It makes Christian Science formidable. It is "restricted" to ninety-nine one-hundredths of the human race, and must be reckoned with by regular Christianity. And will be, as soon as it is too late.

BOOK II

THERE were remarkable things about the stranger called the Man-Mystery—things so very extraordinary that they monopolized attention and made *all* of him seem extraordinary; but this was not so, the most of his qualities being of the common, every-day size and like anybody else's. It was curious. He was of the ordinary stature, and had the ordinary aspects; yet in him were hidden such strange contradictions and disproportions! He was majestically fearless and heroic; he had the strength of thirty men and the daring of thirty thousand; handling armies, organizing states, administering governments—these were pastimes to him; he publicly and ostentatiously accepted the human race at its own valuation—as demigods—and privately and successfully dealt with it at quite another and juster valuation—as children and slaves; his ambitions were stupendous, and his dreams had no commerce with the humble plain, but moved with the cloud-rack among the snow-summits. These features of him were, indeed, extraordinary, but the rest of him was ordinary and usual. He was so mean-minded, in the matter of jealousy, that it was thought he was descended from a god; he was vain in little ways, and had a pride in trivialities; he doted on ballads about moonshine and bruised hearts; in education he was deficient, he was indifferent to literature, and knew nothing of art; he was dumb upon all subjects but one, indifferent to all except that one—the Nebular Theory. Upon that one his flow of words was full and free, he was a geyser. The official astronomers disputed his facts and derided his views, and said that he had invented both, they not being findable in any of the books. But many of the laity, who wanted their nebulosities fresh, admired his doctrine and adopted it, and it attained to great prosperity in spite of the hostility of the experts."—*The Legend of the Man-Mystery*, ch. i.

CHAPTER I

JANUARY, 1903. When we do not know a
public man personally, we guess him out by the
facts of his career. When it is Washington, we
all arrive at about one and the same result. We
agree that his words and his acts clearly inter-
pret his character to us, and that they never
leave us in doubt as to the motives whence the
words and acts proceeded. It is the same with
Joan of Arc, it is the same with two or three or
five or six others among the immortals. But
in the matter of motives and of a few details of
character we agree to disagree upon Napoleon,
Cromwell, and all the rest; and to this list we
must add Mrs. Eddy. I think we can peacefully agree as to two or three extraordinary
features of her make-up, but not upon the
other features of it. We cannot peacefully
agree as to her motives, therefore her character
must remain crooked to some of us and straight
to the others.

No matter, she is interesting enough without
an amicable agreement. In several ways she
is the most interesting woman that ever lived,
and the most extraordinary. The same may
be said of her career, and the same may be said
of its chief result. She started from nothing.
Her enemies charge that she surreptitiously
took from Quimby a peculiar system of healing
which was mind-cure with a Biblical basis.
She and her friends deny that she took anything from him. This is a matter which we
can discuss by-and-by. Whether she took it
or invented it, it was—materially—a sawdust
mine when she got it, and she has turned it
into a Klondike; its spiritual dock had next
to no custom, if any at all: from it she has
launched a world-religion which has now six
hundred and sixty - three churches, and she
charters a new one every four days. When
we do not know a person — and also when
we do — we have to judge his size by the
size and nature of his achievements, as compared with the achievements of others in his
special line of business — there is no other
way. Measured by this standard, it is thir-

teen hundred years since the world has produced any one who could reach up to Mrs.
Eddy's waistbelt.

Figuratively speaking, Mrs. Eddy is already
as tall as the Eiffel tower. She is adding surprisingly to her stature every day. It is quite
within the probabilities that a century hence
she will be the most imposing figure that has
cast its shadow across the globe since the inau-
guration of our era. I grant that after saying
these strong things, it is necessary that I offer
some details calculated to satisfactorily demonstrate the proportions which I have claimed
for her. I will do that presently; but before
exhibiting the matured *sequoia gigantea*, I believe it will be best to exhibit the sprout from
which it sprang. It may save the reader from
making miscalculations. The person who imagines that a Big Tree sprout is bigger than
other kinds of sprouts is quite mistaken.
It is the ordinary thing; it makes no show,
it compels no notice, it hasn't a detectible
quality in it that entitles it to attention, or
suggests the future giant its sap is suckling.
That is the kind of sprout Mrs. Eddy was.

From her childhood days up to where she was running a half-century a close race and gaining on it, she was most humanly commonplace.

She is the witness I am drawing this from. She has revealed it in her autobiography. Not intentionally, of course — I am not claiming that. An autobiography is the most treacherous thing there is. It lets out every secret its author is trying to keep; it lets the truth shine unobstructed through every harmless little deception he tries to play; it pitilessly exposes him as a tin hero worshipping himself as Big Metal every time he tries to do the modest-unconsciousness act before the reader. This is not guessing; I am speaking from autobiographical personal experience; I was never able to refrain from mentioning, with a studied casualness that could deceive none but the most incautious reader, that an ancestor of mine was sent ambassador to Spain by Charles I., nor that in a remote branch of my family there exists a claimant to an earldom, nor that an uncle of mine used to own a dog that was descended from the dog that was in the Ark;

and at the same time I was never able to persuade myself to call a gibbet by its right name
when accounting for other ancestors of mine,
but always spoke of it as the "platform"—
puerilely intimating that they were out lecturing when it happened.

It is Mrs. Eddy over again. As regards her
minor half, she is as commonplace as the rest
of us. Vain of trivial things all the first half of
her life, and still vain of them at seventy and
recording them with naïve satisfaction—even
rescuing some early rhymes of hers of the sort
that we all scribble in the innocent days of our
youth—rescuing them and printing them without pity or apology, just as the weakest and
commonest of us do in our gray age. More—
she still frankly admires them; and in her introduction of them profanely confers upon them
the holy name of "poetry." Sample:

> " And laud the land whose talents rock
>   The cradle of her power,
>   And wreaths are twined round Plymouth Rock
>   From erudition's bower."

> " Minerva's silver sandals still
>   Are loosed and not effete."

You note it is not a shade above the thing which all human beings churn out in their youth.

You would not think that in a little wee primer — for that is what the *Autobiography* is—a person with a tumultuous career of seventy years behind her could find room for two or three pages of padding of this kind, but such is the case. She evidently puts narrative together with difficulty and is not at home in it, and is glad to have something ready-made to fill in with. Another sample:

" Here fame-honored Hickory rears his bold form,
And bears[1] a brave breast to the lightning and storm,
While Palm, Bay, and Laurel in classical glee,
Chase Tulip, Magnolia, and fragrant Fringe-tree."

Vivid? You can fairly see those trees galloping around. That she could still treasure up, and print, and manifestly admire those Poems, indicates that the most daring and masculine and masterful woman that has appeared in the earth in centuries has the same soft, girly-girly places in her that the rest of us have.

[1] Meaning *bares?* I think so.—M. T.

When it comes to selecting her ancestors she is still human, natural, vain, commonplace—as commonplace as I am myself when I am sorting ancestors for my autobiography. She combs out some creditable Scots, and labels them and sets them aside for use, not overlooking the one to whom Sir William Wallace gave "a heavy sword encased in a brass scabbard," and naïvely explaining *which* Sir William Wallace it was, lest we get the wrong one by the hassock;[1] this is the one "from whose patriotism and bravery comes that heart-stirring air, 'Scots wha hae wi' Wallace bled.'" Hannah More was related to her ancestors. She explains who Hannah More was.

Whenever a person informs us who Sir William Wallace was, or who wrote "Hamlet," or where the Declaration of Independence was fought, it fills us with a suspicion wellnigh amounting to conviction, that that person would not suspect us of being so empty of knowledge if he wasn't suffering from the same "claim" himself. Then we turn to page 20 of

[1] I am in some doubt as to what a hassock is, but any way it sounds good.—M. T.

8

the *Autobiography* and happen upon this passage, and that hasty suspicion stands rebuked:

" I gained book-knowledge with far less labor than is usually requisite. At ten years of age I was as familiar with Lindley Murray's Grammar as with the Westminster Catechism; and the latter I had to repeat every Sunday. My favorite studies were Natural Philosophy, Logic, and Moral Science. From my brother Albert I received lessons in the ancient tongues, Hebrew, Greek, and Latin."

You catch your breath in astonishment, and feel again and still again the pang of tnat rebuke. But then your eye falls upon the next sentence but one, and the pain passes away and you set up the suspicion again with evil satisfaction:

" *After my discovery of Christian Science, most of the knowledge I had gleaned from school-books vanished like a dream.*"

That disappearance accounts for much in her miscellaneous writings. As I was saying, she

handles her "ancestral shadows," as she calls
them, just as I do mine. It is remarkable.
When she runs across "a relative of my Grandfather Baker, General Henry Knox, of Revolutionary fame," she sets him down; when she
finds another good one, "the late Sir John
Macneill, in the line of my Grandfather Baker's
family," she sets him down, and remembers
that he "was prominent in British politics, and
at one time held the position of ambassador to
Persia"; when she discovers that her grand-
parents "were likewise connected with Captain
John Lovewell, whose gallant leadership and
death in the Indian troubles of 1722–25 caused
that prolonged contest to be known historically
as Lovewell's War," she sets the Captain down;
when it turns out that a cousin of her grand-
mother "was John Macneill, the New Hampshire general, who fought at Lundy's Lane and
won distinction in 1814 at the battle of Chippewa," she catalogues the General. (And tells
where Chippewa was.) And then she skips *all*
her platform people; never mentions one of
them. It shows that she is just as human as
any of us.

Yet, after all, there is something very touching in her pride in these worthy small-fry, and something large and fine in her modesty in not caring to remember that their kinship to her can confer no distinction upon her, whereas her mere mention of their names has conferred upon them a fadeless earthly immortality.

CHAPTER II

WHEN she wrote this little biography her great life-work had already been achieved, she was become renowned; to multitudes of reverent disciples she was a sacred personage, a familiar of God, and His inspired channel of communication with the human race. Also, to them these following things were facts, and not doubted:

She had written a Bible in middle age, and had published it; she had recast it, enlarged it, and published it again; she had not stopped there, but had enlarged it further, polished its phrasing, improved its form, and published it yet again. It was at last become a compact, grammatical, dignified, and workman-like body of literature. This was good training, persistent training; and in all arts it is training that brings the art to perfection. We are now confronted with one of the most teasing and baffling riddles of Mrs. Eddy's history—a riddle which may be formulated thus:

How is it that a primitive literary gun which began as a hundred-yard flint-lock smooth-bore muzzle-loader, and in the course of forty years has acquired one notable improvement after another—percussion cap; fixed cartridge; rifled barrel; efficiency at half a mile—how is it that such a gun, sufficiently good on an elephant-hunt (Christian Science) from the beginning, and growing better and better all the time during forty years, has *always* collapsed back to its original flint-lock estate the moment the huntress trained it on any other creature than an elephant?

Something more than a generation ago Mrs. Eddy went out with her flint-lock on the rabbit-range, and this was a part of the result:

"After his decease, and a severe casualty deemed fatal by skilful physicians, we discovered that the Principle of all healing and the law that governs it is God, a divine Principle, and a spiritual not material law, and regained health."—Preface to *Science and Health*, first revision, 1883.

N. B. Not from the book *itself;* from the *Preface.*

You will notice the awkwardness of that English. If you should carry that paragraph up to the Supreme Court of the United States in order to find out for good and all whether the fatal casualty happened to the dead man—as the paragraph almost asserts—or to some person or persons not even hinted at in the paragraph, the Supreme Court would be obliged to say that the evidence established nothing with certainty except that *there had been a casualty*—victim not known.

The context thinks it explains who the victim was, but it does nothing of the kind. It furnishes some guessing-material of a sort which enables you to infer that it was "we" that suffered the mentioned injury, but if you should carry the language to a court you would not be able to prove that it necessarily meant that. "We" are Mrs. Eddy; a funny little affectation. She replaced it later with the more dignified third person.

The quoted paragraph is from Mrs. Eddy's preface to the first revision of *Science and Health* (1883). Sixty-four pages further along —in the body of the book (the elephant-range), she went out with that same flint-lock and got this following result. Its English is very nearly as straight and clean and competent as is the English of the latest revision of *Science and Health* after the gun has been improved from smooth-bore musket up to globe-sighted, long-distance rifle:

"Man controlled by his Maker has no physical suffering. His body is harmonious, his days are multiplying instead of diminishing, he is journeying towards Life instead of death, and bringing out the new man and crucifying the old affections, cutting them off in every material direction until he learns the utter supremacy of Spirit and yields obedience thereto."

In the latest revision of *Science and Health* (1902), the perfected gun furnishes the following. The English is clean, compact, dignified, almost perfect. But it is observable that it is not prominently better than it is in the above paragraph, which was a product of the primitive flint-lock:

" How unreasonable is the belief that we are

wearing out life and hastening to death, and at the same time we are communing with immortality? If the departed are in rapport with mortality, or matter, they are not spiritual, but must still be mortal, sinful, suffering, and dying. Then wherefore look to them—even were communication possible—for proofs of immortality and accept them as oracles?"—*Edition of* 1902, *page* 78.

With the above paragraphs compare these that follow. It is Mrs. Eddy writing—after a good long twenty years of pen-practice. Compare also with the alleged Poems already quoted. The prominent characteristic of the Poems is affectation, artificiality; their make-up is a complacent and pretentious outpour of false figures and fine writing, in the sophomoric style. The same qualities and the same style will be found, unchanged, unbettered, in these following paragraphs—after a lapse of more than fifty years, and after—as aforesaid —long literary training. The italics are mine:

1. "What plague spot or bacilli were [*sic*] gnawing [*sic*] at the heart of this metropolis . . .

and bringing it [the heart] on bended knee? Why, it was an *institute* that had entered its *vitals*—that, among other things, taught games," et cetera.—*C. S. Journal*, p. 670, article entitled " A Narrative—by Mary Baker G. Eddy."

2. "Parks sprang up [*sic*] . . . electric-cars run [*sic*] merrily through several streets, concrete sidewalks and macadamized roads dotted [*sic*] the place," et cetera.—*Ibid.*

3. "Shorn [*sic*] of its suburbs it had indeed little left to admire, save to [*sic*] such as fancy a skeleton above ground *breathing* [*sic*] slowly through a barren [*sic*] breast."—*Ibid.*

This is not English—I mean, grown-up English. But it is fifteen-year-old English, and has not grown a month since the same mind produced the Poems. The standard of the Poems and of the plague-spot-and-bacilli effort is exactly the same. It is most strange that the same intellect that worded the simple and self-contained and clean-cut paragraph beginning with " How unreasonable is the belief," should in the very same lustrum discharge upon the world such a verbal chaos as the utterance concerning that plague-spot or bacilli which were gnawing at the insides of the metropolis and bringing its heart on bended knee, thus exposing to the eye the rest of the skeleton breathing slowly through a barren breast.

The immense contrast between the legitimate English of *Science and Health* and the bastard English of Mrs. Eddy's miscellaneous work, and between the maturity of the one diction and the juvenility of the other, suggests—compels— the question, Are there *two* guns? It would seem so. Is there a poor, foolish, old, scattering flint-lock for rabbit, and a long-range, centre-driving, up-to-date Mauser-magazine for elephant? It looks like it. For it is observable that in *Science and Health* (the elephant-ground) the practice was good at the start and has remained so, and that the practice in the miscellaneous, outside, small-game field was very bad at the start and was never less bad at any later time.

I wish to say that of Mrs. Eddy I am not requiring perfect English, but only good English. No one can write perfect English and keep it up through a stretch of ten chapters. It has never been done. It was approached in the " well of

English undefiled "; it has been approached in Mrs. Eddy's Annex to that Book; it has been approached in several English grammars; I have even approached it myself; but none of us has made port.

Now, the English of *Science and Health* is good. In passages to be found in Mrs. Eddy's *Autobiography* (on pages 53, 57, 101, and 113), and on page 6 of her squalid preface to *Science and Health*, first revision, she seems to me to claim the whole and sole authorship of the book. That she wrote the *Autobiography*, and *that preface*,[1] and the Poems, and the Plague-spot-Bacilli, we are not permitted to doubt. Indeed, we know she wrote them. But the very certainty that she wrote these things compels a doubt that she wrote *Science and Health*. She is guilty of little awkwardnesses of expression in the *Autobiography* which a practised pen would hardly allow to go uncorrected in even a hasty private letter, and could not dream of passing by uncorrected in passages intended for print. But she passes them placidly by; as placidly as if she did not suspect that they were

[1] See Appendix A for it.—M. T.

offences against third-class English. I think that that placidity was born of that very un-awareness, so to speak. I will cite a few in-stances from the *Autobiography*. The italics are mine:

"I remember reading in my childhood cer-tain manuscripts containing Scriptural Sonnets, besides *other* verses and enigmas," etc. Page 7.
[On page 27.] "Many pale cripples went into the Church leaning on crutches who came out carrying them on their shoulders."

It is awkward, because at the first glance it seems to say that the cripples went in leaning on crutches which went out carrying the crip-ples on their shoulders. It would have cost her no trouble to put her "who" after her "cripples." I blame her a little; I think her proof-reader should have been shot. We may let her capital C pass, but it is another awk-wardness, for she is talking about a building, not about a religious society.

"Marriage and Parentage" [Chapter-head-ing. Page 30]. You imagine that she is going to begin a talk about her marriage and finish with some account of her father and mother. And so you will be deceived. "Marriage" was right, but "Parentage" was not the best word for the rest of the record. It refers to the birth of her own child. After a certain period of time "my babe was born." Marriage and Motherhood—Marriage and Maternity—Marriage and Product—Marriage and Dividend—either of these would have fitted the facts and made the matter clear.

"Without my knowledge he was appointed a guardian." Page 32.

She is speaking of her child. She means that a guardian *for* her child was appointed, but that isn't what she says.

"If spiritual conclusions are separated from their premises, the nexus is lost, and the argument with its rightful conclusions, becomes correspondingly obscure." Page 34.

We shall never know why she put the word "correspondingly" in there. Any fine, large word would have answered just as well: psychosuperintangibly — electroincandescently — oligarcheologically — sanchrosynchrostereoptically—any of these would have answered, any of these would have filled the void.

"His spiritual noumenon and phenomenon silenced portraiture." Page 34.

Yet she says she forgot everything she knew, when she discovered Christian Science. I realize that noumenon is a daisy; and I will not deny that I shall use it whenever I am in a company which I think I can embarrass with it; but, at the same time, I think it is out of place among friends in an autobiography. There, I think a person ought not to have anything up his sleeve. It undermines confidence. But my dissatisfaction with the quoted passage is not on account of noumenon; it is on account of the misuse of the word "silenced." You cannot silence portraiture with a noumenon; if portraiture should make a noise, a way could be found to silence it, but even then it could not be done with a noumenon. Not even with a brick, some authorities think.

"It may be that the mortal life-battle still wages," etc. Page 35.

That is clumsy. Battles do not wage, battles are waged. Mrs. Eddy has one very curious and interesting peculiarity: whenever she notices that she is chortling along without saying anything, she pulls up with a sudden "God is over us all," or some other sounding irrelevancy, and for the moment it seems to light up the whole district; then, before you can recover from the shock, she goes flitting pleasantly and meaninglessly along again, and you hurry hopefully after her, thinking you are going to get something this time; but as soon as she has led you far enough away from her turkeylet she takes to a tree. Whenever she discovers that she is getting pretty disconnected, she couples-up with an ostentatious "*But*" which has nothing to do with anything that went before or is to come after, then she hitches some empties to the train—unrelated verses from the Bible, usually—and steams out of sight and leaves you wondering how she did that clever thing. For striking instances, see bottom paragraph on page 34 and the paragraph on page 35 of her *Autobiography*. She has a purpose—a deep and dark and artful purpose—in what she is saying in the first paragraph, and you guess what it is, but that is due to your own talent, not hers; she has made it as obscure as language could do it. The other paragraph has no meaning and no discoverable intention. It is merely one of her God-over-alls. I cannot spare room for it in this place.[1]

"I beheld with ineffable awe our great Master's marvellous skill in demanding neither obedience to hygienic laws nor," etc. Page 41.

The word is loosely chosen — skill. She probably meant judgment, intuition, penetration, or wisdom.

"Naturally, my first jottings were but efforts to express in feeble diction Truth's ultimate." Page 42.

One understands what she means, but she should have been able to say what she meant—

[1] See Appendix B.—M. T.

9

at any time before she discovered Christian Science and forgot everything she knew—and after it, too. If she had put "feeble" in front of "efforts" and then left out "in" and "diction," she would have scored.

". . . its written expression increases in perfection under the guidance of the great Master." Page 43.

It is an error. Not even in those advantageous circumstances can increase be added to perfection.

"Evil is not mastered by evil; it can only be overcome with Good. This brings out the nothingness of evil, and the eternal Somethingness vindicates the Divine Principle and improves the race of Adam." Page 76.

This is too extraneous for me. That is the trouble with Mrs. Eddy when she sets out to explain an over-large exhibit: the minute you think the light is bursting upon you the candle goes out and your mind begins to wander.

"No one else can drain the cup which I have
drunk to the dregs, as the discoverer and teacher
of Christian Science." Page 47.

That is saying we cannot empty an empty
cup. We knew it before; and we know she
meant to tell us that that particular cup is going to remain empty. That is, we think that
that was the idea, but we cannot be sure. She
has a perfectly astonishing talent for putting
words together in such a way as to make
successful inquiry into their intention impossible.

She generally makes us uneasy when she begins to tune up on her fine-writing timbrel. It
carries me back to her Plague-Spot and Poetry
days, and I just dread those:

"Into mortal mind's material obliquity I
gazed and stood abashed. Blanched was the
cheek of pride. My heart bent low before the
omnipotence of Spirit, and a tint of humility
soft as the heart of a moonbeam mantled the
earth. Bethlehem and Bethany, Gethsemane
and Calvary, spoke to my chastened sense as
by the tearful lips of a babe." Page 48.

The heart of a moonbeam is a pretty enough Friendship's - Album expression — let it pass, though I do think the figure a little strained; but humility has no tint, humility has no complexion, and if it had it could not mantle the earth. A moonbeam might—I do not know— but she did not say it was the moonbeam. But let it go, I cannot decide it, she mixes me up so. A babe hasn't "tearful lips," it's its eyes. You find none of Mrs. Eddy's kind of English in *Science and Health*—not a line of it.

SETTING aside title-page, index, etc., the little *Autobiography* begins on page 7 and ends on page 130. My quotations are from the first forty pages. They seem to me to prove the presence of the 'prentice hand. The style of the forty pages is loose and feeble and 'prentice-like. The movement of the narrative is not orderly and sequential, but rambles around, and skips forward and back and here and there and yonder, 'prentice-fashion. Many a journeyman has broken up his narrative and skipped about and rambled around, but he did it for a purpose, for an advantage; there was art in it, and points to be scored by it; the observant reader perceived the game, and enjoyed it and respected it, if it was well played. But Mrs. Eddy's performance was without intention, and destitute of art. She could score no points by it on those terms, and almost any reader can see that her work was the uncalculated puttering of a novice.

In the above paragraph I have described the first third of the booklet. That third being completed, Mrs. Eddy leaves the rabbit-range, crosses the frontier, and steps out upon her far-spreading big-game territory—Christian Science—and there is an instant change! The style smartly improves, and the clumsy little technical offences disappear. In these two-thirds of the booklet I find only one such offence, and it has the look of being a printer's error.

I leave the riddle with the reader. Perhaps he can explain how it is that a person—trained or untrained—who on the one day can write nothing better than Plague-Spot-Bacilli and feeble and stumbling and wandering personal history littered with false figures and obscurities and technical blunders, can on the next day sit down and write fluently, smoothly, compactly, capably, and confidently on a great big thundering subject, and do it as easily and comfortably as a whale paddles around the globe.

As for me, I have scribbled so much in fifty years that I have become saturated with convictions of one sort and another concerning a scribbler's limitations; and these are so strong that when I am familiar with a literary person's work I feel perfectly sure that I know enough about his limitations to know what he can *not* do. If Mr. Howells should pretend to me that he wrote the Plague - Spot - Bacilli rhapsody, I should receive the statement courteously, but I should know it for a—well, for a perversion. If the late Josh Billings should rise up and tell me that he wrote Herbert Spencer's philosophies, I should answer and say that the spelling casts a doubt upon his claim. If the late Jonathan Edwards should rise up and tell me he wrote Mr. Dooley's books, I should answer and say that the marked difference between his style and Dooley's is argument against the soundness of his statement. You see how much I think of *circumstantial evidence*. In literary matters—in my belief—it is often better than any person's word, better than any shady character's oath. It is difficult for me to believe that the same hand that wrote the Plague-Spot-Bacilli and the first third of the little Eddy biography wrote also *Science and Health.* Indeed, it is more than difficult, it is impossible.

Largely speaking, I have read acres of what purported to be Mrs. Eddy's writings, in the past two months. I cannot know, but I am convinced, that the circumstantial evidence shows that her actual share in the work of composing and phrasing these things was so slight as to be inconsequential. Where she puts her literary foot down, her trail across her paid polisher's page is as plain as the elephant's in a Sunday-school procession. Her verbal output, when left undoctored by her clerks, is quite unmistakable. It always exhibits the strongly distinctive features observable in the virgin passages from her pen already quoted by me:

Desert vacancy, as regards thought.

Self-complacency.

Puerility.

Sentimentality.

Affectations of scholarly learning.

Lust after eloquent and flowery expression.

Repetition of pet poetic picturesquenesses.

Confused and wandering statement.

Metaphor gone insane.

Meaningless words, used because they are pretty, or showy, or unusual.

Sorrowful attempts at the epigrammatic.

Destitution of originality.

The fat volume called *Miscellaneous Writings of Mrs. Eddy* contains several hundred pages. Of the five hundred and fifty-four pages of prose in it I find ten lines, on page 319, to be Mrs. Eddy's; also about a page of the preface or " Prospectus"; also about fifteen pages scattered along through the book. If she wrote any of the rest of the prose, it was rewritten after her by another hand. Here I will insert two-thirds of her page of the prospectus. It is evident that whenever, under the inspiration of the Deity, she turns out a book, she is always allowed to do some of the preface. I wonder why that is? It always mars the work. I think it is done in humorous malice. I think the clerks like to see her give herself away. They know she will, her stock of usable materials being limited and her procedure in employing them always the same, substantially. They know that when the initiated come upon her first erudite allusion, or upon any one of her other stage-properties, they can shut their eyes and tell what will follow. She usually throws off an easy remark all sodden with Greek or Hebrew or Latin learning; she usually has a person watching for a star—she can seldom get away from that poetic idea—sometimes it is a Chaldee, sometimes a Walking Delegate, sometimes an entire stranger, but be he what he may, he is generally there when the train is ready to move, and has his pass in his hat-band; she generally has a Being with a Dome on him, or some other cover that is unusual and out of the fashion; she likes to fire off a Scripture-verse where it will make the handsomest noise and come nearest to breaking the connection; she often throws out a Forefelt, or a Foresplendor, or a Foreslander where it will have a fine nautical foreto'gallant sound and make the sentence sing; after which she is nearly sure to throw discretion away and take to her deadly passion, Intoxicated Metaphor. At such a time the Mrs. Eddy that does not hesitate is lost:

"The ancient Greek looked longingly for the Olympiad. The Chaldee watched the appearing of a star; to him no higher destiny dawned on the dome of being than that foreshadowed by signs in the heavens. The meek Nazarene, the scoffed of all scoffers, said, 'Ye can discern the face of the sky; but can ye not discern the signs of the times?'—for He forefelt and foresaw the ordeal of a perfect Christianity, hated by sinners.

"To kindle all minds with a gleam of gratitude, the new idea that comes welling up from infinite Truth needs to be understood. The seer of this age should be a sage.

"Humility is the stepping-stone to a higher recognition of Deity. The mounting sense gathers fresh forms and strange fire from the ashes of dissolving self, and drops the world. Meekness heightens immortal attributes, only by removing the dust that dims them. Goodness reveals another scene and another self seemingly rolled up in shades, but brought to light by the evolutions of advancing thought, whereby we discern the power of Truth and Love to heal the sick.

"Pride is ignorance; those assume most who have the least wisdom or experience; and they

steal from their neighbor, because they have so
little of their own."—*Miscellaneous Writings*,
page 1, and six lines at top of page 2.

It is not believable that the hand that wrote
those clumsy and affected sentences wrote the
smooth English of *Science and Health*.

It is often said in print that Mrs. Eddy claims that God was the Author of *Science and Health*. Mr. Peabody states in his pamphlet that "she says not she but God was the Author." I cannot find that in her autobiography she makes this transference of the authorship, but I think that in it she definitely claims that she did her work under His inspiration—definitely for her; for as a rule she is not a very definite person, even when she seems to be trying her best to be clear and positive. Speaking of the early days when her Science was beginning to unfold itself and gather form in her mind, she says (*Autobiography*, page 43):

"The divine hand led me into a new world of light and Life, a fresh universe—old to God, but new to His 'little one.'"

She being His little one, as I understand it.

The divine hand led her. It seems to mean "God inspired me"; but when a person uses metaphors instead of statistics—and that is Mrs. Eddy's common fashion—one cannot always feel sure about the intention.

[Page 56.] "Even the Scripture gave no direct interpretation of the Scientific basis for demonstrating the spiritual Principle of healing, until our Heavenly Father saw fit, through the *Key to the Scriptures*, in *Science and Health*, to unlock this 'mystery of godliness.'"

Another baffling metaphor. If she had used plain forecastle English, and said "God wrote the *Key* and I put it in my book"; or if she had said "God furnished me the solution of the mystery and I put it on paper"; or if she had said "God did it all," then we should understand; but her phrase is open to any and all of those translations, and is a Key which unlocks nothing—for us. However, it seems to at least mean "God inspired me," if nothing more.

There was personal and intimate communion, at any rate—we get that much out of the

riddles. The connection extended to business,
after the establishment of the teaching and
healing industry.

[Page 71.] "When God impelled me to set
a price on my instruction," etc. Further down:
"God has since shown me, in multitudinous
ways, the wisdom of this decision."

She was not able to think of a "financial
equivalent"—meaning a pecuniary equivalent
—for her "instruction in Christian Science
Mind-healing." In this emergency she was
"led" to charge three hundred dollars for a
term of "twelve half-days." She does not say
who led her, she only says that the amount
greatly troubled her. I think it means that
the price was suggested from above, "led" being a theological term identical with our commercial phrase "personally conducted." She
"shrank from asking it, but was finally led, by
a strange providence, to accept this fee."
"Providence" is another theological term.
Two leds and a providence, taken together,
make a pretty strong argument for inspiration.
I think that these statistics make it clear that

the price was arranged above. This view is constructively supported by the fact, already quoted, that God afterwards approved, "in multitudinous ways," her wisdom in accepting the mentioned fee. "Multitudinous ways"— multitudinous encoring—suggests enthusiasm. Business enthusiasm. And it suggests nearness. God's nearness to his "little one." Nearness, and a watchful personal interest. A warm, palpitating, Standard - Oil interest, so to speak. All this indicates inspiration. We may assume, then, two inspirations: one for the book, the other for the business.

The evidence for inspiration is further augmented by the testimony of Rev. George Tomkins, D.D., already quoted, that Mrs. Eddy and her book were foretold in Revelation, and that Mrs. Eddy "*is* God's brightest thought to this age, giving us the spiritual interpretation of the Bible in the 'little book'" of the Angel.

I am aware that it is not Mr. Tomkins that is speaking, but Mrs. Eddy. The commissioned lecturers of the Christian Science Church have to be members of the Board of Lectureship. (By-laws, Sec. 2, p. 70.) The Board of Lectureship is selected by the Board of Directors of the Church. (By-laws, Sec. 3, p. 70.) The Board of Directors of the Church is the property of Mrs. Eddy. (By-laws, p. 22.) Mr. Tomkins did not make that statement without authorization from headquarters. He necessarily got it from the Board of Directors, the Board of Directors from Mrs. Eddy, Mrs. Eddy from the Deity. Mr. Tomkins would have been turned down by that procession if his remarks had been unsatisfactory to it.

It may be that there is evidence somewhere —as has been claimed—that Mrs. Eddy has charged upon the Deity the verbal authorship of *Science and Health.* But if she ever made the charge, she has withdrawn it (as it seems to me), and in the most formal and unqualified of all ways. See *Autobiography,* page 57:

"When the demand for this book increased . . . the copyright was infringed. I entered a suit at Law, and my copyright was protected."

Thus it is plain that she did not plead that the Deity was the (verbal) Author; for if she

had done that, she would have lost her case—
and with rude promptness. It was in the old
days before the Berne Convention and before
the passage of our amended law of 1891, and
the court would have quoted the following
stern clause from the existing statute and
frowned her out of the place:

"No Foreigner can acquire copyright in the
United States."

To sum up. The evidence before me indicates three things:

1. That Mrs. Eddy claims the verbal authorship for herself.

2. That she denies it to the Deity.

3. That—in her belief—she wrote the book
under the inspiration of the Deity, but furnished the language herself.

In one place in the *Autobiography* she claims
both the language and the *ideas;* but when this
witness is testifying, one must draw the line
somewhere, or she will prove both sides of her
case—nine sides, if desired.

It is too true. Much too true. Many, many
times too true. She is a most trying witness—
the most trying witness that ever kissed the

Book, I am sure. There is no keeping up with
her erratic testimony. As soon as you have
got her share of the authorship nailed where
you half hope and half believe it will stay and
cannot be joggled loose any more, she joggles it
loose again—or seems to; you cannot be sure,
for her habit of dealing in meaningless metaphors instead of in plain, straightforward statistics, makes it nearly always impossible to tell
just what it is she is trying to say. She was
definite when she claimed both the language
and the ideas of the book. That seemed to
settle the matter. It seemed to distribute the
percentages of credit with precision between
the collaborators: ninety-two per cent. to Mrs.
Eddy, who did all the work, and eight per cent.
to the Deity, who furnished the inspiration—
not enough of it to damage the copyright in
a country closed against Foreigners, and yet
plenty to advertise the book and market it at
famine rates. Then Mrs. Eddy does not keep
still, but fetches around and comes forward
and testifies again. It is most injudicious. For
she resorts to metaphor this time, and it makes
trouble, for she seems to reverse the percent-

ages and claim only the eight per cent. for herself. I quote from Mr. Peabody's book (*Eddyism, or Christian Science.* Boston: 15 Court Square, price twenty-five cents):

"Speaking of this book, Mrs. Eddy, in January last (1901) said: 'I should blush to write of *Science and Health, with Key to the Scriptures,* as I have, were it of human origin, and I, apart from God, its author; but as I was only a scribe echoing the harmonies of Heaven in divine metaphysics, I cannot be supermodest of the Christian Science text-book.'"

Mr. Peabody's comment:

"Nothing could be plainer than that. Here is a distinct avowal that the book entitled *Science and Health* was the work of Almighty God."

It does seem to amount to that. She was only a "scribe." Confound the word, it is just a confusion, it has no determinable meaning there, it leaves us in the air. A scribe is merely a person who writes. He may be a copyist, he may be an amanuensis, he may be a writer of originals, and furnish both the language and the ideas. As usual with Mrs. Eddy, the connection affords no help—"echoing" throws no light upon "scribe." A rock can reflect an echo, a wall can do it, a mountain can do it, many things can do it, but a scribe can't. A scribe that could reflect an echo could get over thirty dollars a week in a side-show. Many impresarios would rather have him than a cow with four tails. If we allow that this present scribe was *setting down* the "harmonies of Heaven"—and certainly that seems to have been the case—then there was only one way to do it that I can think of: listen to the music and put down the notes one after another as they fell. In that case Mrs. Eddy did not invent the tune, she only entered it on paper. Therefore—dropping the metaphor—she was merely an amanuensis, and furnished neither the language of *Science and Health* nor the ideas. It reduces her to eight per cent. (and the dividends on that and the rest).

Is that it? We shall never know. For Mrs. Eddy is liable to testify again at any time. But until she does it, I think we must conclude that the Deity was Author of the whole book, and Mrs. Eddy merely His telephone and stenographer. Granting this, her claim as the Voice of God stands—for the present—justified and established.

POSTSCRIPT

I overlooked something. It appears that there was more of that utterance than Mr. Peabody has quoted in the above paragraph. It will be found in Mrs. Eddy's organ, the *Christian Science Journal* (January, 1901) and reads as follows:

"It was not myself . . . which dictated *Science and Health, with Key to the Scriptures.*"

That is certainly clear enough. The words which I have removed from that important sentence explain Who it was that did the dictating. It was done by

"the divine power of Truth and Love, infinitely above me."

Certainly that is definite. At last, through her personal testimony, we have a sure grip upon the following vital facts, and they settle the authorship of *Science and Health* beyond peradventure:

1. Mrs. Eddy furnished "the ideas and the language."

2. God furnished the ideas and the language.

It is a great comfort to have the matter authoritatively settled.

CHAPTER V

IT is hard to locate her, she shifts about so much. She is a shining drop of quicksilver which you put your finger on and it isn't there. There is a paragraph in the *Autobiography* (page 96) which places in seemingly darkly significant procession three Personages:

1. The Virgin Mary.
2. Jesus of Nazareth.
3. Mrs. Eddy.

This is the paragraph referred to:

"No person can take the individual place of the Virgin Mary. No person can compass or fulfil the individual mission of Jesus of Nazareth. No person can take the place of the author of *Science and Health*, the discoverer and founder of Christian Science. Each individual must fill his own niche in time and eternity."

I have read it many times, but I still cannot be sure that I rightly understand it. If the

Saviour's name had been placed first and the Virgin Mary's second and Mrs. Eddy's third, I should draw the inference that a descending scale from First Importance to Second Importance and then to Small Importance was indicated; but to place the Virgin first, the Saviour second, and Mrs. Eddy third, seems to turn the scale the other way and make it an ascending scale of Importances, with Mrs. Eddy ranking the other two and holding first place.

I think that that was perhaps the intention, but none but a seasoned Christian Scientist can examine a literary animal of Mrs. Eddy's creation and tell which end of it the tail is on. She is easily the most baffling and bewildering writer in the literary trade.

EDDY is a commonplace name, and would have an unimpressive aspect in the list of the reformed Holy Family. She has thought of that. In the book of By-laws written by her —"impelled by a power not one's own "—there is a paragraph which explains how and when her disciples came to confer a title upon her;

and this explanation is followed by a warning
as to what will happen to any female Scientist
who shall desecrate it:

"*The title of Mother.* Therefore if a student
of Christian Science shall apply this title, either
to herself or to others, except as the term for
kinship according to the flesh, it shall be regarded by the Church as an indication of disrespect for their Pastor Emeritus, and unfitness
to be a member of the Mother-Church."

She is the Pastor Emeritus.

While the quoted paragraph about the Procession seems to indicate that Mrs. Eddy is
expecting to occupy the First Place in it, that
expectation is not definitely avowed. In an
earlier utterance of hers she is clearer—clearer,
and does not claim the first place all to herself,
but only the half of it. I quote from Mr.
Peabody's book again:

"In the *Christian Science Journal* for April,
1889, when it was her property, and published
by her, it was claimed for her, and *with her
sanction*, that she was equal with Jesus, and

elaborate effort was made to establish the claim.

"Mrs. Eddy has distinctly *authorized* the claim in her behalf that she herself was the chosen successor to and equal of Jesus."

In her *Miscellaneous Writings* (using her once favorite "We" for "I") she says that "While we entertain decided views . . . and shall express them as duty demands, we shall claim no especial gift from our divine origin," etc.

Our divine origin. It suggests Equal again. It is inferable, then, that in the near by-and-by the new Church will officially rank the Holy Family in the following order:

1. Jesus of Nazareth.—1. Our Mother.
2. The Virgin Mary.

SUMMARY

I am not playing with Christian Science and its founder, I am examining them; and I am doing it because of the interest I feel in the inquiry. My results may seem inadequate to the reader, but they have for me clarified a muddle and brought a sort of order out of a chaos, and so I value them.

My readings of Mrs. Eddy's uninspired miscellaneous literary efforts have convinced me of several things:

1. That she did not write *Science and Health.*

2. That the Deity did (or did not) write it.

3. That She thinks She wrote it.

4. That She believes She wrote it under the Deity's inspiration.

5. That She believes She is a Member of the Holy Family.

6. That She believes She is the equal of the Head of it.

Finally, I think She is now entitled to the capital S—on her own evidence.

CHAPTER VI

THUS far we have a part of Mrs. Eddy's portrait. Not made of fictions, surmises, reports, rumors, innuendoes, dropped by her enemies; no, she has furnished all of the materials herself, and laid them on the canvas, under my general superintendence and direction. As far as she has gone with it, it is the presentation of a complacent, commonplace, illiterate New England woman who "forgot everything she knew" when she discovered her discovery, then wrote a Bible in good English under the inspiration of God, and climbed up it to the supremest summit of earthly grandeur attainable by man— where she sits serene to-day, beloved and worshipped by a multitude of human beings of as good average intelligence as is possessed by those that march under the banner of any competing cult. This is not intended to flatter the competing cults, it is merely a statement of cold fact.

That a commonplace person should go climbing aloft and become a god or a half-god or a quarter-god and be worshipped by men and women of average intelligence, is nothing. It has happened a million times, it will happen a hundred million more. It has been millions of years since the first of these supernaturals appeared, and by the time the last one—in that inconceivably remote future—shall have performed his solemn little high-jinks on the stage and closed the business, there will be enough of them accumulated in the museum on the Other Side to start a heaven of their own—and jam it.

Each in his turn those little supernaturals of our by-gone ages and æons joined the monster procession of his predecessors and marched horizonward, disappeared, and was forgotten. They changed nothing, they built nothing, they left nothing behind them to remember them by, nothing to hold their disciples together, nothing to solidify their work and enable it to defy the assaults of time and the weather. They passed, and left a vacancy. They made one fatal mistake; they all made it, each in his turn: they failed to *organize* their forces, they failed to *centralize* their strength, they failed to provide a fresh Bible and a sure and perpetual cash income for business, and often they failed to provide a new and accepted Divine Personage to worship.

Mrs. Eddy is not of that small fry. The materials that go to the making of the rest of her portrait will prove it. She will furnish them herself:

She published her book. She copyrighted it. She copyrights everything. If she should say, "Good-morning; how do you do?" she would copyright it; for she is a careful person, and knows the value of small things.

She began to teach her Science, she began to heal, she began to gather converts to her new religion — fervent, sincere, devoted, grateful people. A year or two later she organized her first Christian Science "Association," with six of her disciples on the roster.

She continued to teach and heal. She was charging nothing, she says, although she was very poor. She taught and healed gratis four years altogether, she says.

Then, in 1879–81 she was become strong enough, and well enough established, to venture a couple of impressively important moves. The first of these moves was to aggrandize the "Association" to a "*Church*." Brave? It is the right name for it, I think. The former name suggests nothing, invited no remark, no criticism, no inquiry, no hostility; the new name invited them all. She must have made this intrepid venture on her own motion. She could have had no important advisers at that early day. If we accept it as her own idea and her own act—and I think we *must*—we have one key to her character. And it will explain subsequent acts of hers that would merely stun us and stupefy us without it. Shall we call it courage? Or shall we call it recklessness? Courage observes; reflects; calculates; surveys the whole situation; counts the cost, estimates the odds, makes up its mind; then goes at the enterprise resolute to win or perish. Recklessness does not reflect, it plunges fearlessly in with a hurrah, and takes the risks, whatever they may be, regardless of expense. Recklessness often fails, Mrs. Eddy has never failed—

from the point of view of her followers. The point of view of other people is naturally not a matter of weighty importance to her.

The new Church was not born loose-jointed and featureless, but had a defined plan, a definite character, definite aims, and a name which was a challenge, and defied all comers. It was "a Mind-healing Church." It was "*without a creed.*" Its name, "The Church of Christ, Scientist."

Mrs. Eddy could not copyright her Church, but she chartered it, which was the same thing and relieved the pain. It had twenty-six charter members. Mrs. Eddy was at once installed as its pastor.

The other venture, above referred to, was Mrs. Eddy's Massachusetts Metaphysical College, in which was taught "the pathology of spiritual power." She could not copyright it, but she got it chartered. For faculty it had herself, her husband of the period (Dr. Eddy), and her adopted son, Dr. Foster-Eddy. The college term was "barely three weeks," she says. Again she was bold, brave, rash, reckless —choose for yourself—for she not only began to charge the student, but charged him *a hundred dollars a week* for the enlightenments. And got it? some may ask. Easily. Pupils flocked from far and near. They came by the hundred. Presently the term was cut down nearly half, but the price remained as before. To be exact, the term-cut was to seven lessons—price, three hundred dollars. The college "yielded a large income." This is believable. In seven years Mrs. Eddy taught, as she avers, over four thousand students in it. (Preface to 1902 edition of *Science and Health*.) Three hundred times four thousand is—but perhaps you can cipher it yourself. I could do it ordinarily, but I fell down yesterday and hurt my leg. Cipher it; you will see that it is a grand sum for a woman to earn in seven years. Yet that was not all she got out of her college in the seven.

At the time that she was charging the primary student three hundred dollars for twelve lessons she was not content with this tidy assessment, but had other ways of plundering him. By advertisement she offered him privileges whereby he could add eighteen lessons to his store for five hundred dollars more. That is to say, he could get a total of thirty lessons in her college for eight hundred dollars.

Four thousand times eight hundred is—but it is a difficult sum for a cripple who has not been "demonstrated over" to cipher; let it go. She taught "over" four thousand students in seven years. "Over" is not definite, but it probably represents a non-paying surplus of learners over and above the paying four thousand. Charity students, doubtless. I think that as interesting an advertisement as has been printed since the romantic old days of the other buccaneers is this one from the *Christian Science Journal* for September, 1886:

"MASSACHUSETTS METAPHYSICAL COLLEGE

"REV. MARY BAKER G. EDDY, PRESIDENT

"571 Columbus Avenue, Boston

"The collegiate course in Christian Science metaphysical healing includes twelve lessons. Tuition, three hundred dollars.

"Course in metaphysical obstetrics includes

six daily lectures, and is open only to students from this college. Tuition, one hundred dollars.

" Class in theology, open (like the above) to graduates, receives six additional lectures on the Scriptures, and summary of the principle and practice of Christian Science, two hundred dollars.

" Normal class is open to those who have taken the first course at this college; six daily lectures complete the Normal course. Tuition, two hundred dollars.

" No invalids, and only persons of good moral character, are accepted as students. All students are subject to examination and rejection; and they are liable to leave the class if found unfit to remain in it.

" A limited number of clergymen received free of charge.

" Largest discount to indigent students, one hundred dollars on the first course.

" No deduction on the others.

" Husband and wife, entered together, three hundred dollars.

"Tuition for all strictly in advance."

There it is—the horse-leech's daughter alive again, after a three-century vacation. Fifty or sixty hours' lecturing for eight hundred dollars.

I was in error as to one matter: there are no charity students. Gratis-taught clergymen must not be placed under that head; they are merely an advertisement. Pauper students can get into the infant class on a two - third rate (cash in advance), but not even an archangel can get into the rest of the game at anything short of par, cash down. For it is "in the spirit of Christ's charity, as one who is joyful to bear healing to the sick "[1] that Mrs. Eddy is working the game. She sends the healing to them outside.

She cannot bear it to them inside the college, for the reason that she does not allow a sick candidate to get in. It is true that this smells of inconsistency,[2] but that is nothing; Mrs. Eddy would not be Mrs. Eddy if she should ever chance to be consistent about anything two days running.

Except in the matter of the Dollar. The

[1] Mrs. Eddy's Introduction to *Science and Health.*
[2] "There is no disease"; "sickness is a belief only."— *Science and Health*, vol. ii., page 173, edition of 1884.—M. T.

Dollar, and appetite for power and notoriety. English must also be added; she is always consistent, she is always Mrs. Eddy, in her English: it is always and consistently confused and crippled and poor. She wrote the Advertisement; her literary trade-marks are there. When she says all "students" are subject to examination, she does not mean students, she means candidates for that lofty place. When she says students are "liable" to leave the class if found unfit to remain in it, she does not mean that if they find themselves unfit, or be found unfit by others, they will be likely to ask permission to leave the class; she means that if *she* finds them unfit she will be "liable" to fire them out. When she nobly offers "tuition for all strictly in advance," she does not mean "*instruction* for all in advance—payment for it later." No, that is only what she says, it is not what she means. If she had written *Science and Health*, the oldest man in the world would not be able to tell with certainty what any passage in it was intended to mean.

CHAPTER VII

HER Church was on its legs.

She was its pastor. It was prospering.

She was appointed one of a committee to draught By-laws for its government. It may be observed, without overplus of irreverence, that this was larks for her. *She did all of the draughting herself.* From the very beginning she was always in the front seat when there was business to be done; in the front seat, with both eyes open, and looking sharply out for Number One; in the front seat, working Mortal Mind with fine effectiveness and giving Immortal Mind a rest for Sunday. When her Church was reorganized, by-and-by, the By-laws were retained. She saw to that. In these Laws for the government of her Church, her empire, her despotism, Mrs. Eddy's character is embalmed for good and all. I think a particularized examination of these Church-laws will be found interesting. And not the less so if we keep in mind that they were "impelled by a power not one's own," as she says—*Anglice.* the inspiration of God.

It is a Church "without a creed." Still, it has one. Mrs. Eddy draughted it—and copyrighted it. In her own name. You cannot become a member of the Mother-Church (nor of any Christian Science Church) without signing it. It forms the first chapter of the By-laws, and is called "Tenets." "Tenets of The Mother-Church, The First Church of Christ, Scientist." It has no hell in it—it throws it overboard.

THE PASTOR EMERITUS

About the time of the reorganization, Mrs. Eddy retired from her position of pastor of her Church, abolished the office of pastor in all branch Churches, and appointed her *book, Science and Health,* to be *pastor-universal.* Mrs. Eddy did not disconnect herself from the office entirely, when she retired, but appointed herself Pastor Emeritus. It is a misleading title, and belongs to the family of that phrase "without a creed." It advertises her as being a

merely honorary official, with nothing to do,
and no authority. The Czar of Russia is Em-
peror Emeritus on the same terms. Mrs. Eddy
was Autocrat of the Church before, with limitless authority, and she kept her grip on that
limitless authority when she took that fictitious
title.

It is curious and interesting to note with what
an unerring instinct the Pastor Emeritus has
thought out and forecast all possible encroach-
ments upon her planned autocracy, and barred
the way against them, in the By-laws which
she framed and copyrighted—under the guidance of the Supreme Being.

THE BOARD OF DIRECTORS

For instance, when Article I. speaks of a
President and Board of Directors, you think
you have discovered a formidable check upon
the powers and ambitions of the honorary pastor, the ornamental pastor, the functionless pastor, the Pastor Emeritus, but it is a mistake.
These great officials are of the phrase-family of
the Church-Without-a-Creed and the Pastor-

With-Nothing-to-Do; that is to say, of the family of Large-Names-Which-Mean-Nothing. The Board is of so little consequence that the By-laws do not state how it is chosen, nor who does it; but they do state, most definitely, that the Board cannot fill a vacancy in its number *"except the candidate is approved by the Pastor Emeritus."*

The *"candidate."* The Board cannot even proceed to an election until the Pastor Emeritus has examined the list and squelched such candidates as are not satisfactory to her.

Whether the original first Board began as the personal property of Mrs. Eddy or not, it is foreseeable that in time, under this By-law, she would own it. Such a first Board might chafe under such a rule as that, and try to legislate it out of existence some day. But Mrs. Eddy was awake. She foresaw that danger, and added this ingenious and effective clause:

"This By-law can neither be amended nor annulled, except by consent of Mrs. Eddy, the Pastor Emeritus."

THE PRESIDENT

The Board of Directors, or Serfs, or Ciphers, elects the President.

On these clearly worded terms: "*Subject to the approval of the Pastor Emeritus.*"

Therefore *She* elects him.

A long term can invest a high official with influence and power, and make him dangerous. Mrs. Eddy reflected upon that; so she limits the President's term to *a year*. She has a capable commerical head, an organizing head, a head for government.

TREASURER AND CLERK

There are a Treasurer and a Clerk. They are elected by the Board of Directors. That is to say, *by Mrs. Eddy.*

Their terms of office expire on the first Tuesday in June of each year, "*or* upon the election of their successors." They must be watchfully obedient and satisfactory to her, or she will elect and install their successors with a suddenness that can be unpleasant to them. It goes without saying that the Treasurer manages the Treasury to suit Mrs. Eddy, and is in fact merely Temporary Deputy Treasurer.

Apparently the Clerk has but two duties to perform: to read messages from Mrs. Eddy to First Members assembled in solemn Council, and provide lists of candidates for Church membership. The select body entitled First Members are the aristocracy of the Mother-Church, the Charter Members, the Aborigines, a sort of stylish but unsalaried little College of Cardinals, good for show, but not indispensable. *Nobody* is indispensable in Mrs. Eddy's empire; she sees to that.

When the Pastor Emeritus sends a letter or message to that little Sanhedrin, it is the Clerk's "imperative duty" to read it "at the place and time specified." Otherwise, the world might come to an end. These are fine, large frills, and remind us of the ways of emperors and such. Such do not use the penny-post, they send a gilded and painted special messenger, and he strides into the Parliament, and business comes to a sudden and solemn and awful stop; and in the impressive hush that follows, the Chief

Clerk reads the document. It is his "imperative duty." If he should neglect it, his official life would end. It is the same with this Mother·Church Clerk; "if he fail to perform this important function of his office," certain majestic and unshirkable solemnities *must* follow: a special meeting "shall" be called; a member of the Church "shall" make formal complaint; then the Clerk "shall" be "removed from office." Complaint is sufficient, no trial is necessary.

There is something very sweet and juvenile and innocent and pretty about these little tinsel vanities, these grave apings of monarchical fuss and feathers and ceremony, here on our ostentatiously democratic soil. She is the same lady that we found in the *Autobiography*, who was so naively vain of all that little ancestral military riffraff that she had dug up and annexed. A person's nature never changes. What it is in childhood, it remains. Under pressure, or a change of interest, it can partially or wholly disappear from sight, and for considerable stretches of time, but nothing can ever permanently modify it, nothing can ever remove it.

BOARD OF TRUSTEES

There isn't any—now.   But with power and
money piling up higher and higher every day
and the Church's dominion spreading daily
wider and farther, a time could come when the
envious and ambitious could start the idea that
it would be wise and well to put a watch upon
these assets—a watch equipped with properly
large authority.   By custom, a Board of Trustees.   Mrs. Eddy has foreseen that probability
—for she is a woman with a long, long look
ahead, the longest look ahead that ever a woman had—and she has provided for that emergency.   In Art. I., Sec. 5, she has decreed that
no Board of Trustees shall ever exist in the
Mother-Church "*except it be constituted by the
Pastor Emeritus.*"

The magnificence of it, the daring of it! Thus
far, she is

The Massachusetts Metaphysical College;
Pastor Emeritus;
President;
Board of Directors;
Treasurer;

Clerk; and future
Board of Trustees;
and is still moving onward, ever onward. When
I contemplate her from a commercial point of
view, there are no words that can convey my
admiration of her.

READERS

These are a feature of *first* importance in the
church-machinery of Christian Science. For
they occupy the pulpit. They hold the place
that the preacher holds in the other Christian
Churches. They hold that place, but *they do
not preach.* Two of them are on duty at a time
—a man and a woman. One reads a passage
from the Bible, the other reads the explanation
of it from *Science and Health*—and so they go
on alternating. This constitutes the service—
this, with choir-music. *They utter no word of
their own.* Art. IV., Sec. 6, closes their mouths
with this uncompromising gag:

" *They shall make no remarks explanatory of
the Lesson-Sermon at any time during the service.*"

It seems a simple little thing. One is not
startled by it at a first reading of it; nor at the
second, nor the third. One may have to read
it a dozen times before the whole magnitude of
it rises before the mind. It far and away over-
sizes and outclasses the best business-idea yet
invented for the safe-guarding and perpetuating of a religion. If it had been thought of
and put in force eighteen hundred and seventy
years ago, there would be but one Christian
sect in the world now, instead of ten dozens
of them.

There are many varieties of men in the world,
consequently there are many varieties of minds
in its pulpits. This insures many differing in-
terpretations of important Scripture texts, and
this in turn insures the splitting up of a religion
into many sects. It is what has happened; it
was sure to happen.

Mrs. Eddy has noted this disastrous result
of preaching, and has put up the bars. She
will have no preaching in her Church. *She* has
explained all essential Scriptures, and set the
explanations down in her book. In her belief
her underlings cannot improve upon those ex-

planations, and in that stern sentence *"they shall make no explanatory remarks"* she has barred them for all time from trying. She will be obeyed; there is no question about that.

In arranging her government she has borrowed ideas from various sources—not poor ones, but the best in the governmental market —but this one is new, this one came out of no ordinary business-head, this one must have come out of her own, there has been no other commercial skull in a thousand centuries that was equal to it. She has borrowed freely and wisely, but I am sure that this idea is many times larger than all her borrowings bulked together. One must respect the business-brain that produced it—the splendid pluck and impudence that ventured to promulgate it, anyway.

ELECTION OF READERS

Readers are not taken at hap-hazard, any more than preachers are taken at hap-hazard for the pulpits of other sects. No, Readers are elected by the Board of Directors. *But—*

12

"*Section* 3. The Board shall inform the Pastor Emeritus of the names of *candidates* for Readers before they are elected, and *if she objects to the nomination, said candidates shall not be chosen.*"

Is *that* an election—by the *Board?* Thus far I have not been able to find out what that Board of Spectres is for. It certainly has no real function, no duty which the hired girl could not perform, no office beyond the mere recording of the autocrat's decrees.

There are no dangerously long office-terms in Mrs. Eddy's government. The Readers are elected for but one year. This insures their subserviency to their proprietor.

Readers are not allowed to copy out passages and read them from the *manuscript* in the pulpit; they must read from *Mrs. Eddy's book* itself. She is right. Slight changes could be slyly made, repeated, and in time get acceptance with congregations. Branch sects could grow out of these practices. Mrs. Eddy knows the human race, and how far to trust it. Her limit is not over a quarter of an inch. It is all that a wise person will risk.

Mrs. Eddy's inborn disposition to copyright everything, charter everything, secure the rightful and proper credit to herself for everything she does, and everything she thinks she does, and everything she thinks, and everything she thinks she thinks or has thought or intends to think, is illustrated in Sec. 5 of Art. IV., defining the duties of official Readers —in church:

"*Naming Book and Author.* The Reader of *Science and Health, with Key to the Scriptures,* before commencing to read from this book, shall *distinctly announce its full title and give the author's name.*"

Otherwise the congregation might get the habit of forgetting who (ostensibly) wrote the book.

THE ARISTOCRACY

This consists of First Members and their apostolic succession. It is a close corporation, and its membership limit is one hundred. Forty will answer, but if the number fall below that, there must be an election, to fill **the grand** quorum.

This Sanhedrin can't *do* anything of the slightest importance, but it can *talk*. It can "discuss." That is, it can discuss "important questions relative to Church members"; evidently persons who are already Church members. This affords it amusement, and does no harm.

It can "fix the salaries of the Readers."

Twice a year it "votes on" admitting candidates. That is, for Church membership. But its work is cut out for it beforehand, by Sec. 2, Art. IX.:

"Every recommendation for membership in the Church 'shall be countersigned by a loyal student of Mrs. Eddy's, by a Director of this Church, or by a First Member.'"

All these three classes of beings are the personal property of Mrs. Eddy. She has absolute control of the elections.

Also it must "transact any Church business that may properly come before it."

"Properly" is a thoughtful word. *No im-*

portant business can come before it. The By-laws have attended to that. No important business goes before *any* one for the final word except Mrs. Eddy. She has looked to that.

The Sanhedrin "votes on" candidates for admission to its own body. But is its vote worth any more than mine would be? No, it isn't. Sec. 4, of Art. V.—Election of First Members —makes this quite plain:

"Before being elected, the candidates for First Members *shall be approved by the Pastor Emeritus over her own signature.*"

Thus the Sanhedrin is the personal property of Mrs. Eddy. She owns it. It has no functions, no authority, no real existence. It is another Board of Shadows. Mrs. Eddy is the Sanhedrin herself.

But it is time to foot up again and "see where we are at." Thus far, Mrs. Eddy is

The Massachusetts Metaphysical College;

Pastor Emeritus;

President;

Board of Directors;

Treasurer;
Clerk;
Future Board of Trustees;
Proprietor of the Priesthood;
Dictator of the Services;
Proprietor of the Sanhedrin.
She has come far, and is still on her way.

CHURCH MEMBERSHIP

In this Article there is another exhibition of a couple of the large features of Mrs. Eddy's remarkable make-up: her business-talent and her knowledge of human nature.

She does not beseech and implore people to join her Church. She knows the human race better than that. She gravely goes through the motions of reluctantly granting admission to the applicant as a favor to him. The idea is worth untold shekels. She does not stand at the gate of the fold with welcoming arms spread, and receive the lost sheep with glad emotion and set up the fatted calf and invite the neighbor and have a time. No, she looks upon him coldly, she snubs him, she says:

"Who are you? Who is your sponsor? Who asked you to come here? Go away, and don't come again until you are invited."

It is calculated to strikingly impress a person accustomed to Moody and Sankey and Sam Jones revivals; accustomed to brain-turning appeals to the unknown and unendorsed sinner to come forward and enter into the joy, etc.— "just as he is"; accustomed to seeing him do it; accustomed to seeing him pass up the aisle through sobbing seas of welcome, and love, and congratulation, and arrive at the mourner's bench and be received like a long-lost government bond.

No, there is nothing of that kind in Mrs. Eddy's system. She knows that if you wish to confer upon a human being something which he is not sure he wants, the best way is to make it apparently difficult for him to get it—then he is no son of Adam if that apple does not assume an interest in his eyes which it lacked before. In time this interest can grow into desire. Mrs. Eddy knows that when you cannot get a man to try—free of cost—a new and effective remedy for a disease he is afflicted with, you can generally sell it to him if you will put a price upon it which he cannot afford.[1] When, in the beginning, she taught Christian Science gratis (for good reasons), pupils were few and reluctant, and required persuasion; it was when she raised the limit to three hundred dollars for a dollar's worth that she could not find standing room for the invasion of pupils that followed.

With fine astuteness she goes through the motions of making it difficult to get membership in her Church. There is a twofold value in this system: it gives membership a high value in the eyes of the applicant; and at the same time the requirements exacted enable Mrs. Eddy to keep him out if she has doubts about

---

[1] I offered to cure of his passion—gratis—a victim of the drinking habit, by a simple and (as it seemed to me) not difficult intellectual method which I had successfully tried upon the tobacco habit. I failed to get him interested. I think my proposition couldn't rouse him, couldn't strongly appeal to him, could not electrify him, because it offered a thing so easy to get, and which could be had for nothing. Within a month afterwards a famous Drink-Cure opened, and at my suggestion he willingly went there, at once, and got himself (temporarily) cured of his habit. Because he had to pay one hundred and fifty dollars. One values a thing when one can't afford it.—M. T.

his value to her. A word further as to applications for membership:

" Applications of students of the Metaphysical College must be signed by the *Board of Directors*."

That is safe. Mrs. Eddy is proprietor of that Board.

Children of twelve may be admitted if invited by "one of Mrs. Eddy's loyal students, or by a First Member, or by a Director."

These sponsors are the property of Mrs. Eddy, therefore her Church is safeguarded from the intrusion of undesirable children.

Other Students. Applicants who have not studied with Mrs. Eddy can get in only "by invitation and recommendation from students of Mrs. Eddy . . . or from members of the Mother-Church."

Other paragraphs explain how two or three other varieties of applicants are to be challenged and obstructed, and tell us who is authorized to invite them, recommend them, endorse them, and all that.

The safeguards are definite, and would seem to be sufficiently strenuous—to Mr. Sam Jones, at any rate. Not for Mrs. Eddy. She adds this clincher:

" The candidates shall be elected by a majority vote of the First Members present."

That is the aristocracy, the aborigines, the Sanhedrin. It is Mrs. Eddy's property. She *herself* is the Sanhedrin. No one can get into the Church if she wishes to keep him out.

This veto power could some time or other have a large value for her, therefore she was wise to reserve it.

It is likely that it is not frequently used. It is also probable that the difficulties attendant upon getting admission to membership have been instituted more to invite than to deter, more to enhance the value of membership and make people long for it than to make it really difficult to get. I think so, because the Mother-Church has many thousands of members more than its building can accommodate.

'ANDSOME ENGLISH REQUIRED

Mrs. Eddy is very particular as regards one detail—curiously so, for her, all things considered. The Church Readers must be "good English scholars"; they must be "thorough English scholars."

She is thus sensitive about the English of her subordinates for cause, possibly. In her chapter defining the duties of the Clerk there is an indication that she harbors resentful memories of an occasion when the hazy quality of her own English made unforeseen and mortifying trouble:

"*Understanding Communications. Sec. 2.* If the Clerk of this Church shall receive a communication from the Pastor Emeritus which he does not fully understand, he shall inform her of this fact before presenting it to the Church, and obtain a clear understanding of the matter —then act in accordance therewith."

She should have waited to calm down, then, but instead she added this, which lacks sugar:

"Failing to adhere to this By-law, the Clerk
must *resign*."

I wish I could see that communication that
broke the camel's back. It was probably the
one beginning: "What plague spot or bacilli
were gnawing at the heart of this metropolis
and bringing it on bended knee?" and I think
it likely that the kindly disposed Clerk tried
to translate it into English and lost his mind
and had to go to the hospital. That By-
law was not the offspring of a forecast, an
intuition, it was certainly born of a sorrowful experience. Its temper gives the fact
away.

The little book of By-laws has manifestly
been tinkered by one of Mrs. Eddy's "thorough
English scholars," for in the majority of cases
its meanings are clear. The book is not even
marred by Mrs. Eddy's peculiar specialty—
lumbering clumsinesses of speech. I believe
the salaried polisher has weeded them all
out but one. In one place, after referring
to *Science and Health*, Mrs. Eddy goes on
to say "the Bible and the above-named

book, with other works by the same author,"
etc.

It is an unfortunate sentence, for it could
mislead a hasty or careless reader for a moment. Mrs. Eddy framed it—it is her very
own—it bears her trade-mark. "The Bible
and *Science and Health*, with other works by the
same author," could have come from no literary vacuum but the one which produced the
remark (in the *Autobiography*): "I remember
reading, in my childhood, certain manuscripts
containing Scriptural Sonnets, besides other
verses and enigmas."

We know what she means, in both instances,
but a low-priced Clerk would not necessarily
know, and on a salary like his he could quite
excusably aver that the Pastor Emeritus had
commanded him to come and make proclama-
tion that she was author of the Bible, and that
she was thinking of discharging some Scriptural
sonnets and other enigmas upon the congregation. It could lose him his place, but it would
not be fair, if it happened before the edict about
"Understanding Communications" was promulgated.

"READERS" AGAIN

The By-law book makes a showy pretence
of orderliness and system, but it is only a pretence.   I will not go so far as to say it is a
harum-scarum jumble, for it is not that, but I
think it fair to say it is at least jumbulacious in
places.   For instance, Articles III. and IV. set
forth in much detail the qualifications and duties
of Readers, she then skips some thirty pages and
takes up the subject again.   It looks like slov-
enliness, but it may be only art.   The belated
By-law has a sufficiently quiet look, but it has
a ton of dynamite in it.   *It makes all the Christian Science Church Readers on the globe the
personal chattels of Mrs. Eddy.*   Whenever she
chooses, she can stretch her long arm around
the world's fat belly and flirt a Reader out of
his pulpit, though he be tucked away in seeming
safety and obscurity in a lost village in the middle of China:

"*In any Church.   Sec. 2.*   The Pastor Emeritus of the Mother-Church shall have the right
(through a *letter* addressed to the individual

and Church of which he is the Reader) to remove a Reader from this office in any Church
of Christ, Scientist, both in America and in for-
eign nations; or to appoint the Reader to fill
any office belonging to the Christian Science
denomination."

She does not have to prefer charges against
him, she does not have to find him lazy, careless, incompetent, untidy, ill-mannered, unholy,
dishonest, she does not have to discover a fault
of any kind in him, she does not have to tell
him nor his congregation why she dismisses and
disgraces him and insults his meek flock, she
does not have to explain to his family why she
takes the bread out of their mouths and turns
them out-of-doors homeless and ashamed in a
strange land; she does not have to do anything
but send a *letter* and say: "Pack!—and ask no
questions!"

Has the Pope this power?—the other Pope—
the one in Rome. Has **he** anything approaching it? Can he turn a priest out of his pulpit
and strip him of his office and his livelihood
just upon a whim, a caprice, and meanwhile
furnishing no reasons to the parish? Not in

America. And not elsewhere, we may believe.

It is odd and strange, to see intelligent and
educated people among us worshipping this self-
seeking and remorseless tyrant as a God. This
worship is denied—by persons who are themselves worshippers of Mrs. Eddy. I feel quite
sure that it is a worship which will continue
during ages.

That Mrs. Eddy wrote that amazing By-law
with her own hand we have much better evidence than her word. We have her English.
It is there. It cannot be imitated. She ought
never to go to the expense of copyrighting her
verbal discharges. When any one tries to
claim them she should call me; I can always
tell them from any other literary apprentice's
at a glance. It was like her to call America a
"nation"; she would call a sand-bar a nation if
it should fall into a sentence in which she was
speaking of peoples, for she would not know
how to untangle it and get it out and classify it
by itself. And the closing arrangement of that
By-law is in true Eddysonian form, too. In
it she reserves authority to make a Reader fill

any office connected with a Science church—
sexton, grave-digger, advertising-agent, Annex-
polisher, leader of the choir, President, Director, Treasurer, Clerk, etc. She did not mean
that. She already possessed that authority.
She meant to clothe herself with power, despotic
and unchallengeable, to appoint all Science
Readers to their offices, both at home and
abroad. The phrase " or to appoint " is another
miscarriage of intention; she did not mean
" or," she meant " and."

That By-law puts into Mrs. Eddy's hands *absolute command* over the most formidable force
and influence existent in the Christian Science
kingdom outside of herself, and it does this *un-
conditionally* and (by auxiliary force of Laws
already quoted) *irrevocably.* Still, she is not
quite satisfied. Something might happen, she
doesn't know what. Therefore she drives in
one more nail, to make sure, and drives it
deep:

*" This By-law can neither be amended nor
annulled, except by consent of the Pastor Emeritus."*
13

Let some one with a wild and delirious fancy try and see if he can imagine her furnishing that consent.

MONOPOLY OF SPIRITUAL BREAD

Very properly, the first qualification for membership in the Mother-Church is belief in the doctrines of Christian Science.

But these doctrines must not be gathered from secondary sources. There is but *one* recognized source. The candidate must be a believer in the doctrines of Christian Science *"according to the platform and teaching contained in the Christian Science text-book, 'Science and Health, with Key to the Scriptures,' by Rev. Mary Baker G. Eddy."*

That is definite, and is final. There are to be no commentaries, no labored volumes of exposition and explanation by anybody except Mrs. Eddy. Because such things could sow error, create warring opinions, split the religion into sects, and disastrously cripple its power. Mrs. Eddy will do the *whole* of the explaining, herself—has done it, in fact. She has written several books. They are to be had (for cash in advance); they are all sacred; additions to them can never be needed and will never be permitted. They tell the candidate how to instruct himself, how to teach others, how to do all things comprised in the business—and they close the door against all would-be competitors, and monopolize the trade:

"The Bible and the above-named book [*Science and Health*], with other works by the same author," must be his *only* text-books for the commerce—he cannot forage outside.

Mrs. Eddy's words are to be the *sole* elucidators of the Bible and *Science and Health*—forever. Throughout the ages, whenever there is doubt as to the meaning of a passage in either of these books the inquirer will not dream of trying to explain it to himself; he would shudder at the thought of such temerity, such profanity; he would be haled to the Inquisition and thence to the public square and the stake if he should be caught studying into text-meanings on his own hook; he will be prudent and seek the meanings at the only permitted source, *Mrs. Eddy's commentaries*.

Value of this Strait-jacket. One must not un-
derrate the magnificence of this long-headed
idea, one must not underestimate its giant possibilities in the matter of hooping the Church
solidly together and keeping it so. It squelches
independent inquiry, and makes such a thing
impossible, profane, criminal, it authoritatively
settles every dispute that can arise. It *starts*
with *finality*—a point which the Roman Church
has travelled towards fifteen or sixteen centuries, stage by stage, and has not yet reached.
The matter of the Immaculate Conception of
the Virgin Mary was not authoritatively settled until the days of Pius IX.—yesterday, so
to speak.

As already noticed, the Protestants are broken up into a long array of sects, a result of
disputes about the meanings of texts, disputes
made unavoidable by the absence of an infallible authority to submit doubtful passages to.
A week or two ago (I am writing in the middle
of January, 1903), the clergy and others here-
abouts had a warm dispute in the papers over
this question: Did Jesus anywhere claim to
be God? It seemed an easy question, but it

turned out to be a hard one. It was ably and elaborately discussed, by learned men of several denominations, but in the end it remained unsettled.

A week ago, another discussion broke out. It was over this text:

"Sell all that thou hast and distribute unto the poor."

One verdict was worded as follows:

"When Christ answered the rich young man and said for him to give to the poor all he possessed or he could not gain everlasting life, He did not mean it in the literal sense. My interpretation of His words is that we should part with what comes between us and Christ.

"There is no doubt that Jesus believed that the rich young man thought more of his wealth than he did of his soul, and, such being the case, it was his duty to give up the wealth.

"Every one of us knows that there is something we should give up for Christ. Those who are true believers and followers know what they have given up, and those who are not yet followers know down in their hearts what they must give up.''

Ten clergymen of various denominations were interviewed, and nine of them agreed with that verdict. That did not settle the matter, because the tenth said the language of Jesus was so strait and definite that it explained *itself:* "Sell *all*," not a percentage.

There is a most unusual feature about that dispute: the nine persons who decided alike, quoted not a single authority in support of their position. I do not know when I have seen trained disputants do the like of that before. The nine merely furnished their own opinions, founded upon—nothing at all. In the other dispute ("Did Jesus anywhere claim to be God?") the same kind of men—trained and learned clergymen — backed up their arguments with chapter and verse. On both sides. Plenty of verses. Were no reinforcing verses to be found in the present case? It looks that way.

The opinion of the nine seems strange to me, for it is unsupported by authority, while there was at least constructive authority for the opposite view.

It is hair-splitting differences of opinion over disputed text-meanings that have divided into many sects a once united Church. One may infer from some of the names in the following list that some of the differences are very slight —so slight as to be not distinctly important, perhaps—yet they have moved groups to withdraw from communions to which they belonged and set up a sect of their own. The list—accompanied by various Church statistics for 1902, compiled by Rev. Dr. H. K. Carroll—was published, January 8, 1903, in the New York *Christian Advocate:*

Adventists (6 bodies),
Baptists (13 bodies),
Brethren (Plymouth) (4 bodies),
Brethren (River) (3 bodies),
Catholics (8 bodies),
Catholic Apostolic,
Christadelphians,
Christian Connection,
Christian Catholics (Dowie),
Christian Missionary Association,
Christian Scientists,
Church of God (Winebrennarian),

Church of the New Jerusalem,
Congregationalists,
Disciples of Christ,
Dunkards (4 bodies),
Evangelical (2 bodies),
Friends (4 bodies),
Friends of the Temple,
German Evangelical Protestant,
German Evangelical Synod,
Independent congregations.
Jews (2 bodies),
Latter-day Saints (2 bodies),
Lutherans (22 bodies),
Mennonites (12 bodies),
Methodists (17 bodies),
Moravians,
Presbyterians (12 bodies),
Protestant Episcopal (2 bodies),
Reformed (3 bodies),
Schwenkfeldians,
Social Brethren,
Spiritualists,
Swedish Evangelical Miss. Covenant (Waldenstromians),
Unitarians,
United Brethren (2 bodies),
Universalists,

Total of sects and splits—139.

In the present month (February), Mr. E. I. Lindh, A.M., has communicated to the Boston *Transcript* a hopeful article on the solution of the problem of the " divided church." Divided is not too violent a term. Subdivided could have been permitted if he had thought of it. He came near thinking of it, for he mentions some of the subdivisions himself: "the 12 kinds of Presbyterians, the 17 kinds of Methodists, the 13 kinds of Baptists, etc." He overlooked the 12 kinds of Mennonites and the 22 kinds of Lutherans, but they are in Rev. Mr. Carroll's list. Altogether, 76 splits under 5 flags. *The Literary Digest* (February 14th) is pleased with Mr. Lindh's optimistic article, and also with the signs of the times, and perceives that "the idea of Church unity is in the air."

Now, then, is not Mrs. Eddy profoundly wise in forbidding, for all time, all explanations of her religion except such as she shall let on to be her own?

I think so. I think there can be no doubt of it. In a way, they will be her own; for, no matter which member of her clerical staff shall furnish the explanations, not a line of them will she ever allow to be printed until she shall have approved it, accepted it, copyrighted it, cabbaged it. We may depend on that with a four-ace confidence.

THE NEW INFALLIBILITY

All in proper time Mrs. Eddy's factory will take hold of that Commandment, and explain it for good and all. It may be that one member of the shift will vote that the word "all" means *all;* it may be that ten members of the shift will vote that "all" means only a percentage; but it is *Mrs. Eddy,* not the eleven, who will do the *deciding.* And if she says it is percentage, then percentage it is, forevermore —and that is what I am expecting, for she doesn't sell all herself, nor any considerable part of it, and as regards the poor, she doesn't declare any dividend; but if she says "all" means all, then all it is, to the end of time, and no follower of hers will ever be allowed to reconstruct that text, or shrink it, or inflate it, or meddle with it in any way at all. Even to-day—right here in the beginning—she is the sole person who, in the matter of Christian Science exegesis, is privileged to exploit the Spiral Twist.[1] The Christian world has *two* Infallibles now.

[1] That is a technicality—that phrase. I got it of an uncle of mine. He had once studied in a theological cem-

Of equal power? For the present only. When Leo XIII. passes to his rest another Infallible will ascend his throne;[1] others, and yet others, and still others will follow him, and be as infallible as he, and decide questions of doctrine as long as they may come up, all down the far future; but Mary Baker G. Eddy is the *only* Infallible that will ever occupy the Science throne. Many a Science Pope will succeed her, but she has closed their mouths; they will repeat and reverently praise and adore her infallibilities, but venture none themselves. In her grave she will still outrank all other Popes, be they of what Church they may. She will hold the supremest of earthly titles, The Infallible—with a capital T. Many in the world's history have had a hunger for such nuggets and slices of power as they might reasonably hope to grab out of an empire's or a religion's assets, but Mrs. Eddy is the only person alive

---

etery, he said, and he called the Department of Biblical Exegesis the Spiral Twist "for short." He said it was always difficult to drive a straight text through an unaccommodating cork, but that if you twisted it it would go. He had kept bar in his less poetical days.—M. T.

[1] It has since happened.—M. T.

or dead who has ever struck for the *whole* of
them. For small things she has the eye of a
microscope, for large ones the eye of a telescope,
and whatever she sees, she wants. Wants it
all.

THE SACRED POEMS

When Mrs. Eddy's "sacred revelations"
(that is the language of the By-laws) are read
in public, their authorship must be named.
The By-laws twice command this, therefore
we mention it twice, to be fair.

But it is also commanded that when a member publicly quotes "from the poems of our
Pastor Emeritus" the authorship shall be
named. For these are sacred, too. There are
kindly people who may suspect a hidden generosity in that By-law; they may think it is
there to protect the Official Reader from the
suspicion of having written the poems himself.
Such do not know Mrs. Eddy. She does an in-
ordinate deal of protecting, but in no distinctly
named and specified case in her history has
Number Two been the object of it. Instances

have been claimed, but they have failed of proof, and even of plausibility.

"Members shall also instruct their students" to look out and advertise the authorship when they read those poems and things. Not on Mrs. Eddy's account, but "for the good of our Cause."

THE CHURCH EDIFICE

1. Mrs. Eddy gave the land. It was not of much value at the time, but it is very valuable now.

2. Her people built the Mother-Church edifice on it, at a cost of two hundred and fifty thousand dollars.

3. Then they gave the whole property to her.

4. Then she gave it to the Board of Directors. *She* is the Board of Directors. She took it out of one pocket and put it in the other.

5. *Sec.* 10 (*of the deed*). "Whenever said Directors shall determine that it is inexpedient to maintain preaching, reading, or speaking in said church in accordance with the terms of

this deed, they are authorized and *required* to re-
convey *forthwith* said lot of land with the building thereon to Mary Baker G. Eddy, her heirs and
assigns forever, by a proper deed of conveyance."

She is never careless, never slipshod, about
a matter of business. Owning the property
through her Board of Waxworks was safe
enough, still it was sound business to set another grip on it to cover accidents, and she did it.

Her barkers (what a curious name; I wonder
if it is copyrighted); her barkers persistently
advertise to the public her generosity in giving
away a piece of land which cost her a trifle, and
a two - hundred - and - fifty - thousand - dollar
church which cost her nothing; and they can
hardly speak of the unselfishness of it without
breaking down and crying; yet they know she
gave nothing away, and never intended to.
However, such is the human race. Often it
does seem such a pity that Noah and his party
did not miss the boat.

Some of the hostiles think that Mrs. Eddy's
idea in protecting this property in the interest
of her heirs, and in accumulating a great money-

fortune, is, that she may leave her natural heirs well provided for when she goes. I think it is a mistake. I think she is of late years giving herself large concern about only one interest—her power and glory, and the perpetuation and worship of her Name — with a capital N. Her Church is her pet heir, and I think it will get her wealth. It is the torch which is to light the world and the ages with her glory.

I think she once prized money for the ease and comfort it could bring, the showy vanities it could furnish, and the social promotion it could command; for we have seen that she was born into the world with little ways and instincts and aspirations and affectations that are duplicates of our own. I do not think her money-passion has ever diminished in ferocity, I do not think that she has ever allowed a dollar that had no friends to get by her alive, but I think her reason for wanting it has changed. I think she wants it now to increase and establish and perpetuate her power and glory with, not to add to her comforts and luxuries, not to furnish paint and fuss and feathers for vain display. I think her ambitions have soared away above the fuss-and-feather stage. She still likes the little shows and vanities—a fact which she exposed in a public utterance two or three days ago when she was not noticing[1]—but I think she does not place a large value upon them now. She could build a mighty and far-shining brass-mounted palace if she wanted to, but she does not do it. She would have had that kind of an ambition in the early scrabbling times. She could go to England to-day and be worshipped by earls, and get a comet's attention from the million, if she cared for such things. She would have gone in the early scrabbling days for much less than an earl, and been vain of it, and glad to show off before the remains of the Scotch kin. But those things are very small to her now—next to invisible, observed through the cloud-rack from the dizzy summit where she perches in these great days. She does not want that church property for herself. It is worth but a quarter of a million—a sum she could call in from her far-spread flocks to-morrow with a lift of her hand. Not a

[1] This is a reference to her public note of January 17th. See Appendix.—M. T.

squeeze of it, just a lift. It would come without a murmur; come gratefully, come gladly. And if her glory stood in more need of the money in Boston than it does where her flocks are propagating it, she would lift the hand, I think.

She is still reaching for the Dollar, she will continue to reach for it; but not that she may spend it upon herself; not that she may spend it upon charities; not that she may indemnify an early deprivation and clothe herself in a blaze of North Adams gauds; not that she may have nine breeds of pie for breakfast, as only the rich New-Englander can; not that she may indulge any petty material vanity or appetite that once was hers and prized and nursed, but that she may apply that Dollar to statelier uses, and place it where it may cast the metallic sheen of her glory farthest across the receding expanses of the globe.

PRAYER

A brief and good one is furnished in the book of By-laws. The Scientist is required to pray it every day.

14

THE LORD'S PRAYER—AMENDED

This is not in the By-laws, it is in the first chapter of *Science and Health*, edition of 1902. I do not find it in the edition of 1884. It is probable that it had not at that time been handed down. *Science and Health's* (latest) rendering of its "spiritual sense" is as follows:

"Our Father-Mother God, all-harmonious, adorable One. Thy kingdom is within us, Thou art ever-present. Enable us to know— as in heaven, so on earth—God is supreme. Give us grace for to-day; feed the famished affections. And infinite Love is reflected in love. And Love leadeth us not into temptation, but delivereth from sin, disease, and death. For God is now and forever all Life, Truth, and Love."[1]

If I thought my opinion was desired and would be properly revered, I should say that in my judgment that is as good a piece of carpentering as any of those eleven Commandment-

---

[1] For the latest version, see Appendix.—M. T.

experts could do with the material, after all their practice. I notice only one doubtful place. "Lead us not into temptation" seems to me to be a very definite request, and that the new rendering turns the definite request into a definite assertion. I shall be glad to have that turned back to the old way and the marks of the Spiral Twist removed, or varnished over; then I shall be satisfied, and will do the best I can with what is left. At the same time, I do feel that the shrinkage in our spiritual assets is getting serious. First the Commandments, now the Prayer. I never expected to see these steady old reliable securities watered down to this. And this is not the whole of it. Last summer the Presbyterians extended the Calling and Election suffrage to nearly everybody entitled to salvation. They did not even stop there, but let out all the unbaptized American infants we had been accumulating for two hundred years and more. There are some that believe they would have let the Scotch ones out, too, if they could have done it. Everything is going to ruin; in no long time we shall have nothing left but the love of God.

THE NEW UNPARDONABLE SIN

"*Working Against the Cause. Sec. 2.* If a member of this Church shall work against the accomplishment *of what the Discoverer and Founder of Christian Science understands is advantageous* to the individual, to this Church, and to the Cause of Christian Science"—out he goes. *Forever.*

The member may *think* that what he is doing will advance the Cause, but he is not invited to do any thinking. More than that, he is not *permitted* to do any—as he will clearly gather from this By-law. When a person joins Mrs. Eddy's Church he must leave his thinker at home. Leave it permanently. To make sure that it will not go off some time or other when he is not watching, it will be safest for him to spike it. If he should forget himself and think just *once*, the By-law provides that he shall be fired out—instantly—forever—no return.

"It shall be the duty of this Church immediately to call a meeting, and *drop forever the name of this member from its records.*"

My, but it breathes a **towering indignation!**

There are forgivable offences, but this is not one of them; there are admonitions, probations, suspensions, in several minor cases; mercy is shown the derelict, in those cases he is gently used, and in time he can get back into the fold —even when he has repeated his offence. But let him *think*, just *once*, without getting his thinker set to Eddy time, and that is enough; his head comes off. There is no second offence, and there is no gate open to that lost sheep, ever again.

" This rule cannot be changed, amended, or an-nulled, except by unanimous vote of all the First Members."

The same being *Mrs. Eddy.* It is naïvely sly and pretty to see her keep putting forward First Members, and Boards of This and That, and other broideries and ruffles of her raiment, as if they were independent entities, instead of a part of her clothes, and could do things all by themselves when she was outside of them.

Mrs. Eddy did not need to copyright the sen-

tence just quoted, its English would protect it.
None but she would have shovelled that com-
ically superfluous " all " in there.

The former Unpardonable Sin has gone out
of service. We may frame the new Christian
Science one thus:

" Whatsoever Member shall think, and without Our Mother's permission act upon his think,
the same shall be cut off from the Church forever."

It has been said that I make many mistakes
about Christian Science through being ignorant
of the spiritual meanings of its terminology. I
believe it is true. I have been misled all this
time by that word Member, because there was
no one to tell me that its spiritual meaning was
Slave.

AXE AND BLOCK

There is a By-law which forbids Members to
practise hypnotism; the penalty is excommunication.

1. If a member is found to be a mental practitioner—

2. Complaint is to be entered against him—

3. By the Pastor Emeritus, and by *none else;*

4. No member is allowed to make complaint to *her* in the matter;

5. *Upon Mrs. Eddy's mere "complaint"—unbacked by evidence or proof, and without giving the accused a chance to be heard—*"his name shall be dropped from this Church."

Mrs. Eddy has only to *say* a member is guilty —that is all. That ends it. It is not a case of he "may" be cut off from Christian Science salvation, it is a case of he "*shall*" be. Her serfs must see to it, and not say a word.

Does the other Pope possess this prodigious and irresponsible power? Certainly not in our day.

Some may be curious to know how Mrs. Eddy *finds out* that a member is practising hypnotism, since no one is allowed to come before her throne and accuse him. She has explained this in *Christian Science History*, first and second editions, page 16:

"I possess *a spiritual sense of what the malicious mental practitioner is mentally arguing* which cannot be deceived; I can discern in the human mind thoughts, motives, and purposes; and neither mental arguments nor psychic power can affect this spiritual insight.''

A marvellous woman; with a hunger for power such as has never been seen in the world before. No thing, little or big, that contains any seed or suggestion of power escapes her avaricious eye; and when once she gets that eye on it, her remorseless grip follows. There isn't a Christian Scientist who isn't ecclesiastically as much her property as if she had bought him and paid for him, and copyrighted him and got a charter. She cannot be satisfied when she has handcuffed a member, and put a leg-chain and ball on him and plugged his ears and removed his thinker, she goes on wrapping needless chains round and round him, just as a spider would. For she trusts no one, believes in no one's honesty, judges every one by herself. Although we have seen that she has absolute and irresponsible command over her spectral Boards and over every official and servant of her Church, at home and abroad, over every minute detail of her Church's government, *present and future*, and can purge her membership of guilty or suspected persons by various plausible formalities and whenever she will, she is still not content, but must set her queer mind to work and invent a way by which she can take a member—any member—by neck and crop and fling him out without anything resembling a formality at all.

She is sole accuser and sole witness, and her testimony is final and carries uncompromising and irremediable doom with it.

The Sole-Witness Court! It should make the Council of Ten and the Council of Three turn in their graves for shame, to see how little they knew about satanic concentrations of irresponsible power. Here we have one Accuser, one Witness, one Judge, one Headsman—and all four bunched together in Mrs. Eddy, the Inspired of God, His Latest Thought to His People, New Member of the Holy Family, the Equal of Jesus.

When a Member is not satisfactory to Mrs. Eddy, and yet is blameless in his life and faultless in his membership and in his Christian Science walk and conversation, shall he hold up his head and tilt his hat over one ear and imagine himself safe because of these perfections? Why, in that very moment Mrs. Eddy will cast that spiritual X-ray of hers through his dungarees and say:

"I see his hypnotism working, among his insides—remove him to the block!"

What shall it profit him to know it isn't so? Nothing. His testimony is of no value. No one wants it, no one will ask for it. He is not present to offer it (he does not know he has been accused), and if he were there to offer it, it would not be listened to.

It was out of powers approaching Mrs. Eddy's —though not equalling them—that the Inquisition and the devastations of the Interdict grew. She will transmit hers. The man born two centuries from now will think he has arrived in hell; and all in good time he will think he knows it. Vast concentrations of irresponsible power have never in any age been used mercifully, and there is nothing to suggest that the Christian Science Papacy is going to spend money on novelties.

Several Christian Scientists have asked me

to refrain from prophecy. There *is* no prophecy in our day but history. But history is a trustworthy prophet. History is always repeating itself, because *conditions* are always repeating themselves. Out of duplicated conditions history always gets a duplicate product.

READING LETTERS AT MEETINGS

I wonder if there is anything a Member *can* do that will not raise Mrs. Eddy's jealousy? The By-laws seem to hunt him from pillar to post all the time, and turn all his thoughts and acts and words into sins against the meek and lowly new deity of his worship. Apparently her jealousy never sleeps. Apparently any trifle can offend it, and but one penalty appease it — excommunication. The By-laws might properly and reasonably be entitled Laws for the Coddling and Comforting of Our Mother's Petty Jealousies. The By-law named at the head of this paragraph reads its transgressor out of the Church if he shall carry a letter from Mrs. Eddy to the congregation and forget to read it or fail to read the whole of it.

HONESTY REQUISITE

Dishonest members are to be admonished; if they continue in dishonest practices, excommunication follows. Considering who it is that draughted this law, there is a certain amount of humor in it.

FURTHER APPLICATIONS OF THE AXE

Here follow the titles of some more By-laws whose infringement is punishable by excommunication:

Silence Enjoined.
Misteaching.
Departure from Tenets.
Violation of Christian Fellowship.
Moral Offences.
Illegal Adoption.
Broken By-laws.
Violation of By-laws. (What is the difference?)
Formulas Forbidden.
Official Advice. (Forbids Tom, Dick, and Harry's clack.)

Unworthy of Membership.
Final Excommunication.
Organizing Churches.

This looks as if Mrs. Eddy had devoted a large share of her time and talent to inventing ways to get rid of her Church members. Yet in another place she seems to invite membership. Not in any urgent way, it is true, still she throws out a bait to such as like notice and distinction (in other words, the Human Race). Page 82:

"It is important that these seemingly strict conditions be complied with, as *the names of the Members of the Mother-Church will be recorded in the history* of the Church and become a part thereof."

We all want to be historical.

MORE SELF-PROTECTIONS

The Hymnal. There is a Christian Science Hymnal. Entrance to it was closed in 1898. Christian Science students who make hymns

nowadays may possibly get them sung in the
Mother-Church, "*but not unless approved by the
Pastor Emeritus.*" Art. XXVII., Sec. 2.

Solo Singers. Mrs. Eddy has contributed the
words of three of the hymns in the Hymnal.
Two of them appear in it six times altogether,
each of them being set to three original forms of
musical anguish. Mrs. Eddy, always thoughtful, has promulgated a By-law requiring the
singing of one of her three hymns in the Mother-
Church "as often as once each month." It is a
good idea. A congregation could get tired of
even Mrs. Eddy's muse in the course of time,
without the cordializing incentive of compulsion. We all know how wearisome the sweet-
est and touchingest things can become, through
rep-rep-repetition, and still rep-rep-repetition,
and more rep-rep-repetition—like "the sweet
by-and-by, *in* the sweet by-and-by," for instance, and "Tah-rah-rah boom-de-aye"; and
surely it is not likely that Mrs. Eddy's machine
has turned out goods that could outwear those
great heart-stirrers, without the assistance of
the lash. "O'er Waiting Harpstrings of the
Mind" is pretty good, quite fair to middling—

the whole seven of the stanzas—but repetition
would be certain to take the excitement out of
it in the course of time, even if there were fourteen, and then it would sound like the multipli-
cation table, and would cease to save. The
congregation would be perfectly sure to get
tired; in fact, *did* get tired—hence the compul-
sory By-law. It is a measure born of experience, not foresight.

The By-laws say that "if a solo singer shall
neglect or refuse to sing alone" one of those
three hymns as often as once a month, and
oftener if so directed by the Board of Directors
—which is Mrs. Eddy—the singer's salary shall
be stopped. It is circumstantial evidence that
some soloists neglected this sacrament and
others refused it. At least that is the charitable view to take of it. There is only one other
view to take: that Mrs. Eddy did really foresee
that there would be singers who would some
day get tired of doing her hymns and proclaim-
ing the authorship, unless persuaded by a By-
law, with a penalty attached. The idea could
of course occur to her wise head, for she would
know that a seven-stanza break might well be a

calamitous strain upon a soloist, and that he might therefore avoid it if unwatched. He could not curtail it, for the whole of anything that Mrs. Eddy does is sacred, and cannot be cut.

BOARD OF EDUCATION

It consists of four members, one of whom is President of it. Its members are elected annually. *Subject to Mrs. Eddy's approval.* Art. XXX., Sec. 2.

She owns the Board—*is* the Board.

Mrs. Eddy is President of the Metaphysical College. If at any time she shall vacate that office, the Directors of the College (that is to say, Mrs. Eddy) "*shall*" elect to the vacancy the President of the Board of Education (which is merely re-electing herself).

It is another case of "Pastor Emeritus." She gives up the shadow of authority, but keeps a good firm hold on the substance.

PUBLIC TEACHERS

Applicants for admission to this industry must pass a thorough three days' examination before the Board of Education "in *Science and Health,* chapter on 'Recapitulation'; the Platform of Christian Science; page 403 of *Christian Science Practice,* from line second to the second paragraph of page 405; and page 488, second and third paragraphs."

BOARD OF LECTURESHIP

The lecturers are exceedingly important servants of Mrs. Eddy, and she chooses them with great care. Each of them has an appointed territory in which to perform his duties—in the North, the South, the East, the West, in Canada, in Great Britain, and so on—and each must stick to his own territory and not forage beyond its boundaries. I think it goes without saying—from what we have seen of Mrs. Eddy —that no lecture is delivered until she has examined and approved it, and that the lecturer is not allowed to change it afterwards.

The members of the Board of Lectureship are elected annually—

"*Subject to the approval of Rev. Mary Baker G. Eddy.*"

15′

MISSIONARIES

There are but four. They are elected—like the rest of the domestics—annually. So far as I can discover, not a single servant of the Sacred Household has a steady job except Mrs. Eddy. It is plain that she trusts no human being but herself.

THE BY-LAWS

The branch Churches are strictly forbidden to use them.

So far as I can see, they could not do it if they wanted to. The By-laws are merely the voice of the master issuing commands to the servants. There is nothing and nobody for the servants to re-utter them to.

That useless edict is repeated in the little book, a few pages farther on. There are several other repetitions of prohibitions in the book that could be spared—they only take up room for nothing.

THE CREED

It is copyrighted. I do not know why, but I suppose it is to keep adventurers from some day claiming that they invented it, and not Mrs. Eddy and that "strange Providence" that has suggested so many clever things to her.

No Change. It is forbidden to change the Creed. That is important, at any rate.

COPYRIGHT

I can understand why Mrs. Eddy copyrighted the early editions and revisions of *Science and Health*, and why she had a mania for copyrighting every scrap of every sort that came from her pen in those jejune days when to be in print probably seemed a wonderful distinction to her in her provincial obscurity, but why she should continue this delirium in these days of her godship and her far-spread fame, I cannot explain to myself. And particularly as regards *Science and Health*. She knows, now, that that Annex is going to live for many centuries; and so, what good is a fleeting forty-two-year copyright going to do it?

Now a *perpetual* copyright would be quite another matter. I would like to give her a hint. Let her strike for a perpetual copyright on that

book. There is precedent for it. There is one
book in the world which bears the charmed life
of perpetual copyright (a fact not known to
twenty people in the world). By a hardy perversion of privilege on the part of the law-
making power the Bible has perpetual copyright in Great Britain. There is no justification
for it in fairness, and no explanation of it except
that the Church is strong enough there to have
its way, right or wrong. The recent Revised
Version enjoys perpetual copyright, too — a
stronger precedent, even, than the other one.

Now, then, what is the Annex but a Revised
Version itself? Which of course it is—Lord's
Prayer and all. With that pair of formidable
British precedents to proceed upon, what Con-
gress of ours—

But how short-sighted I am. Mrs. Eddy has
thought of it long ago. She thinks of everything. She knows she has only to keep her
copyright of 1902 alive through its first stage of
twenty-eight years, and perpetuity is assured.
A Christian Science Congress will reign in the
Capitol then. She probably attaches small value
to the first edition (1875). Although it was a

Revelation from on high, it was slim, lank, incomplete, padded with bales of refuse rags, and puffs from lassoed celebrities to fill it out, an uncreditable book, a book easily sparable, a book not to be mentioned in the same year with the sleek, fat, concise, compact, compressed, and competent Annex of to-day, in its dainty flexible covers, gilt - edges, rounded corners, twin screw, spiral twist, compensation balance, Testament-counterfeit, and all that; a book just born to curl up on the hymn-book-shelf in church and look just too sweet and holy for anything.   Yes, I see now what she was copyrighting that child for.

CHRISTIAN SCIENCE PUBLISHING ASSOCIATION

It is true—in matters of business Mrs. Eddy thinks of everything.   She thought of an organ, to disseminate the Truth as it was in Mrs. Eddy. Straightway she started one — the *Christian Science Journal.*

It is true—in matters of business Mrs. Eddy thinks of everything.   As soon as she had got the *Christian Science Journal* sufficiently in debt to make its presence on the premises disagreeable to her, it occurred to her to make somebody a present of it. Which she did, along with its debts. It was in the summer of 1889. The victim selected was her Church—called, in those days, The National Christian Scientist Association.

She delivered this sorrow to those lambs as a "gift" in consideration of their "loyalty to our great cause."

Also—still thinking of everything—she told them to retain Mr. Bailey in the editorship and make Mr. Nixon publisher. We do not know what it was she had against those men; neither do we know whether she scored on Bailey or not, we only know that God protected Nixon, and for that I am sincerely glad, although I do not know Nixon and have never even seen him.

Nixon took the *Journal* and the rest of the Publishing Society's liabilities, and demonstrated over them during three years, then brought in his report:

"On assuming my duties as publisher, there was not a dollar in the treasury; but on the contrary the Society owed unpaid printing and paper bills to the amount of several hundred dollars, not to mention a contingent liability of many more hundreds"—represented by advance-subscriptions paid for the *Journal* and the "Series," the which goods Mrs. Eddy had not delivered. And couldn't, very well, perhaps, on a Metaphysical College income of but a few thousand dollars a day, or a week, or whatever it was in those magnificently flourishing times. The struggling *Journal* had swallowed up those advance-payments, but its "claim" was a severe one and they had failed to cure it. But Nixon cured it in his diligent three years, and joyously reported the news that he had cleared off all the debts and now had a fat six thousand dollars in the bank.

It made Mrs. Eddy's mouth water.

At the time that Mrs. Eddy had unloaded that dismal gift on to her National Association, she had followed her inveterate custom: she had tied a string to its hind leg, and kept one end of it hitched to her belt. We have seen her do that in the case of the Boston Mosque. When she deeds property, she puts in **that** string-clause. It provides that under certain conditions she can pull the string and land the property in the cherished home of its happy youth. In the present case she believed that she had made provision that if at any time the National Christian Science Association should dissolve itself by a formal vote, she could pull.

A year after Nixon's handsome report, she writes the Association that she has a "unique request to lay before it." It has dissolved, and she is not quite sure that the *Christian Science Journal* has "already fallen into her hands" by that act, though it "seems" to her to have met with that accident; so she would like to have the matter decided by a formal vote. But whether there is a doubt or not, "I see the wisdom," she says, "of again owning this Christian Science waif."

I think that that is unassailable evidence that the waif was making money, hands down.

She pulled her gift in. A few years later she donated the Publishing Society, along with its real estate, its buildings, its plant, its publications, and its money—the whole worth twenty-two thousand dollars, and free of debt—to—

Well, *to the Mother-Church!*

That is to say, to herself. There is an account of it in the *Christian Science Journal*, and of how she had already made some other handsome gifts—to her Church—and others to—to her Cause—besides "an almost countless number of private charities" of cloudy amount and otherwise indefinite. This landslide of generosities overwhelmed one of her literary domestics. While he was in that condition he tried to express what he felt:

"Let us endeavor to lift up our hearts in thankfulness to . . . our Mother in Israel for these evidences of generosity and self-sacrifice that appeal to our deepest sense of gratitude, even while surpassing our comprehension."

A year or two later, Mrs. Eddy promulgated some By-laws of a self-sacrificing sort which assuaged him, perhaps, and perhaps enabled his surpassed comprehension to make a sprint and catch up. These are to be found in Art. XII., entitled

THE CHRISTIAN SCIENCE PUBLISHING SOCIETY

This Article puts the whole publishing business into the hands of a publishing Board—special. *Mrs. Eddy appoints to its vacancies.*

The profits go semi-annually to the Treasurer of the Mother - Church. *Mrs. Eddy owns the Treasurer.*

Editors and publishers of the *Christian Science Journal cannot be elected or removed without Mrs. Eddy's knowledge and consent.*

Every candidate for employment in a high capacity or a low one, on the other periodicals or in the publishing house, *must first be "accepted by Mrs. Eddy as suitable."* And "by the Board of Directors"—which is surplusage, since Mrs. Eddy owns the Board.

If at any time a weekly shall be started, "*it shall be owned by The First Church of Christ, Scientist*"—which is Mrs. Eddy.

I THINK that any one who will carefully examine the By-laws (I have placed all of the
important ones before the reader), will arrive
at the conclusion that of late years the master-
passion in Mrs. Eddy's heart is a hunger for
power and glory; and that while her hunger for
money still remains, she wants it now for the
expansion and extension it can furnish to that
power and glory, rather than what it can do for
her towards satisfying minor and meaner ambitions.

I wish to enlarge a little upon this matter. I
think it is quite clear that the reason why Mrs.
Eddy has concentrated in herself all powers,
all distinctions, all revenues that are within the
command of the Christian Science Church Universal is that she desires and intends to devote
them to the purpose just suggested—the up-
building of her personal glory—hers, and no
one else's; that, and the continuing of her

name's glory after she shall have passed away. *If she has overlooked a single power, howsoever minute, I cannot discover it. If she has found one, large or small, which she has not seized and made her own, there is no record of it, no trace of it.* In her foragings and depredations she usually puts forward the Mother-Church—a lay figure—and hides behind it. Whereas, she is in manifest reality the Mother-Church herself. ˙It has an impressive array of officials, and committees, and Boards of Direction, of Education, of Lectureship, and so on—geldings, every one, shadows, spectres, apparitions, wax-figures: she is supreme over them all, she can abolish them when she will; blow them out as she would a candle. She is herself the Mother-Church. Now there is one By-law which says that the Mother-Church

"shall be officially controlled by no other church."

That does not surprise us—we know by the rest of the By-laws that that is a quite irrelevant remark. Yet we do vaguely and hazily wonder why she takes the trouble to say it; why she wastes the words; what her object can be—seeing that that emergency has been in so many, many ways, and so effectively and drastically barred off and made impossible. Then presently the object begins to dawn upon us. That is, it does after we have read the rest of the By-law three or four times, wondering and admiring to see Mrs. Eddy—Mrs. Eddy—Mrs. Eddy, of all persons—throwing away power!— making a fair exchange—doing a fair thing for once—more, an almost generous thing! Then we look it through yet once more—unsatisfied, a little suspicious—and find that it is nothing but a sly, thin make-believe, and that even the very title of it is a sarcasm and embodies a falsehood—"self" government:

"*Local Self-Government.* The First Church of Christ, Scientist, in Boston, Massachusetts, shall assume no official control of other churches of this denomination. It shall be officially controlled by no other church."

It has a most pious and deceptive give-and-take air of perfect fairness, unselfishness, magnanimity—almost godliness, indeed. But it is all art.

In the By-laws, Mrs. Eddy, speaking by the mouth of her other self, the Mother-Church, proclaims that she will assume no official control of other churches—branch churches. We examine the other By-laws, and they answer some important questions for us:

1. What *is* a branch Church? It is a body of Christian Scientists, organized in the one and only permissible way — by a member, in good standing, of the Mother-Church, and who is also a pupil of one of Mrs. Eddy's accredited students. That is to say, one of her properties. *No other can do it.* There are other indispensable requisites; what are they?

2. The new Church cannot enter upon its functions until its members have individually signed, and pledged allegiance to, a *Creed furnished by Mrs. Eddy.*

3. *They are obliged to study her books, and order their lives by them.* And they must read *no outside religious works.*

4. *They must sing the hymns and pray the*

prayers provided by her, and use no others in the services, except by her permission.

5. They cannot have preachers and pastors. *Her law.*

6. In their Church they must have two Readers—a man and a woman.

7. They must read the services framed and appointed by *her.*

8. *She*—not the branch Church—*appoints* those Readers.

9. *She*—not the branch Church—*dismisses* them and *fills the vacancies.*

10. She can do this *without consulting the branch Church, and without explaining.*

11. The branch Church can have a religious lecture from time to time. *By applying to Mrs. Eddy.* There is no other way.

12. But the branch Church cannot select the lecturer. *Mrs. Eddy does it.*

13. The branch Church pays his fee.

14. The harnessing of all Christian Science wedding-teams, members of the branch Church, must be done by duly authorized and consecrated Christian Science functionaries. *Her factory is the only one that makes and licenses them.*

[15. **Nothing** is said about christenings. It is inferable from this that a Christian Science child is born a Christian Scientist and requires no tinkering.

[16. Nothing is said about funerals. It is inferable, then, that a branch Church is privileged to do in that matter as it may choose.]

To sum up. Are *any* important Church-functions absent from the list? I cannot call any to mind. Are there any lacking ones whose exercise could make the branch in any noticeable way independent of the Mother-Church?—even in any trifling degree? I think of none. If the named functions were abolished would there still be a Church left? Would there be even a shadow of a Church left? Would there be anything at all left?—even the bare *name* ?

Manifestly not. There isn't a single vital and essential Church-function of any kind, that is not named in the list. And over every one of them the Mother-Church has permanent and unchallengeable control, upon every one of them Mrs. Eddy has set her irremovable grip. *She holds, in perpetuity, autocratic and indis-*

putable sovereignty and control over every branch Church in the earth; and yet says, in that sugary, naïve, angel-beguiling way of hers, that the Mother-Church

"*shall assume no official control of other churches of this denomination.*"

Whereas in truth the unmeddled-with liberties of a branch Christian Science Church are but very, very few in number, and are these:

1. It can appoint its own furnace - stoker, winters.

2. It can appoint its own fan-distributors, summers.

3. It can, in accordance with its own choice in the matter, burn, bury, or preserve members who are pretending to be dead—whereas there is no such thing as death.

4. It can take up a collection.

The branch Churches have *no* important liberties, none that give them an important voice in their own affairs. Those are all locked up, and Mrs. Eddy has the key. "Local Self-Government" is a large name and sounds well; but

16

the branch Churches have no more of it than have the privates in the King of Dahomey's army.

"MOTHER-CHURCH UNIQUE"

Mrs. Eddy, with an envious and admiring eye upon the solitary and rivalless and world-shadowing majesty of St. Peter's, reveals in her By-laws her purpose to set the Mother-Church apart by itself in a stately seclusion and make it duplicate that lone sublimity under the Western sky. The By-law headed " Mother-Church Unique" says—

" In its relation to other Christian Science churches, the Mother-Church stands alone.

" It occupies a position that no other Church can fill.

" Then for a branch Church to assume such position would be disastrous to Christian Science.

" Therefore—"

Therefore no branch Church is allowed to have branches. There shall be no Christian Science St. Peter's in the earth but just one— the Mother-Church in Boston.

"NO FIRST MEMBERS"

But for the thoughtful By-law thus entitled, every Science branch in the earth would imitate the Mother-Church and set up an aristocracy. Every little group of ground-floor Smiths and Furgusons and Shadwells and Simpsons that organized a branch would assume that great title, of "First Members," along with its vast privileges of "discussing" the weather and casting blank ballots, and soon there would be such a locust-plague of them burdening the globe that the title would lose its value and have to be abolished.

But where business and glory are concerned, Mrs. Eddy thinks of everything, and so she did not fail to take care of her Aborigines, her stately and exclusive One Hundred, her college of functionless cardinals, her Sanhedrin of Privileged Talkers (Limited). After taking away *all* the liberties of the branch Churches, and in the same breath disclaiming all official control over their affairs, she smites them on the mouth with this—the very mouth that was watering for those nobby ground-floor honors—

"*No First Members.*   Branch Churches shall not organize with First Members, that special method of organization being adapted to the Mother-Church alone."

And so, first members being prohibited, we pierce through the cloud of Mrs. Eddy's English and perceive that they must then necessarily organize with Subsequent Members.   There is no other way.   It will occur to them by-and-by to found an aristocracy of Early Subsequent Members.   There is no By-law against it.

"THE."

I uncover to that imperial word.   And to the mind, too, that conceived the idea of seizing and monopolizing it as a title.   I believe it is Mrs. Eddy's dazzlingest invention.   For show, and style, and grandeur, and thunder and lightning and fireworks it outclasses all the previous inventions of man, and raises the limit on the Pope.   He can never put his avid hand on that word of words—it is pre-empted.   And copyrighted, of course.   It lifts the Mother-

Church away up in the sky, and fellowships it with the rare and select and exclusive little company of the THE's of deathless glory—persons and things whereof history and the ages could furnish only single examples, not two: *the* Saviour, *the* Virgin, *the* Milky Way, *the* Bible, *the* Earth, *the* Equator, *the* Devil, *the* Missing Link —and now *The* First Church, Scientist. And by clamor of edict and By-law Mrs. Eddy gives personal notice to all branch Scientist Churches on this planet to leave that THE alone.

She has demonstrated over it and made it sacred to the Mother-Church:

" The article ' The' must not be used before the titles of branch Churches—
" Nor written on applications for membership in naming such churches."

Those are the terms. There can and will be a million First Churches of Christ, Scientist, scattered over the world, in a million towns and villages and hamlets and cities, and each may call itself (suppressing the ˏarticle), " First Church of Christ, Scientist "—it is permissible,

and no harm; but there is only one *The* Church
of Christ, Scientist, and there will never be another. And whether that great word fall in
the middle of a sentence or at the beginning of
it, it must always have its capital T.

I do not suppose that a juvenile passion for
fussy little worldly shows and vanities can furnish a match to this, anywhere in the history
of the nursery. Mrs. Eddy does seem to be a
shade fonder of little special distinctions and
pomps than is usual with human beings.

She instituted that immodest "The" with
her own hand; she did not wait for somebody
else to think of it.

A LIFE-TERM MONOPOLY

There is but *one* human Pastor in the whole
Christian Science world; she reserves that exalted place to herself.

A PERPETUAL ONE

There is but *one other* object in the whole
Christian Science world honored with that title
and holding that office: it is her *book*, the Annex

—permanent Pastor of The First Church, and of all branch Churches.

With her own hand she draughted the By-laws which make her the only really absolute sovereign that lives to-day in Christendom.[1]

She does not allow any objectionable pictures to be exhibited in the room where her book is sold, nor any indulgence in idle gossip there; and from the general look of that By-law I judge that a lightsome and improper person can be as uncomfortable in that place as he could be in heaven.

THE SANCTUM SANCTORUM AND SACRED CHAIR

In a room in The First Church of Christ, Scientist, there is a museum of objects which

[1] Even that ideal representative of irresponsible power, the General of the Jesuits, is not in the running with Mrs. Eddy. He is authentically described as follows:

"The Society of Jesus has really but one head, the General. He must be a professed Jesuit of the four vows, and it is the professed Jesuits of the four vows only who take part in his election, which is by secret ballot. He has four 'assistants' to help him, and an 'admonisher,' elected in the same way as himself, to keep him in, or, if need be, to bring him back to the right path. The electors of the General have the right of *deposing* him if he is guilty of a serious fault."

have attained to holiness through contact with Mrs. Eddy—among them an electrically lighted oil-picture of a *chair* which she used to sit in—and disciples from all about the world go softly in there, in restricted groups, under proper guard, and reverently gaze upon those relics. It is worship. Mrs. Eddy could stop it if she was not fond of it, for her sovereignty over that temple is supreme.

The fitting-up of that place as a shrine is not an accident, nor a casual, unweighed idea; it is imitated from age-old religious custom. In Treves the pilgrim reverently gazes upon the Seamless Robe, and humbly worships; and does the same in that other continental church where they keep a duplicate; and does likewise in the Church of the Holy Sepulchre, in Jerusalem, where memorials of the Crucifixion are preserved; and now, by good fortune we have our Holy Chair and things, and a market for our adorations nearer home.

But is there not a detail that is new, fresh, original? Yes, whatever old thing Mrs. Eddy touches gets something new by the contact—something not thought of before by any one—

something original, all her own, and copyright-
able. The new feature is *self* worship—exhibited in permitting this shrine to be installed
during her lifetime, and winking her sacred eye
at it.

A prominent Christian Scientist has assured
me that the Scientists do not worship Mrs. Eddy,
and I think it likely that there may be five or
six of the cult in the world who do not worship
her; but she herself is certainly not of that company. Any healthy-minded person who will
examine Mrs. Eddy's little *Autobiography* and
the Manual of By-laws written by her will be
convinced that she worships herself; and that
she brings to this service a fervor of devotion
surpassing even that which she formerly laid at
the feet of the Dollar, and equalling any which
rises to the Throne of Grace from any quarter.

I think this is as good a place as any to salve
a hurt which I was the means of inflicting upon
a Christian Scientist lately. The first third of
this book was written in 1899 in Vienna. Until
last summer I had supposed that that third
had been printed in a book which I published
about a year later—a hap which had not hap-

pened. I then sent the chapters composing it to the *North American Review*, but failed, in one instance, to date them. And so, in an undated chapter I said a lady told me "last night" so and so. There was nothing to indicate to the reader that that "last night" was several years old, therefore the phrase seemed to refer to a night of very recent date. What the lady had told me was, that in a part of the Mother-Church in Boston she had seen Scientists worshipping a portrait of Mrs. Eddy before which a light was kept constantly burning.

A Scientist came to me and wished me to retract that "untruth." He said there was no such portrait, and that if I wanted to be sure of it I could go to Boston and see for myself. I explained that my "last night" meant a good while ago; that I did not doubt his assertion that there was no such portrait there now, but that I should continue to believe it had been there at the time of the lady's visit until she should retract her statement herself. I was at no time vouching for the truth of the remark, nevertheless I considered it worth par.

And yet I am sorry the lady told me, since a

wound which brings me no happiness has resulted. I am most willing to apply such salve as I can. The best way to set the matter right and make everything pleasant and agreeable all around will be to print in this place a description of the shrine as it appeared to a recent visitor, Mr. Frederick W. Peabody, of Boston. I will copy his newspaper account, and the reader will see that Mrs. Eddy's portrait is not there now:

"We lately stood on the threshold of the Holy of Holies of the Mother-Church, and with a crowd of worshippers patiently waited for admittance to the hallowed precincts of the 'Mother's Room.' Over the doorway was a sign informing us that but four persons at a time would be admitted; that they would be permitted to remain but five minutes only, and would please retire from the 'Mother's Room' at the ringing of the bell. Entering with three of the faithful, we looked with profane eyes upon the consecrated furnishings. A show-woman in attendance monotonously announced the character of the different appointments. Set in a recess of the wall and illumined with electric light was an oil-painting the show-woman seriously declared to be a lifelike and realistic picture of the Chair in which the Mother sat when she composed her 'inspired' work. It was a picture of an old-fashioned, country, hair-cloth rocking-chair, and an exceedingly commonplace-looking table with a pile of manuscript, an ink-bottle, and pen conspicuously upon it. On the floor were sheets of manuscript. 'The mantel-piece is of pure onyx,' continued the show-woman, 'and the beehive upon the window-sill is made from one solid block of onyx; the rug is made of a hundred breasts of eider-down ducks, and the toilet-room you see in the corner is of the latest design, with gold-plated drain-pipes; the painted windows are from the Mother's poem, "Christ and Christmas," and that case contains complete copies of all the Mother's books.' The chairs upon which the sacred person of the Mother had reposed were protected from sacrilegious touch by a broad band of satin ribbon. My companions expressed their admiration in subdued and reverent tones, and at the tinkling of the bell we reverently tiptoed out of the room to admit another delegation of the patient waiters at the door.''

Now, then, I hope the wound is healed. I am willing to relinquish the portrait, and compromise on the Chair. At the same time, if I were going to worship either, I should not choose the Chair.

As a picturesquely and persistently interesting personage, there is no mate to Mrs. Eddy, the accepted Equal of the Saviour. But some of her tastes are so different from His! I find it quite impossible to imagine Him, in life, standing sponsor for that museum there, and taking pleasure in its sumptuous shows. I believe He would put that Chair in the fire, and the bell along with it; and I think He would make the show-woman go away. I think He would break those electric bulbs, and the "mantel-piece of pure onyx," and say reproachful things about the golden drain-pipes of the lavatory, and give the costly rug of duck-breasts to the poor, and sever the satin ribbon and invite the weary to rest and ease their aches in the consecrated chairs. What He would do with the painted windows we can better conjecture when we come presently to examine their peculiarities.

THE CHRISTIAN SCIENCE PASTOR-UNIVERSAL

When Mrs. Eddy turned the pastors out of all the Christian Science churches and abolished the office for all time—as far as human occupancy is concerned—she appointed the Holy Ghost to fill their place. If this language be blasphemous, I did not invent the blasphemy, I am merely stating a fact. I will quote from page 227 of *Science and Health* (edition 1899), as a first step towards an explanation of this startling matter—a passage which sets forth and classifies the Christian Science Trinity:

"Life, Truth, and Love constitute the triune God, or triply divine Principle. They represent a trinity in unity, three in one—the same in essence, though multiform in office: God the Father; Christ the type of Sonship; Divine Science, or the Holy Comforter. . . .

"The *Holy Ghost*, or Spirit, *reveals* this triune Principle, and (*the Holy Ghost*) is expressed in *Divine Science*, which is *the Comforter*, leading into all Truth, and revealing the divine Principle of the universe—universal and perpetual harmony."

I will cite another passage. Speaking of Jesus—

"His students then *received the Holy Ghost.* By this is meant, that by all they had witnessed and suffered they were roused to an enlarged *understanding of Divine Science,* even to the *spiritual interpretation . . . of His teachings,"* etc.

Also, page 579, in the chapter called the Glossary:

"HOLY GHOST. *Divine Science;* the developments of Life, Truth, and Love."

The Holy Ghost *reveals* the massed spirit of the fused trinity; this massed spirit is *expressed* in Divine Science, and is the *Comforter;* Divine Science *conveys* to men the "*spiritual interpretation*" of the Saviour's teachings. That seems to be the meaning of the quoted passages.

Divine Science is Christian Science; the book *Science and Health* is a "*revelation*" of the whole spirit of the Trinity, and is therefore "*The Holy Ghost*"; it conveys to men the "*spiritual inter-*

pretation" of the Bible's teachings, and there-fore is " the *Comforter*."

I do not find this analyzing work easy, I would rather saw wood; and a person can never tell whether he has added up a *Science and Health* sum right or not, anyway, after all his trouble. Neither can he easily find out whether the texts are still on the market or have been discarded from the Book; for two hundred and fifty-eight editions of it have been issued, and no two editions seem to be alike. The annual changes—in technical terminology; in matter and wording; in transpositions of chapters and verses; in leaving out old chapters and verses and putting in new ones—seem to be next to innumerable, and as there is no index, there is no way to find a thing one wants without read-ing the book through. If ever I inspire a Bible-Annex I will not rush at it in a half-digested, helter-skelter way and have to put in thirty-eight years trying to get some of it the way I want it, I will sit down and think it out and know what it is I want to say before I begin. An inspirer cannot inspire for Mrs. Eddy and keep his reputation. I have never seen such

slipshod work, bar the ten that interpreted for
the home market the "sell all thou hast." I
have quoted one "spiritual" rendering of the
Lord's Prayer, I have seen one other one, and
am told there are five more.[1] Yet the inspirer
of Mrs. Eddy the new Infallible casts a complacent critical stone at the other Infallible for being
unable to make up its mind about such things.
Science and Health, edition 1899, page 33:

"The decisions, by vote of Church Councils,
as to what should and should not be considered
Holy Writ, the manifest mistakes in the ancient
versions: the thirty thousand different readings
in the Old Testament and the three hundred
thousand in the New—these facts show how a
mortal and material sense stole into the divine
record, darkening, to some extent, the inspired
pages with its own hue."

To some extent, yes — speaking cautiously.
But it is nothing, really nothing; Mrs. Eddy is
only a little way behind, and if her inspirer
lives to get her Annex to suit him that Catholic

[1] See a second rendering in Appendix. (Lord's Prayer.)
—M. T.
17

record will have to "go 'way back and set down," as the ballad says. Listen to the boastful song of Mrs. Eddy's organ, the *Christian Science Journal* for March, 1902, about that year's revamping and half-soling of *Science and Health*, whose official name is the Holy Ghost, the Comforter, and who is now the Official Pastor and Infallible and Unerring Guide of every Christian Science church in the two hemispheres, hear Simple Simon that met the pieman brag of the Infallible's fallibility:

"Throughout the entire book the verbal changes are so numerous as to indicate the vast amount of time and labor Mrs. Eddy has devoted to this revision. The time and labor thus bestowed is relatively as great as that of the committee who revised the Bible. . . . Thus we have additional evidence of the herculean efforts our beloved Leader has made and is constantly making for the promulgation of Truth and the furtherance of her divinely bestowed mission," etc.

It is a steady job. I could help inspire if desired; I am not doing much now, and would

THE FIRST CHURCH OF CHRIST, SCIENTIST, CENTRAL PARK
WEST AND 96TH STREET, NEW YORK

work for half-price, and should not object to the country.

PRICE OF THE PASTOR-UNIVERSAL

The price of the Pastor-Universal, *Science and Health,* called in Science literature the Comforter—and by that other sacred Name—is three dollars in cloth, as heretofore, six when it is finely bound, and shaped to imitate the Testament, and is broken into verses. Margin of profit above cost of manufacture, from five hundred to seven hundred per cent., as already noted. In the profane subscription-trade, it costs the publisher heavily to canvass a three-dollar book; he must pay the general agent *sixty per cent.* commission—that is to say, one dollar and eighty cents. Mrs. Eddy escapes this blistering tax, because she owns the Christian Science canvasser, and can compel him to work for nothing. Read the following *command*—not request —fulminated by Mrs. Eddy, over her signature, in the *Christian Science Journal* for March, 1897, and quoted by Mr. Peabody in his book. The book referred to is *Science and Health:*

" It shall be the duty of all Christian Scientists to circulate and to sell as many of these books as they can."

That is flung at all the elect, everywhere that the sun shines, but no penalty is shaken over their heads to scare them. The same command was issued to the members (numbering to-day twenty-five thousand) of The Mother-Church, also, but with it went a *threat*, of the infliction, in case of disobedience, of the most dreaded punishment that has a place in the Church's list of penalties for transgressions of Mrs. Eddy's edicts — excommunication:

" If a member of The First Church of Christ, Scientist, shall fail to obey this injunction, it will render him liable to lose his membership in this Church.   MARY BAKER EDDY."

It is the spirit of the Spanish Inquisition.

None but accepted and well-established *gods* can venture an affront like that and do it with confidence. But the human race will take anything from that class. Mrs. Eddy knows the human race; knows it better than any mere human being has known it in a thousand centuries. My confidence in her human-beingship is getting shaken, my confidence in her godship is stiffening.

SEVEN HUNDRED PER CENT.

A Scientist out West has visited a bookseller—with intent to find fault with me—and has brought away the information that the price at which Mrs. Eddy sells *Science and Health* is not an unusually high one for the size and make of the book. That is true. But in the book-trade—that profit-devourer unknown to Mrs. Eddy's book—a three-dollar book that is made for thirty-five or forty cents in large editions is put at three dollars because the publisher has to pay author, middleman, and advertising, and if the price were much below three the profit accruing would not pay him fairly for his time and labor. At the same time, if he could get ten dollars for the book he would take it, and his morals would not fall under criticism.

But if he were an inspired person commissioned by the Deity to receive and print and spread broadcast among sorrowing and suffering and poor men a precious message of healing and cheer and salvation, he would have to do as Bible Societies do—sell the book at a pinched margin above cost to such as could pay, and give it free to all that couldn't; and his name would be praised. But if he sold it at seven hundred per cent. profit and put the money in his pocket, his name would be mocked and derided. Just as Mrs. Eddy's is. And most justifiably, as it seems to me.

The complete Bible contains one million words. The New Testament by itself contains two hundred and forty thousand words.

My '84 edition of *Science and Health* contains one hundred and twenty thousand words—just half as many as the New Testament.

Science and Health has since been so inflated by later inspirations that the 1902 edition contains one hundred and eighty thousand words—not counting the thirty thousand at the back, devoted by Mrs. Eddy to advertising the book's healing abilities—and the inspiring continues right along.

If you have a book whose market is so sure and so great that you can give a printer an everlasting order for thirty or forty or fifty thousand copies a year he will furnish them at a cheap rate, because whenever there is a slack time in his press-room and bindery he can fill the idle intervals on your book and be making something instead of losing. That is the kind of contract that can be let on *Science and Health* every year. I am obliged to doubt that the three-dollar *Science and Health* costs Mrs. Eddy above fifteen cents, or that the six-dollar copy costs her above eighty cents. I feel quite sure that the average profit to her on these books, above cost of manufacture, is all of seven hundred per cent.

Every proper Christian Scientist has to buy and own (and canvass for) *Science and Health* (one hundred and eighty thousand words), and he must also own a Bible (one million words). He can buy the one for from three to six dollars, and the other for fifteen cents. Or, if three dollars is all the money he has, he can get his

Bible for *nothing*. When the Supreme Being disseminates a saving Message through uninspired agents—the New Testament, for instance —it can be done for five cents a copy; but when He sends one containing only two-thirds as many words through the shop of a Divine Personage, it costs *sixty times as much*. I think that in matters of such importance it is bad economy to employ a wild-cat agency.

Here are some figures which are perfectly authentic, and which seem to justify my opinion:

"These [Bible] societies, inspired only by a sense of religious duty, are issuing the Bible at a price so small that they have made it *the cheapest book printed*. For example, the American Bible Society offers an edition of *the whole Bible as low as fifteen cents* and the *New Testament at five cents*, and the British Society at *sixpence and one penny, respectively*. These low prices, made possible by their policy of selling the books *at cost or below cost*," etc.—New York *Sun*, February 25, 1903.

CHAPTER IX

WE may now make a final footing-up of Mrs. Eddy, and see what she is, in the fulness of her powers. She is

The Massachusetts Metaphysical College;

Pastor Emeritus;

President;

Board of Directors;

Board of Education;

Board of Lectureships;

Future Board of Trustees;

Proprietor of the Publishing - House and Periodicals;

Treasurer;

Clerk;

Proprietor of the Teachers;

Proprietor of the Lecturers;

Proprietor of the Missionaries;

Proprietor of the Readers;

Dictator of the Services: sole Voice of the Pulpit;

Proprietor of the Sanhedrin;

Sole Proprietor of the Creed.   (Copyrighted.)

Indisputable Autocrat of the Branch Churches, with their life and death in her hands;

Sole Thinker for The First Church (and the others);

Sole and Infallible Expounder of Doctrine, in life and in death;

Sole permissible Discoverer, Denouncer, Judge, and Executioner of Ostensible Hypnotists;

Fifty-handed God of Excommunication—with a thunderbolt in every hand;

Appointer and Installer of the Pastor of all the Churches—the Perpetual Pastor-Universal, *Science and Health*, "the Comforter."

CHAPTER X

THERE she stands—painted by herself. No witness but herself has been allowed to testify. She stands there painted by her *acts*, and decorated by her words. When she talks, she has only a decorative value as a witness, either for or against herself, for she deals mainly in unsupported assertion; and in the rare cases where she puts forward a verifiable fact she gets out of it a meaning which it refuses to furnish to anybody else. Also, when she talks, she is unstable; she wanders, she is incurably inconsistent; what she says to-day she contradicts to-morrow.

But her *acts* are consistent. They are always faithful to her, they never misinterpret her, they are a mirror which always reflects her exactly, precisely, minutely, unerringly, and always the same, to date, with only those progressive little natural changes in stature, dress, complexion, mood, and carriage that mark—

exteriorly—the march of the years and record the accumulations of experience, while—interiorly—through all this steady drift of evolution the one essential detail, the commanding detail, the master detail of the make-up remains as it was in the beginning, suffers no change and *can* suffer none; the *basis* of the character; the temperament, the disposition, that indestructible iron framework upon which the character is *built*, and whose shape it must take, and keep, throughout life. We call it a person's *nature*.

The man who is born stingy can be taught to give liberally—with his hands; but not with his heart. The man born kind and compassionate can have that disposition crushed down out of sight by embittering experience; but if it were an organ the post-mortem would find it still in his corpse. The man born ambitious of power and glory may live long without finding it out, but when the opportunity comes he will know, will strike for the largest thing within the limit of his chances at the time—constable, perhaps—and will be glad and proud when he gets it, and will write home about it. But he will not stop with that start; his appetite will come again; and by-and-by again, and yet again; and when he has climbed to police commissioner it will at last begin to dawn upon him that what his Napoleon soul wants and was born for is something away higher up— he does not quite know what, but Circumstance and Opportunity will indicate the direction and he will cut a road through and find out.

I think Mrs. Eddy was born with a far-seeing business-eye, but did not know it; and with a great organizing and executive talent, and did not know it; and with a large appetite for power and distinction, and did not know it. I think the reason that her make did not show up until middle life was that she had General Grant's luck—Circumstance and Opportunity did not come her way when she was younger. The qualities that were born in her had to wait for circumstance and opportunity—but they were there: they were there to stay, whether they ever got a chance to fructify or not. If they had come early, they would have found her ready and competent. And they—not she —would have determined what they would set

her at and what they would make of her. If
they had elected to commission her as second-
assistant cook in a bankrupt boarding-house, I
know the rest of it—I know what would have
happened. She would have owned the boarding-house within six months; she would have
had the late proprietor on salary and hump-
ing himself, as the worldly say; she would have
had that boarding-house spewing money like a
mint; she would have worked the servants and
the late landlord up to the limit; she would have
squeezed the boarders till they wailed, and by
some mysterious quality born in her she would
have kept the affections of certain of the lot
whose love and esteem she valued, and flung
the others down the back area; in two years she
would own all the boarding-houses in the town,
in five all the boarding-houses in the State, in
twenty all the hotels in America, in forty all the
hotels on the planet, and would sit at home with
her finger on a button and govern the whole
combination as easily as a bench-manager governs a dog-show.

It would be a grand thing to see, and I feel a
kind of disappointment—but never mind, a

religion is better and larger; and there is more *to* it. And I have not been steeping myself in Christian Science all these weeks without finding out that the one sensible thing to do with a disappointment is to put it out of your mind and think of something cheerfuler.

We outsiders cannot conceive of Mrs. Eddy's Christian Science Religion as being a sudden and miraculous birth, but only as a growth from a seed planted by circumstances, and developed stage by stage by command and compulsion of the same force. What the stages were we cannot know, but are privileged to guess. She may have gotten the mental-healing idea from Quimby—it had been experimented with for ages, and was no one's special property. [For the present, for convenience' sake, let us proceed upon the hypothesis that that was *all* she got of him, and that she put up the rest of the assets herself. This will strain us, but let us try it.] In each and all its forms and under all its many names, mental healing had had limits, always, and they were rather narrow ones— Mrs. Eddy, let us imagine, removed the fence, abolished the frontiers. Not by expanding mental-healing, but by absorbing its small bulk into the vaster bulk of Christian Science—Divine Science, The Holy Ghost, the Comforter —which was a quite different and sublimer force, and one which had long lain dormant and unemployed.

The Christian Scientist believes that the Spirit of God (life and love) pervades the universe like an atmosphere; that whoso will study *Science and Health* can get from it the secret of how to inhale that transforming air; that to breathe it is to be made new; that from the new man all sorrow, all care, all miseries of the mind vanish away, for that only peace, contentment and measureless joy can live in that divine fluid; that it purifies the body from disease, which is a vicious creation of the gross human mind, and cannot continue to exist in the presence of the Immortal Mind, the renewing Spirit of God.

The Scientist finds this reasonable, natural, and not harder to believe than that the disease-germ, a creature of darkness, perishes when exposed to the light of the great sun—a new revelation of profane science which no one doubts.

He reminds us that the actinic ray, shining upon lupus, cures it—a horrible disease which was incurable fifteen years ago, and had been incurable for ten million years before; that this wonder, unbelievable by the physicians at first, is believed by them now; and so he is tranquilly confident that the time is coming when the world will be educated up to a point where it will comprehend and grant that the light of the Spirit of God, shining unobstructed upon the soul, is an actinic ray which can purge both mind and body from disease and set them free and make them whole.

It is apparent, then, that in Christian Science it is not one man's mind acting upon another man's mind that heals; that it is solely the Spirit of God that heals; that the healer's mind performs no office but to convey that force to the patient; that it is merely the wire which carries the electric fluid, so to speak, and delivers the message. Therefore, if these things be true, mental-healing and Science-healing are separate and distinct processes, and no kinship exists between them.

To heal the body of its ills and pains is a

18

mighty benefaction, but in our day our physicians and surgeons work a thousand miracles—prodigies which would have ranked as miracles fifty years ago—and they have so greatly extended their domination over disease that we feel so well protected that we are able to look with a good deal of composure and absence of hysterics upon the claims of new competitors in that field.

But there is a mightier benefaction than the healing of the body, and that is the healing of the spirit—which is Christian Science's other claim. So far as I know, so far as I can find out, it makes it good. Personally I have not known a Scientist who did not seem serene, contented, unharassed. I have not found an outsider whose observation of Scientists furnished him a view that differed from my own. Buoyant spirits, comfort of mind, freedom from care—these happinesses we all have, at intervals; but in the spaces between, dear me, the black hours! They have put a curse upon the life of every human being I have ever known, young or old. I concede not a single exception. Unless it might be those Scientists just referred to. They may have been playing a part with me; I hope they were not, and I believe they were not.

Time will test the Science's claim. If time shall make it good; if time shall prove that the Science can heal the persecuted spirit of man and banish its troubles and keep it serene and sunny and content—why, then Mrs. Eddy will have a monument that will reach above the clouds. For if she did not hit upon that imperial idea and evolve it and deliver it, its discoverer can never be identified with certainty, now, I think. It is the giant feature, it is the sun that rides in the zenith of Christian Science; the auxiliary features are of minor consequence. [Let us still leave the large "if" aside, for the present, and proceed as if it had no existence.]

It is not supposable that Mrs. Eddy realized, at first, the size of her plunder. (No, *find*— that is the word; she did not realize the size of her find, at first.) It had to grow upon her, by degrees, in accordance with the inalterable custom of Circumstance, which works by stages, and by stages only, and never furnishes any mind with all the materials for a large idea at one time.

In the beginning, Mrs. Eddy was probably interested merely in the mental-healing detail. And perhaps mainly interested in it pecuniarily, for she was poor.

She would succeed in anything she undertook. She would attract pupils, and her commerce would grow. She would inspire in patient and pupil confidence in her earnestness; her history is evidence that she would not fail of that.

There probably came a time, in due course, when her students began to think there was something deeper in her teachings than they had been suspecting — a mystery beyond mental-healing, and higher. It is conceivable that by consequence their manner towards her changed little by little, and from respectful became reverent. It is conceivable that this would have an influence upon her; that it would incline her to wonder if their secret thought—that she was inspired—might not be a well-grounded guess. It is conceivable that as time went on the thought in their minds and its reflection in hers might solidify into conviction.

She would remember, then, that as a child

she had been called, more than once, by a mysterious voice—just as had happened to little Samuel. (Mentioned in her *Autobiography*.) She would be impressed by that ancient reminiscence, now, and it could have a prophetic meaning for her.

It is conceivable that the persuasive influences around her and within her would give a new and powerful impulse to her philosophizings, and that from this, in time, would result that great birth, the healing of body and mind by the inpouring of the Spirit of God—the central and dominant idea of Christian Science—and that when this idea came she would not doubt that it was an inspiration direct from Heaven.

CHAPTER XI

I MUST rest a little, now. To sit here and painstakingly spin out a scheme which imagines Mrs. Eddy, of all people, working her mind on a plane above commercialism; imagines her thinking, philosophizing, discovering majestic things; and even imagines her dealing in sincerities—to be frank, I find it a large contract. But I have begun it, and I will go through with it.

CHAPTER XII

It is evident that she made disciples fast, and
that their belief in her and in the authenticity
of her heavenly ambassadorship was not of the
lukewarm and half - way sort, but was profoundly earnest and sincere. Her book was issued from the press in 1875, it began its work
of convert-making, and within six years she had
successfully launched a new Religion and a new
system of healing, and was teaching them to
crowds of eager students in a College of her
own, at prices so extraordinary that we are almost compelled to accept her statement (no,
her guarded intimation) that the rates were arranged on high, since a mere human being un-
acquainted with commerce and accustomed to
think in pennies could hardly put up such a
hand as that without supernatural help.

From this stage onward—Mrs. Eddy being
what she was — the rest of the development-
stages would follow naturally and inevitably.

But if she had been anybody else, there would have been a different arrangement of them, with different results. Being the extraordinary person she was, she realized her position and its possibilities; realized the possibilities, and had the daring to use them for all they were worth.

We have seen what her methods were after she passed the stage where her divine ambassadorship was granted its exequatur in the hearts and minds of her followers; we have seen how steady and fearless and calculated and orderly was her march thenceforth from conquest to conquest; we have seen her strike dead, without hesitancy, any hostile or questionable force that rose in her path: first, the horde of pretenders that sprang up and tried to take her Science and its market away from her—she crushed them, she obliterated them: when her own National Christian Science Association became great in numbers and influence, and loosely and dangerously garrulous, and began to expound the doctrines according to its own uninspired notions, she took up her sponge without a tremor of fear and wiped that Association out;

when she perceived that the preachers in her pulpits were becoming afflicted with doctrine-tinkering, she recognized the danger of it, and did not hesitate nor temporize, but promptly dismissed the whole of them in a day, and abolished their office permanently; we have seen that, as fast as her power grew, she was competent to take the measure of it, and that as fast as its expansion suggested to her gradually awakening native ambition a higher step she took it; and so, by this evolutionary process, we have seen the gross money-lust relegated to second place, and the lust of empire and glory rise above it. A splendid dream; and by force of the qualities born in her she is making it come true.

These qualities—and the capacities growing out of them by the nurturing influences of training, observation, and experience — seem to be clearly indicated by the character of her career and its achievements. They seem to be:

A clear head for business, and a phenomenally long one;

Clear understanding of business situations;

Accuracy in estimating the opportunities they
offer;

Intelligence in planning a business move;

Firmness in sticking to it after it has been
decided upon;

Extraordinary daring;

Indestructible persistency;

Devouring ambition;

Limitless selfishness;

A knowledge of the weaknesses and poverties
and docilities of human nature and how to turn
them to account which has never been surpassed, if ever equalled;

And—necessarily—the foundation-stone of
Mrs. Eddy's character is a never - wavering
confidence in herself.

It is a granite character. And—quite naturally—a measure of the talc of smallnesses
common to human nature is mixed up in it
and distributed through it. When Mrs. Eddy is
not dictating serviiities from her throne in the
clouds to her official domestics in Boston or to
her far-spread subjects round about the planet,
but is down on the ground, she is kin to us and
one of us: sentimental as a girl, garrulous, un-

grammatical, incomprehensible, affected, vain of her little human ancestry, unstable, inconsistent, unreliable in statement, and naïvely and everlastingly self-contradictory—oh, trivial and common and commonplace as the commonest of us! just a Napoleon as Madame de Rémusat saw him, a brass god with clay legs.

CHAPTER XIII

In drawing Mrs. Eddy's portrait it has been my purpose to restrict myself to materials furnished by *herself*, and I believe I have done that. If I have misinterpreted any of her acts, it was not done intentionally.

It will be noticed that in skeletonizing a list of the qualities which have carried her to the dizzy summit which she occupies, I have not mentioned the power which was the commanding force employed in achieving that lofty flight. It did not belong in that list; it was a force that was not a detail of her character, but was an outside one. It was the power which proceeded from her people's recognition of her as a supernatural personage, conveyer of the Latest Word, and divinely commissioned to deliver it to the world. The form which such a recognition takes, consciously or unconsciously, is *worship;* and worship does not question nor criticise, it obeys. The object of it does not need to coddle it, bribe it, beguile it, reason with it, convince it—it commands it; that is sufficient; the obedience rendered is not reluctant, but prompt and whole-hearted. Admiration for a Napoleon, confidence in him, pride in him, affection for him, can lift him high and carry him far; and these are forms of worship, and are strong forces, but they are worship of a mere human being, after all, and are infinitely feeble, as compared with those that are generated by that other worship, the worship of a divine personage. Mrs. Eddy has this efficient worship, this massed and centralized force, this force which is indifferent to opposition, untroubled by fear, and goes to battle singing, like Cromwell's soldiers; and while she has it she can command and it will obey, and maintain her on her throne, and extend her empire.

She will have it until she dies; and then we shall see a curious and interesting further development of her revolutionary work begin.

CHAPTER XIV

THE President and Board of Directors will succeed her, and the government will go on without a hitch. The By-laws will bear that interpretation. All the Mother-Church's vast powers are concentrated in that Board. Mrs. Eddy's unlimited personal reservations make the Board's ostensible supremacy, during her life, a sham, and the Board itself a shadow. But Mrs. Eddy has not made those reservations for any one but herself—they are distinctly personal, they bear her name, they are not usable by another individual. When she dies her reservations die, and the Board's shadow-powers become real powers, without the change of any important By-law, and the Board sits in her place as absolute and irresponsible a sovereign as she was.

It consists of but five persons, a much more manageable Cardinalate than the Roman

Pope's. I think it will elect its Pope from its own body, and that it will fill its own vacancies. An elective Papacy is a safe and wise system, and a long-liver.

CHAPTER XV

WE may take that up now.

It is not a single if, but a several-jointed one; not an oyster, but a vertebrate.

1. Did Mrs. Eddy borrow from Quimby the Great Idea, or only the little one, the old-timer, the ordinary mental-healing—healing by "mortal" mind?

2. If she borrowed the Great Idea, did she carry it away in her head, or in manuscript?

3. Did she hit upon the Great Idea herself?

By the Great Idea I mean, of course, the conviction that the Force involved was still existent, and could be applied now just as it was applied by Christ's Disciples and their converts, and as successfully.

4. Did she philosophize it, systematize it, and write it down in a book?

5. Was it she, and not another, that built a new Religion upon the book and organized it?

I think No. 5 can be answered with a Yes,

and dismissed from the controversy. And I think that the Great Idea, great as it was, would have enjoyed but a brief activity, and would then have gone to sleep again for some more centuries, but for the perpetuating impulse it got from that organized and tremendous force.

As for Nos. 1, 2, and 4, the hostiles contend that Mrs. Eddy got the Great Idea from Quimby and carried it off in manuscript. But their testimony, while of consequence, lacks the most important detail; so far as my information goes, the Quimby manuscript has not been produced. I think we cannot discuss No. 1 and No. 2 profitably. Let them go.

For me, No. 3 has a mild interest, and No. 4 a violent one.

As regards No. 3, Mrs. Eddy was brought up, from the cradle, an old-time, boiler-iron, Westminster - Catechism Christian, and knew her Bible as well as Captain Kydd knew his, "when he sailed, when he sailed," and perhaps as sympathetically. The Great Idea had struck a million Bible-readers before her as being possible of resurrection and application—it must have struck as many as that, and been cogitated, indolently, doubtingly, then dropped and forgotten—and it could have struck *her*, in due course. But how it could *interest* her, how it could appeal to her—with her make—is a thing that is difficult to understand.

For the thing back of it is wholly gracious and beautiful: the power, through loving mercifulness and compassion, to heal fleshly ills and pains and griefs—*all*—with a word, with a touch of the hand! This power was given by the Saviour to the Disciples, and to *all* the converted. All—every one. It was *exercised* for generations afterwards. Any Christian who was in earnest and not a make-believe, not a policy-Christian, not a Christian for revenue only, had that healing power, and could cure with it *any disease or any hurt or damage possible to human flesh and bone.* These things are true, or they are not. If they were true seventeen and eighteen and nineteen centuries ago it would be difficult to satisfactorily explain why or how or by what argument that power should be non-existent in Christians now.[1]

[1] See Appendix.—M. T.

To wish to exercise it could occur to Mrs. Eddy—but would it?

Grasping, sordid, penurious, famishing for everything she sees—money, power, glory— vain, untruthful, jealous, despotic, arrogant, insolent, pitiless where thinkers and hypnotists are concerned, illiterate, shallow, incapable of reasoning outside of commercial lines, immeasurably selfish—

Of course the Great Idea *could* strike her, we have to grant that, but why it should *interest* her is a question which can easily overstrain the imagination and bring on nervous prostration, or something like that, and is better left alone by the judicious, it seems to me—

Unless we call to our help the alleged other side of Mrs. Eddy's make and character—the side which her multitude of followers see, and sincerely believe in. Fairness requires that their view be stated here. It is the opposite of the one which I have drawn from Mrs. Eddy's history and from her By-laws. To her followers she is this:

Patient, gentle, loving, compassionate, noble-hearted, unselfish, sinless, widely cultured, splendidly equipped mentally, a profound thinker, an able writer, a divine personage, an inspired messenger whose acts are dictated from the Throne, and whose every utterance is the Voice of God.

She has delivered to them a religion which has revolutionized their lives, banished the glooms that shadowed them, and filled them and flooded them with sunshine and gladness and peace; a religion which has no hell; a religion whose heaven is not put off to another time, with a break and a gulf between, but begins here and now, and melts into eternity as fancies of the waking day melt into the dreams of sleep.

They believe it is a Christianity that is in the New Testament; that it has always been there; that in the drift of ages it was lost through disuse and neglect, and that this benefactor has found it and given it back to men, turning the night of life into day, its terrors into myths, its lamentations into songs of emancipation and rejoicing.[1]

[1] For a clear understanding of the two claims of Christian Science, read the novel *The Life Within*, published by Lothrops, Boston.—M. T.

There we have Mrs. Eddy as her followers see her. She has lifted them out of grief and care and doubt and fear, and made their lives beautiful; she found them wandering forlorn in a wintry wilderness, and has led them to a tropic paradise like that of which the poet sings:

"O, islands there are on the face of the deep
 Where the leaves never fade and the skies never weep."

To ask them to examine with a microscope the character of such a benefactor; to ask them to examine it at all; to ask them to look at a blemish which another person believes he has found in it—well, in their place could you do it? Would you do it? Wouldn't you be ashamed to do it? If a tramp had rescued your child from fire and death, and saved its mother's heart from breaking, could you see his rags? Could you smell his breath? Mrs. Eddy has done more than that for these people.

They are prejudiced witnesses. To the credit of human nature it is not possible that they should be otherwise. They sincerely believe that Mrs. Eddy's character is pure and perfect and beautiful, and her history without stain or blot or blemish. But that does not settle it. They sincerely believe she did not borrow the Great Idea from Quimby, but hit upon it herself. It may be so, and it could be so. Let it go—there is no way to settle it. They believe she carried away no Quimby manuscripts. Let that go, too—there is no way to settle it. They believe that she, and not another, built the Religion upon the book, and organized it. I believe it, too.

Finally, they believe that she philosophized Christian Science, explained it, systematized it, and wrote it all out with her own hand in the book *Science and Health*.

I am not able to believe that. Let us draw the line there. The known and undisputed products of her pen are a formidable witness against her. They do seem to me to prove, quite clearly and conclusively, that writing, upon even simple subjects, is a difficult labor for her; that she has never been able to write anything above third-rate English; that she is weak in the matter of grammar; that she has but a rude and dull sense of the values of words; that she so lacks in the matter of literary precision that she can seldom put a thought into words that express it lucidly to the reader and leave no doubts in his mind as to whether he has rightly understood or not; that she cannot even draught a Preface that a person can fully comprehend, nor one which can by any art be translated *into* a fully understandable form; that she can seldom inject into a Preface even single sentences whose meaning is uncompromisingly clear—yet Prefaces are her specialty, if she has one.

Mrs. Eddy's known and undisputed writings are very limited in bulk; they exhibit no depth, no analytical quality, no thought above school-composition size, and but juvenile ability in handling thoughts of even that modest magnitude. She has a fine commercial ability, and could govern a vast railway system in great style; she could draught a set of rules that Satan himself would say could not be improved on— for devilish effectiveness—by his staff; but we know, by our excursions among the Mother-Church's By-laws, that their English would discredit the deputy baggage-smasher. I am quite sure that Mrs. Eddy cannot write well upon any subject, even a commercial one.

In the very first revision of *Science and Health* (1883), Mrs. Eddy wrote a Preface which is an unimpeachable witness that the rest of the book was written by somebody else. I have put it in the Appendix[1] along with a page or two taken from the body of the book,[2] and will ask the reader to compare the labored and lumbering and confused gropings of this Preface with the easy and flowing and direct English of the other exhibit, and see if he can believe that the one hand and brain produced both.

And let him take the Preface apart, sentence by sentence, and searchingly examine each sentence word by word, and see if he can find half a dozen sentences whose meanings he is so sure of that he can rephrase them—in words of his own—and reproduce what he takes to be those meanings. Money can be lost on this game. I know, for I am the one that lost it.

Now let the reader turn to the excerpt which I have made from the chapter on "Prayer"[3]

[1] See Appendix A.—M. T.   [2] Appendix B.—M. T.
[3] See Appendix.—M. T.

(last year's edition of *Science and Health*), and compare that wise and sane and elevated and lucid and compact piece of work with the aforesaid Preface, and with Mrs. Eddy's poetry concerning the gymnastic trees, and Minerva's not yet effete sandals, and the wreaths imported from Erudition's bower for the decoration of Plymouth Rock, and the Plague-spot and Bacilli, and my other exhibits (turn back to my Chapters I. and II.) from the *Autobiography*, and finally with the late Communication concerning me,[1] and see if he thinks anybody's affirmation, or anybody's sworn testimony, or any other testimony of any imaginable kind, would ever be likely to convince him that Mrs. Eddy wrote that chapter on Prayer.

I do not wish to impose my opinion on any one who will not permit it, but such as it is I offer it here for what it is worth. I cannot believe, and I do not believe, that Mrs. Eddy originated any of the thoughts and reasonings out of which the book *Science and Health* is con-

[1] See Appendix. This reference is to the article "Mrs. Eddy in Error," in the *North American Review* for April, 1903.—M. T.

structed; and I cannot believe, and do not believe that she ever wrote any part of that book.

I think that if anything in the world stands proven, and well and solidly proven, by unimpeachable testimony — the treacherous testimony of her own pen in her known and undisputed literary productions — it is that Mrs. Eddy is not capable of thinking upon high planes, nor of reasoning clearly nor writing intelligently upon low ones.

Inasmuch as—in my belief—the very first editions of the book *Science and Health* were far above the reach of Mrs. Eddy's mental and literary abilities, I think she has from the very beginning been claiming as her own another person's book, and wearing as her own property laurels rightfully belonging to that person— the *real* author of *Science and Health*. And I think the reason—and the only reason—that he has not protested is because his work was not exposed to print until after he was safely dead.

That with an eye to business, and by grace of her business talent, she has restored to the world neglected and abandoned features of the

Christian religion which her thousands of followers find gracious and blessed and contenting,
I recognize and confess; but I am convinced
that every single detail of the work except
just that one—the delivery of the product to
the world—was conceived and performed by
another.

APPENDIX A

THERE seems a Christian necessity of learning God's power and purpose to heal both mind and body. This thought grew out of our early seeking Him in all our ways, and a hopeless as singular invalidism that drugs increased instead of diminished, and hygiene benefited only for a season. By degrees we have drifted into more spiritual latitudes of thought, and experimented as we advanced until demonstrating fully the power of mind over the body. About the year 1862, having heard of a mesmerist in Portland who was treating the sick by manipulation, we visited him; he helped us for a time, then we relapsed somewhat. After his decease, and a severe casualty deemed fatal by skilful physicians, we discovered that the Principle of all healing and the law that governs it is God, a divine Principle, and a spiritual not material law, and regained health.

It was not an individual or mortal mind acting upon another so-called mind that healed us. It was the glorious truths of Christian Science that we discovered as we neared that verge of so-called material life named death; yea, it was the great Shekinah, the spirit of Life, Truth, and Love illuminating our understanding of the action and might of Omnipotence! The old gentleman to whom we have referred had some very advanced views on healing, but he was not avowedly religious neither scholarly. We interchanged thoughts on the subject of healing the sick. I restored some patients of his that he failed to heal, and left in his possession some manuscripts of mine containing corrections of his desultory pennings, which I am informed at his decease passed into the hands of a patient of his, now residing in Scotland. He died in 1865 and left no published works. The only manuscript that we ever held of his, longer than to correct it, was one of perhaps a dozen pages, most of which we had composed. He manipulated the sick; hence his ostensible method of healing was physical instead of *mental*.

We helped him in the esteem of the public by our writings, but never knew of his stating orally or in writing that he treated his patients *mentally;* never heard him give any directions to that effect; and have it from one of his patients, who now asserts that he was the founder of mental healing, that he never revealed to anyone his method. We refer to these facts simply to refute the calumnies and false claims of our enemies, that we are preferring dishonest claims to the discovery and founding at this period of Metaphysical Healing or Christian Science.

The Science and laws of a purely mental healing and their method of application through spiritual power alone, else a mental argument against disease, are our own discovery at this date. True, the Principle is divine and eternal; but the application of it to heal the sick had been lost sight of, and required to be again spiritually discerned and its science discovered, that man might retain it through the understanding. Since our discovery in 1866 of the divine science of Christian Healing, we have labored with tongue and pen to found this system. In this endeavor every obstacle has been thrown in our path that the envy and revenge of a few disaffected students could devise. The superstition and ignorance of even this period have not failed to contribute their mite towards misjudging us, while its Christian advancement and scientific research have helped sustain our feeble efforts.

Since our first Edition of *Science and Health*, published in 1875, two of the aforesaid students have plagiarized and pirated our works. In the issues of E. J. A., almost exclusively ours, were thirteen paragraphs, without credit, taken verbatim from our books.

Not one of our printed works was ever copied or abstracted from the published or from the unpublished writings of anyone. Throughout our publications of Metaphysical Healing or Christian Science, when writing or dictating them, we have given ourselves to contemplation wholly apart from the observation of the material senses: to look upon a copy would have distracted our thoughts from the subject before us. We were seldom able to copy our own compositions, and have employed an amanuensis for the last six years. Every work that we

have had published has been extemporaneously
written; and out of fifty lectures and sermons
that we have delivered the last year, forty-four
have been extemporaneous. We have distributed many of our unpublished manuscripts;
loaned to one of our youngest students, R.
K . . . . . y, between three and four hundred
pages, of which we were sole author—giving
him liberty to copy but not to publish them.

Leaning on the sustaining Infinite with loving trust, the trials of to-day grow brief, and
to-morrow is big with blessings.

The wakeful shepherd, tending his flocks,
beholds from the mountain's top the first faint
morning beam ere cometh the risen day. So
from Soul's loftier summits shines the pale star
to prophet-shepherd, and it traverses night,
over to where the young child lies, in cradled
obscurity, that shall waken a world. Over the
night of error dawn the morning beams and
guiding star of Truth, and "the wise men" are
led by it to Science, which repeats the eternal
harmony that it reproduced, in proof of immortality. The time for thinkers has come;
and the time for revolutions, ecclesiastical and

civil, must come. Truth, independent of doctrines or time-honored systems, stands at the threshold of history. Contentment with the past, or the cold conventionality of custom, may no longer shut the door on science; though empires fall, "He whose right it is shall reign." Ignorance of God should no longer be the stepping-stone to faith; understanding Him, "whom to know aright is Life eternal," is the only guaranty of obedience.

This volume may not open a new thought, and make it at once familiar. It has the sturdy task of a pioneer, to hack away at the tall oaks and cut the rough granite, leaving future ages to declare what it has done. We made our first discovery of the adaptation of metaphysics to the treatment of disease in the winter of 1866; since then we have tested the Principle on ourselves and others, and never found it to fail to prove the statements herein made of it. We must learn the science of Life, to reach the perfection of man. To understand God as the Principle of all being, and to live in accordance with this Principle, is the Science of Life. But to reproduce this harmony of being, the error of personal sense must yield to science, even as the science of music corrects tones caught from the ear, and gives the sweet concord of sound. There are many theories of physic and theology, and many calls in each of their directions for the right way; but we propose to settle the question of "What is Truth?" on the ground of proof, and let that method of healing the sick and establishing Christianity be adopted that is found to give the most health and to make the best Christians; science will then have a fair field, in which case we are assured of its triumph over all opinions and beliefs. Sickness and sin have ever had their doctors; but the question is, Have they become less because of them? The longevity of our antediluvians would say, No! and the criminal records of to-day utter their voices little in favor of such a conclusion. Not that we would deny to Cæsar the things that are his, but that we ask for the things that belong to Truth; and safely affirm, from the demonstrations we have been able to make, that the science of man understood would have eradicated sin, sickness, and death, in a less period than six thousand years. We find great difficulties in starting this work right. Some shockingly false claims are already made to a metaphysical practice; mesmerism, its very antipodes, is one of them. Hitherto we have never, in a single instance of our discovery, found the slightest resemblance between mesmerism and metaphysics. No especial idiosyncrasy is requisite to acquire a knowledge of metaphysical healing; spiritual sense is more important to its discernment than the intellect; and those who would learn this science without a high moral standard of thought and action, will fail to understand it until they go up higher. Owing to our explanations constantly vibrating between the same points, an irksome repetition of words must occur; also the use of capital letters, genders, and technicalities peculiar to the science. Variety of language, or beauty of diction, must give place to close analysis and unembellished thought. "Hoping all things, enduring all things," to do good to our enemies, to bless them that curse us, and to bear to the sorrowing and the sick consolation and healing, we commit these pages to posterity.

MARY BAKER G. EDDY.

APPENDIX B

THE Gospel narratives bear brief testimony
even to the life of our great Master. His spiritual noumenon and phenomenon, silenced portraiture. Writers, less wise than the Apostles,
essayed in the Apocryphal New Testament, a
legendary and traditional history of the early
life of Jesus. But Saint Paul summarized the
character of Jesus as the model of Christianity,
in these words: "Consider Him who endured
such contradictions of sinners against Himself.
Who for the joy that was set before Him, endured the cross, despising the shame, and is
set down at the right hand of the throne of
God."

It may be that the mortal life-battle still
wages, and must continue till its involved
errors are vanquished by victory-bringing
Science; but this triumph will come! God is
over all. He alone is our origin, aim, and Being. The real man is not of the dust, nor is he

ever created through the flesh; for his father
and mother are the one Spirit, and his brethren
are all the children of one parent, the eternal
Good.

Any kind of literary composition was exces-
sively difficult for Mrs. Eddy. She found it
grinding hard work to dig out anything to say.
She realized, at the above stage in her life, that
with all her trouble she had not been able to
scratch together even material enough for a
child's Autobiography, and also that what she
had secured was in the main not valuable, not
important, considering the age and the fame of
the person she was writing about; and so it occurred to her to attempt, in that paragraph, to
excuse the meagreness and poor quality of the
feast she was spreading, by letting on that she
could do ever so much better if she wanted to,
but was under constraint of Divine etiquette.
To feed with more than a few indifferent crumbs
a plebeian appetite for personal details about
Personages in her class was not the correct
thing, and she blandly points out that there is
Precedent for this reserve. When Mrs. Eddy

tries to be artful—in literature—it is generally after the manner of the ostrich; and with the ostrich's luck. Please try to find the connection between the two paragraphs.—M. T.

APPENDIX C

THE following is the spiritual signification of the Lord's Prayer:

Principle, eternal and harmonious,
Nameless and adorable Intelligence,
Thou art ever present and supreme.
And when this supremacy of Spirit shall appear,
    the dream of matter will disappear.
Give us the understanding of Truth and Love.
And loving we shall learn God, and Truth will
    destroy all error.
And lead us unto the Life that is Soul, and de-
    liver us from the errors of sense, sin, sick-
    ness, and death,
For God is Life, Truth, and Love for ever.
    —*Science and Health*, edition of 1881.

It seems to me that this one is distinctly superior to the one that was inspired for last year's edition. It is strange, but to my mind plain, that inspiring is an art which does not improve with practice.—M. T.

APPENDIX D

For verily I say unto you, That whosoever shall say unto this mountain, Be thou removed, and be thou cast into the sea; and shall not doubt in his heart, but shall believe that those things which he saith shall come to pass; he shall have whatsoever he saith. Therefore I say unto you, What things soever ye desire when ye pray, believe that ye receive them, and ye shall have them.

Your Father knoweth what things ye have need of, before ye ask Him.—CHRIST JESUS.

THE prayer that reclaims the sinner and heals the sick, is an absolute faith that all things are possible to God—a spiritual understanding of Him—an unselfed love. Regardless of what another may say or think on this subject, I speak from experience. This prayer, combined with self-sacrifice and toil, is the means whereby God has enabled me to do what I have done for the religion and health of mankind.

Thoughts unspoken are not unknown to the divine Mind. Desire is prayer; and no less can occur from trusting God with our desires, that they may be moulded and exalted before they take form in audible word, and in deeds.

What are the motives for prayer? Do we pray to make ourselves better, or to benefit those that hear us; to enlighten the Infinite, or to be heard of men? Are we benefited by praying? Yes, the desire which goes forth hungering after righteousness is blessed of our Father, and it does not return unto us void.

God is not moved by the breath of praise to do more than He has already done; nor can the Infinite do less than bestow all good, since He is unchanging Wisdom and Love. We can do more for ourselves by humble fervent petitions; but the All-loving does not grant them simply on the ground of lip-service, for He already knows all.

Prayer cannot change the Science of Being, but it does bring us into harmony with it. Goodness reaches the demonstration of Truth. A request that another may work for us never does our work. The habit of pleading with the divine Mind, as one pleads with a human being, perpetuates the belief in God as humanly circumscribed—an error which impedes spiritual growth.

God is Love. Can we ask Him to be more? God is Intelligence. Can we inform the infinite Mind, or tell Him anything He does not already comprehend? Do we hope to change perfection? Shall we plead for more at the open fount, which always pours forth more than we receive? The unspoken prayer does bring us nearer the Source of all existence and blessedness.

Asking God to *be* God is a "vain repetition." God is "the same yesterday, and to-day, and forever"; and He who is immutably right will do right, without being reminded of His province. The wisdom of man is not sufficient to warrant him in advising God.

Who would stand before a blackboard, and pray the principle of mathematics to work out the problem? The rule is already established, and it is our task to work out the solution. Shall we ask the divine Principle of all goodness to do His own work? His work is done; and we have only to avail ourselves of God's rule, in order to receive the blessing thereof.

The divine Being must be reflected by man— else man is not the image and likeness of the patient, tender, and true, the one "altogether lovely"; but to understand God is the work of eternity, and demands absolute concentration of thought and energy.

How empty are our conceptions of Deity! We admit theoretically that God is good, omnipotent, omnipresent, infinite, and then we try to give information to this infinite Mind; and plead for unmerited pardon, and a liberal outpouring of benefactions. Are we really grateful for the good already received? Then we shall avail ourselves of the blessings we have, and thus be fitted to receive more. Gratitude is much more than a verbal expression of thanks. Action expresses more gratitude than speech.

If we are ungrateful for Life, Truth, and Love, and yet return thanks to God for all blessings, we are insincere; and incur the sharp censure our Master pronounces on hypocrites. In such a case the only acceptable prayer is to put the finger on the lips and remember our blessings. While the heart is far from divine

Truth and Love, we cannot conceal the ingratitude of barren lives, for God knoweth all things.

What we most need is the prayer of fervent desire for growth in grace, expressed in patience, meekness, love, and good deeds. To keep the commandments of our Master and follow his example, is our proper debt to Him, and the only worthy evidence of our gratitude for all He has done. Outward worship is not of itself sufficient to express loyal and heartfelt gratitude, since He has said: "If ye love Me, keep My Commandments."

The habitual struggle to be always good, is unceasing prayer. Its motives are made manifest in the blessings they bring—which, if not acknowledged in audible words, attest our worthiness to be made partakers of Love.

Simply asking that we may love God will never make us love Him; but the longing to be better and holier—expressed in daily watchfulness, and in striving to assimilate more of the divine character — this will mould and fashion us anew, until we awake in His likeness. We reach the Science of Christianity through demonstration of the divine nature; but in this wicked world goodness will "be evil spoken of," and patience must work experience.

Audible prayer can never do the works of spiritual understanding, which regenerates; but silent prayer, watchfulness, and devout obedience, enable us to follow Jesus' example. Long prayers, ecclesiasticism, and creeds, have clipped the divine pinions of Love, and clad religion in human robes. They materialize worship, hinder the Spirit, and keep man from demonstrating his power over error.

Sorrow for wrong-doing is but one step towards reform, and the very easiest step. The next and great step required by Wisdom is the test of our sincerity—namely, reformation. To this end we are placed under the stress of circumstances. Temptation bids us repeat the offence, and woe comes in return for what is done. So it will ever be, till we learn that there is no discount in the law of justice, and that we must pay "the uttermost farthing." The measure ye mete "shall be measured to you again," and it will be full "and running over."

Saints and sinners get their full award, but not always in this world. The followers of Christ drank His cup. Ingratitude and persecution filled it to the brim; but God pours the riches of His love into the understanding and affections, giving us strength according to our day. Sinners flourish "like a green bay-tree"; but, looking farther, the Psalmist could see their end — namely, the destruction of sin through suffering.

Prayer is sometimes used, as a confessional, to cancel sin. This error impedes true religion. Sin is forgiven, only as it is destroyed by Christ —Truth and Life. If prayer nourishes the belief that sin is cancelled, and that man is made better by merely praying, it is an evil. He grows worse who continues in sin because he thinks himself forgiven.

An apostle says that the Son of God (Christ) came to "destroy the works of the devil." We should follow our divine Exemplar, and seek the destruction of all evil works, error and disease included. We cannot escape the penalty due for sin. The Scriptures say, that if we deny Christ, "He also will deny us."

The divine Love corrects and governs man. Men may pardon, but this divine Principle alone reforms the sinner. God is not separate from the wisdom He bestows. The talents He gives we must improve. Calling on Him to forgive our work, badly done or left undone, implies the vain supposition that we have nothing to do but to ask pardon, and that afterwards we shall be free to repeat the offence.

To cause suffering, as the result of sin, is the means of destroying sin. Every supposed pleasure in sin will furnish more than its equivalent of pain, until belief in material life and sin is destroyed. To reach heaven, the harmony of Being, we must understand the divine Principle of Being.

"God is Love." More than this we cannot ask; higher we cannot look; farther we cannot go. To suppose that God forgives or punishes sin, according as His mercy is sought or unsought, is to misunderstand Love and make prayer the safety-valve for wrong-doing.

Jesus uncovered and rebuked sin before He cast it out. Of a sick woman He said that Satan had bound her; and to Peter He said,

"Thou art an offence unto me." He came teaching and showing men how to destroy sin, sickness, and death. He said of the fruitless tree, "It is hewn down."

It is believed by many that a certain magistrate, who lived in the time of Jesus, left this record: "His rebuke is fearful." The strong language of our Master confirms this description.

The only civil sentence which He had for error was, "Get thee behind Me, Satan." Still stronger evidence that Jesus' reproof was pointed and pungent is in His own words— showing the necessity for such forcible utterance, when He cast out devils and healed the sick and sinful. The relinquishment of error deprives material sense of its false claims.

Audible prayer is impressive; it gives momentary solemnity and elevation to thought; but does it produce any lasting benefit? Looking deeply into these things, we find that "a zeal . . . not according to knowledge," gives occasion for reaction unfavorable to spiritual growth, sober resolve, and wholesome perception of God's requirements. The motives for verbal prayer may embrace too much love of applause to induce or encourage Christian sentiment.

Physical sensation, not Soul, produces material ecstasy, and emotions. If spiritual sense always guided men at such times, there would grow out of those ecstatic moments a higher experience and a better life, with more devout self-abnegation, and purity. A self-satisfied ventilation of fervent sentiments never makes a Christian. God is not influenced by man. The "divine ear" is not an auditorial nerve. It is the all-hearing and all-knowing Mind, to whom each want of man is always known, and by whom it will be supplied.

The danger from audible prayer is, that it may lead us into temptation. By it we may become involuntary hypocrites, uttering desires which are not real, and consoling ourselves in the midst of sin, with the recollection that we have prayed over it—or mean to ask forgiveness at some later day. Hypocrisy is fatal to religion.

A wordy prayer may afford a quiet sense of self-justification, though it makes the sinner a

21

hypocrite. We never need despair of an honest heart, but there is little hope for those who
only come spasmodically face to face with their
wickedness, and then seek to hide it. Their
prayers are indexes which do not correspond
with their character. They hold secret fellowship with sin; and such externals are spoken of
by Jesus as "like unto whited sepulchres . . .
full of all uncleanness."

If a man, though apparently fervent and
prayerful, is impure, and therefore insincere,
what must be the comment upon him? If he
had reached the loftiness of his prayer, there
would be no occasion for such comment. If
we feel the aspiration, humility, gratitude, and
love which our words express—this God accepts; and it is wise not to try to deceive ourselves or others, for "there is nothing covered
that shall not be revealed." Professions and
audible prayers are like charity in one respect
—they "cover a multitude of sins." Praying
for humility, with whatever fervency of expression, does not always mean a desire for it.
If we turn away from the poor, we are not
ready to receive the reward of Him who blesses

the poor. We confess to having a very wicked
heart, and ask that it may be laid bare before
us; but do we not already know more of this
heart than we are willing to have our neighbor
see?

We ought to examine ourselves, and learn
what is the affection and purpose of the heart;
for this alone can show us what we honestly
are. If a friend informs us of a fault, do we
listen to the rebuke patiently, and credit what
is said? Do we not rather give thanks that we
are "not as other men?" During many years
the author has been most grateful for merited
rebuke. The sting lies in unmerited censure—
in the falsehood which does no one any good.

The test of all prayer lies in the answer to
these questions: Do we love our neighbor better
because of this asking? Do we pursue the old
selfishness, satisfied with having prayed for
something better, though we give no evidence
of the sincerity of our requests by living consistently with our prayer? If selfishness has
given place to kindness, we shall regard our
neighbor unselfishly, and bless them that curse
us; but we shall never meet this great duty by

simply asking that it may be done. There is a cross to be taken up, before we can enjoy the fruition of our hope and faith.

Dost thou "love the Lord thy God with all thy heart, and with all thy soul, and with all thy mind?" This command includes much— even the surrender of all merely material sensation, affection, and worship. This is the El Dorado of Christianity. It involves the Science of Life, and recognizes only the divine control of Spirit, wherein Soul is our master, and material sense and human will have no place.

Are you willing to leave all for Christ, for Truth, and so be counted among sinners? No! Do you really desire to attain this point? No! Then why make long prayers about it, and ask to be Christians, since you care not to tread in the footsteps of our dear Master? If unwilling to follow His example, wherefore pray with the lips that you may be partakers of His nature? Consistent prayer is the desire to do right. Prayer means that we desire to, and will, walk in the light so far as we receive it, even though with bleeding footsteps, and waiting patiently on the Lord, will leave our real desires to be rewarded by Him.

The world must grow to the spiritual understanding of prayer. If good enough to profit by Jesus' cup of earthly sorrows, God will sustain us under these sorrows. Until we are thus divinely qualified, and willing to drink His cup, millions of vain repetitions will never pour into prayer the unction of Spirit, in demonstration of power, and "with signs following." Christian Science reveals a necessity for overcoming the world, the flesh and evil, and thus destroying all error.

Seeking is not sufficient. It is striving which enables us to enter. Spiritual attainments open the door to a higher understanding of the divine Life.

One of the forms of worship in Thibet is to carry a praying-machine through the streets, and stop at the doors to earn a penny by grinding out a prayer; whereas civilization pays for clerical prayers, in lofty edifices. Is the difference very great, after all?

Experience teaches us that we do not always receive the blessings we ask for in prayer.

There is some misapprehension of the source and means of all goodness and blessedness, or we should certainly receive what we ask for, The Scriptures say: "Ye ask, and receive not, because ye ask amiss, that ye may consume it upon your lusts." What we desire and ask for it is not always best for us to receive. In this case infinite Love will not grant the request. Do you ask Wisdom to be merciful, and not punish sin? Then "ye ask amiss." Without punishment, sin would multiply. Jesus' prayer, "forgive us our debts," specified also the terms of forgiveness. When forgiving the adulterous woman He said, "Go, and sin no more."

A magistrate sometimes remits the penalty, but this may be no moral benefit to the criminal; and at best, it only saves him from one form of punishment. The moral law, which has the right to acquit or condemn, always demands restitution, before mortals can "go up higher." Broken law brings penalty, in order to compel this progress.

Mere legal pardon (and there is no other, for divine Principle never pardons our sins or mistakes till they are corrected) leaves the offender free to repeat the offence; if, indeed, he has not already suffered sufficiently from vice to make him turn from it with loathing. Truth bestows no pardon upon error, but wipes it out in the most effectual manner. Jesus suffered for our sins, not to annul the divine sentence against an individual's sin, but to show that sin must bring inevitable suffering.

Petitions only bring to mortals the results of their own faith. We know that a desire for holiness is requisite in order to gain it; but if we desire holiness above all else, we shall sacrifice everything for it. We must be willing to do this, that we may walk securely in the only practical road to holiness. Prayer alone cannot change the unalterable Truth, or give us an understanding of it; but prayer coupled with a fervent habitual desire to know and do the will of God will bring us into all Truth. Such a desire has little need of audible expression. It is best expressed in thought and life.

APPENDIX E

Reverend Heber Newton on Christian Science:

To begin, then, at the beginning, Christian Science accepts the work of healing sickness as an integral part of the discipleship of Jesus Christ. In Christ it finds, what the Church has always recognized, theoretically, though it has practically ignored the fact—the Great Physician. That Christ healed the sick, we none of us question. It stands plainly upon the record. This ministry of healing was too large a part of His work to be left out from any picture of that life. Such service was not an incident of His career—it was an essential element of that career. It was an integral factor in His mission. The Evangelists leave us no possibility of confusion on this point. Co-equal with his work of instruction and inspiration was His work of healing.

The records make it equally clear that the

Master laid His charge upon His disciples to do as He had done. "When He had called unto Him His twelve disciples, He gave them power over unclean spirits, to cast them out, and to heal all manner of sickness and all manner of disease."[1] In sending them forth, "He commanded them, saying, . . . As ye go, preach, saying, The kingdom of heaven is at hand. Heal the sick, cleanse the lepers, raise the dead, cast out demons."[2]

That the twelve disciples undertook to do the Master's work of healing, and that they, in their measure, succeeded, seems beyond question. They found in themselves the same power that the Master found in Himself, and they used it as He had used His power. The record of The Acts of the Apostles, if at all trustworthy history, shows that they, too, healed the sick.

Beyond the circle of the original twelve, it is equally clear that the early disciples believed themselves charged with the same mission, and that they sought to fulfil it. The records of the early Church make it indisputable that powers of healing were recognized as among the gifts of

[1] Matt. x., 11.   [2] *Ib.*, x., 5, 7, 8.

the Spirit. St. Paul's letters render it certain that these gifts were not a privilege of the original twelve, merely, but that they were the heritage into which all the disciples entered.

Beyond the era of the primitive Church, through several generations, the early Christians felt themselves called to the same ministry of healing, and enabled with the same secret of power. Through wellnigh three centuries, the gifts of healing appear to have been, more or less, recognized and exercised in the Church. Through those generations, however, there was a gradual disuse of this power, following upon a failing recognition of its possession. That which was originally the rule became the exception. By degrees, the sense of authority and power to heal passed out from the consciousness of the Church. It ceased to be a sign of the indwelling Spirit. For fifteen centuries, the recognition of this authority and power has been altogether exceptional. Here and there, through the history of these centuries, there have been those who have entered into this belief of their own privilege and duty, and have used the gift which they recognized.

The Church has never been left without a line of witnesses to this aspect of the discipleship of Christ. But she has come to accept it as the normal order of things that what was once the rule in the Christian Church should be now only the exception. Orthodoxy has framed a theory of the words of Jesus to account for this strange departure of His Church from them. It teaches us to believe that His example was not meant to be followed, in this respect, by all His disciples. The power of healing which was in Him was a purely exceptional power. It was used as an evidence of His divine mission. It was a miraculous gift. The gift of working miracles was not bestowed upon His Church at large. His original disciples, the twelve apostles, received this gift, as a necessity of the critical epoch of Christianity—the founding of the Church. Traces of the power lingered on, in weakening activity, until they gradually ceased, and the normal condition of the Church was entered upon, in which miracles are no longer possible.

We accept this, unconsciously, as the true state of things in Christianity. But it is a conception which will not bear a moment's examination. There is not the slightest suggestion upon record that Christ set any limit to this charge which He gave His disciples. On the contrary, there are not lacking hints that He looked for the possession and exercise of this power wherever His spirit breathed in men.

Even if the concluding paragraph of St. Mark's Gospel were a later appendix, it may none the less have been a faithful echo of words of the Master, as it certainly is a trustworthy record of the belief of the early Christians as to the thought of Jesus concerning His followers. In that interesting passage, Jesus, after His death, appeared to the eleven, and formally commissioned them, again, to take up His work in the world; bidding them, "Go ye into all the world and preach the gospel to every creature." "And these signs," He tells them, "shall follow them that believe"—not the apostles only, but "them that believe," without limit of time; "in My name they shall cast out devils . . . they shall lay hands on the sick and they shall recover."[1] The concluding discourse

[1] Mark xvi., 15, 17, 18.

to the disciples, recorded in the Gospel according to St. John, affirms the same expectation on the part of Jesus; emphasizing it in His solemn way: "Verily, verily, I say unto you, He that believeth on Me, the works that I do shall he do also; and greater works than these shall he do."[1]

[1] John xiv., 12.

APPENDIX F

FEW will deny that an intelligence apart
from man formed and governs the spiritual universe and man; and this intelligence is the eternal
Mind, and neither matter nor man created this
intelligence and divine Principle; nor can this
Principle produce aught unlike itself. All that
we term sin, sickness, and death is comprised
in the belief of matter. The realm of the real
is spiritual; the opposite of Spirit is matter; and
the opposite of the real is unreal or material.
Matter is an error of statement, for there is no
matter. This error of premises leads to error
of conclusion in every statement of matter as a
basis. Nothing we can say or believe regarding matter is true, except that matter is unreal,
simply a belief that has its beginning and end-
ing.

The conservative firm called matter and
mind God never formed. The unerring and
eternal Mind destroys this imaginary copartner-

ship, formed only to be dissolved in a manner and at a period unknown. This copartnership is obsolete. Placed under the microscope of metaphysics matter disappears. Only by understanding there are not two, matter and mind, is a logical and correct conclusion obtained by either one. Science gathers not grapes of thorns or figs of thistles. Intelligence never produced non-intelligence, such as matter: the immortal never produced mortality, good never resulted in evil. The science of Mind shows conclusively that matter is a myth. Metaphysics are above physics, and drag not matter, or what is termed that, into one of its premises or conclusions. Metaphysics resolves things into thoughts, and exchanges the objects of sense for the ideas of Soul. These ideas are perfectly tangible and real to consciousness, and they have this advantage— they are eternal. Mind and its thoughts comprise the whole of God, the universe, and of man. Reason and revelation coincide with this statement, and support its proof every hour, for nothing is harmonious or eternal that is not spiritual: the realization of this will bring out objects from a higher source of thought; hence more beautiful and immortal.

The fact of spiritualization produces results in striking contrast to the farce of materialization: the one produces the results of chastity and purity, the other the downward tendencies and earthward gravitation of sensualism and impurity.

The exalting and healing effects of metaphysics show their fountain. Nothing in pathology has exceeded the application of metaphysics. Through mind alone we have prevented disease and preserved health. In cases of chronic and acute diseases, in their severest forms, we have changed the secretions, renewed structure, and restored health; have elongated shortened limbs, relaxed rigid muscles, made cicatrized joints supple; restored carious bones to healthy conditions, renewed that which is termed the lost substance of the lungs; and restored healthy organizations where disease was organic instead of functional.

MRS. EDDY IN ERROR

I FEEL almost sure that Mrs. Eddy's inspiration-works are getting out of repair. I think so because they made some errors in a statement which she uttered through the press on the 17th of January. Not large ones, perhaps, still it is a friend's duty to straighten such things out and get them right when he can. Therefore I will put my other duties aside for a moment and undertake this helpful service. She said as follows:

"In view of the circulation of certain criticisms from the pen of Mark Twain, I submit the following statement:

"It is a fact, well understood, that I begged the students who first gave me the endearing appellative 'mother' not to name me thus. But, without my consent, that word spread like wildfire. I still must think the name is not applicable to me. I stand in relation to this century as a Christian discoverer, founder, and

leader. I regard self-deification as blasphemous; I may be more loved, but I am less
lauded, pampered, provided for, and cheered
than others before me—and wherefore? Because Christian Science is not yet popular, and
I refuse adulation.

"My visit to the Mother-Church after it was
built and dedicated pleased me, and the situation was satisfactory. The dear members
wanted to greet me with escort and the ringing
of bells, but I declined, and went alone in my
carriage to the church, entered it, and knelt in
thanks upon the steps of its altar. There the
foresplendor of the beginnings of truth fell mys-
teriously upon my spirit. I believe in one
Christ, teach one Christ, know of but one Christ.
I believe in but one incarnation, one Mother
Mary, and know I am not that one, and never
claimed to be. It suffices me to learn the Science of the Scriptures relative to this subject.

"Christian Scientists have no quarrel with
Protestants, Catholics, or any other sect. They
need to be understood as following the divine
Principle—God, Love—and not imagined to be
unscientific worshippers of a human being.

"In the aforesaid article, of which I have
seen only extracts, Mark Twain's wit was not

wasted in certain directions. Christian Science eschews divine rights in human beings. If the individual governed human consciousness, my statement of Christian Science would be disproved, but to understand the spiritual idea is essential to demonstrate Science and its pure monotheism—one God, one Christ, no idolatry, no human propaganda. Jesus taught and proved that what feeds a few feeds all. His life-work subordinated the material to the spiritual, and He left this legacy of truth to mankind. His metaphysics is not the sport of philosophy, religion, or Science; rather it is the pith and finale of them all.

"I have not the inspiration or aspiration to be a first or second Virgin-Mother—her duplicate, antecedent, or subsequent. What I am remains to be proved by the good I do. We need much humility, wisdom, and love to perform the functions of foreshadowing and foretasting heaven within us. This glory is molten in the furnace of affliction."

She still thinks the name of Our Mother not applicable to her; and she is also able to remember that it distressed her when it was conferred upon her, and that she begged to have it suppressed. Her memory is at fault here. If she will take her By-laws, and refer to Section 1 of Article XXII., written with her own hand— she will find that she has reserved that title to herself, and is so pleased with it, and so—may we say jealous?—about it, that she threatens with excommunication any sister Scientist who shall call herself by it. This is that Section 1:

"*The Title of Mother.* In the year 1895 loyal Christian Scientists had given to the author of their text-book, the Founder of Christian Science, the individual, endearing term of Mother. Therefore, if a student of Christian Science shall apply this title, either to herself or to others, except as the term for kinship according to the flesh, it shall be regarded by the Church as an indication of disrespect for their Pastor Emeritus, and unfitness to be a member of the Mother-Church."

Mrs. Eddy is herself the Mother-Church—its powers and authorities are in her possession solely—and she can abolish that title whenever it may please her to do so. She has only to command her people, wherever they may be in the earth, to use it no more, and it will never be uttered again. She is aware of this.

It may be that she "refuses adulation" when she is not awake, but when she is awake she encourages it and propagates it in that museum called "Our Mother's Room," in her Church in Boston. She could abolish that institution with a word, if she wanted to. She is aware of that. I will say a further word about the museum presently.

Further down the column, her memory is unfaithful again:

"I believe in ... but one Mother Mary, and know I am not that one, and never claimed to be."

At a session of the National Christian Science Association, held in the city of New York on the 27th of May, 1890, the secretary was "instructed to send to our Mother greetings and words of affection from her assembled children."[1]

[1] Page 24, Official Report.

Her telegraphic response was read to the Association at next day's meeting:

"All hail! He hath filled the hungry with good things and the sick hath He not sent empty away.—MOTHER MARY."[1]

Which Mother Mary is this one? Are there two? If so, she is both of them; for, when she signed this telegram in this satisfied and unprotesting way, the Mother-title which she was going to so strenuously object to, and put from her with humility, and seize with both hands, and reserve as her sole property, and protect her monopoly of it with a stern By-law, while recognizing with diffidence that it was "not applicable" to her (then and to-day)—*that* Mother-title was not yet born, and would not be offered to her until five years later. The date of the above "Mother Mary" is 1890; the "individual, endearing title of Mother" was given her "in 1895"—according to her own testimony. See her By-law quoted above.

In his opening Address to that Convention of

[1] Page 24, Official Report.

1890, the President recognized this Mary—our Mary—and abolished all previous ones. He said:

"There is but one Moses, one Jesus; and there is but one Mary."[1]

The confusions being now dispersed, we have this clarified result:

There had *been* a Moses at one time, and only one; there had *been* a Jesus at one time, and only one; there *is* a Mary and "only one." She is not a Has Been, she is an Is—the "Author of *Science and Health;* and we cannot ignore her."[2]

1. In 1890, there was but one Mother Mary. The President said so.

2. Mrs. Eddy was that one. She said so, in signing the telegram.

3. Mrs. Eddy was not that one—for she says so, in her Associated Press utterance of January 17th.

4. And has "never claimed to be" that one— unless the signature to the telegram is a claim

---

[1] Page 13, Official Report.   [2] *Ibid.*

Thus it stands proven and established that she is that Mary and isn't, and thought she was and knows she wasn't. That much is clear.

She is also "The Mother," by the election of 1895, and did not want the title, and thinks it is not applicable to her, and will excommunicate any one that tries to take it away from her. So that is clear.

I think that the only really troublesome confusion connected with these particular matters has arisen from the name—Mary. Much vexation, much misunderstanding, could have been avoided if Mrs. Eddy had used some of her other names in place of that one. "Mother Mary" was certain to stir up discussion. It would have been much better if she had signed the telegram "Mother Baker"; then there would have been no Biblical competition, and, of course, that is a thing to avoid. But it is not too late, yet.

I wish to break in here with a parenthesis, and then take up this examination of Mrs. Eddy's Claim[1] of January 17th again.

[1] "Claim." In Christian Science terminology, "Claims" are errors of mortal mind, fictions of the imagination.

The history of her "Mother Mary" telegram
—as told to me by one who ought to be a very
good authority — is curious and interesting.
The telegram ostensibly quotes verse 53 from
the "Magnificat," but really makes some pretty
formidable changes in it. This is St. Luke's
version:

"He hath filled the hungry with good things,
and the *rich* He hath sent empty away."

This is "Mother Mary's" telegraphed version:

"He hath filled the hungry with good things,
and the *sick* hath He *not* sent empty away."[1]

To judge by the Official Report, the bursting
of this bombshell in that massed convention of
trained Christians created no astonishment,
since it caused no remark, and the business of
the convention went tranquilly on, thereafter,
as if nothing had happened.

Did those people detect those changes? We

[1] Page 24, Official Report.

cannot know. I think they must have noticed
them, the wording of St. Luke's verse being as
familiar to all Christians as is the wording of
the Beatitudes; and I think that the reason
the new version provoked no surprise and no
comment was, that the assemblage took it for a
"Key"—a spiritualized explanation of verse
53, newly sent down from heaven through Mrs.
Eddy. For all Scientists study their Bibles
diligently, and they know their Magnificat. I
believe that their confidence in the authenticity
of Mrs. Eddy's inspirations is so limitless and
so firmly established that no change, however
violent, which she might make in a Bible text
could disturb their composure or provoke from
them a protest.

Her improved rendition of verse 53 went into
the convention's report and appeared in a New
York paper the next day. The (at that time)
Scientist whom I mentioned a minute ago, and
who had not been present at the convention,
saw it and marvelled; marvelled and was indignant—indignant with the printer or the
telegrapher, for making so careless and so
dreadful an error. And greatly distressed, too;

for, of course, the newspaper people would fall foul of it, and be sarcastic, and make fun of it, and have a blithe time over it, and be properly thankful for the chance. It shows how innocent he was; it shows that he did not know the limitations of newspaper men in the matter of Biblical knowledge. The new verse 53 raised no insurrection in the press; in fact, it was not even remarked upon; I could have told him the boys would not know there was anything the matter with it. I have been a newspaper man myself, and in those days I had my limitations like the others.

The Scientist hastened to Concord and told Mrs. Eddy what a disastrous mistake had been made, but he found to his bewilderment that she was tranquil about it, and was not proposing to correct it. He was not able to get her to promise to make a correction. He asked her secretary if he had heard aright when the telegram was dictated to him; the secretary said he had, and took the filed copy of it and verified its authenticity by comparing it with the stenographic notes.

Mrs. Eddy did make the correction, two

months later, in her official organ. It attracted
no attention among the Scientists; and, naturally,
none elsewhere, for that periodical's circulation
was practically confined to disciples of the cult.

That is the tale as it was told to me by an
ex-Scientist. Verse 53—renovated and spiritualized—had a narrow escape from a tremendous celebrity. The newspaper men would
have made it as famous as the assassination
of Cæsar, but for their limitations.

To return to the Claim. I find myself greatly
embarrassed by Mrs. Eddy's remark: "I regard
self-deification as blasphemous." If she is
right about that, I have written a half-ream of
manuscript this past week which I must not
print, either in the book which I am writing, or
elsewhere: for it goes into that very matter with
extensive elaboration, citing, in detail, words
and acts of Mrs. Eddy's which seem to me to
prove that she is a faithful and untiring wor-
shipper of herself, and has carried self-deification to a length which has not been before ventured in ages. If ever. There is not room
enough in this chapter for that Survey, but I
can epitomize a portion of it here.

With her own untaught and untrained mind, and without outside help, she has erected upon a firm and lasting foundation the most minutely perfect, and wonderful, and smoothly and exactly working, and best safe-guarded system of government that has yet been devised in the world, as I believe, and as I am sure I could prove if I had room for my documentary evidences here.

It is a despotism (on this democratic soil); a sovereignty more absolute than the Roman Papacy, more absolute than the Russian Czarship; it has not a single power, not a shred of authority, legislative or executive, which is not lodged solely in the sovereign; all its dreams, its functions, its energies, have a single object, a single reason for existing, and only the one—to build to the sky the glory of the sovereign, and keep it bright to the end of time.

Mrs. Eddy is the sovereign; she devised that great place for herself, she occupies that throne.

In 1895, she wrote a little primer, a little body of autocratic laws, called the *Manual of The First Church of Christ, Scientist,* and put those laws in force, in permanence. Her government is all there; all in that deceptively innocent-looking little book, that cunning little devilish book, that slumbering little brown volcano, with hell in its bowels. In that book she has planned out her system, and classified and defined its purposes and powers.

MAIN PARTS OF THE MACHINE

A Supreme Church. At Boston.

Branch Churches. All over the world.

One Pastor for the whole of them: to wit, her book, *Science and Health.* Term of the book's office—*forever.*

In every C. S. pulpit, two " Readers," a man and a woman. *No talkers, no preachers, in any Church*—readers only. *Readers of the Bible and her books*—no others. No commentators allowed to write or print.

A Church Service. She has framed it—for all the C. S. Churches—selected its readings, its prayers, and the hymns to be used, and has appointed the order of procedure. No changes permitted.

A Creed. She wrote it. All C. S. Churches must subscribe to it. No other permitted.

A Treasury. At Boston. She carries the key.

A C. S. Book-Publishing House. For books approved by her. No others permitted.

Journals and Magazines. These are organs of hers, and are controlled by her.

A College. For teaching C. S.

DISTRIBUTION OF THE MACHINE'S POWERS AND DIGNITIES

Supreme Church.
Pastor Emeritus—Mrs. Eddy.
Board of Directors.
Board of Education.
Board of Finance.
College Faculty.
Various Committees.
Treasurer.
Clerk.
First Members (*of the Supreme Church*).
Members of the Supreme Church.
It looks fair, it looks real, but it is **all a fiction.**

Even the little "Pastor Emeritus" is a fiction.
Instead of being merely an honorary and ornamental official, Mrs. Eddy is the only official in
the entire body that has the slightest power.
In her Manual, she has provided a prodigality
of ways and forms whereby she can rid herself
of any functionary in the government whenever she wants to. The officials are all shadows,
save herself; she is the only reality. She allows no one to hold office more than a year—
no one gets a chance to become over-popular
or over-useful, and dangerous. "Excommunication" is the favorite penalty—it is threat-
ened at every turn. It is evidently the pet
dread and terror of the Church's membership.

The member who *thinks*, without getting his
thought from Mrs. Eddy before uttering it, is
banished *permanently*. One or two kinds of sinners can plead their way back into the fold, but
this one, never. To *think*—in the Supreme
Church—is the New Unpardonable Sin.

To nearly every severe and fierce rule, Mrs.
Eddy adds this rivet: "*This By-law shall not
be changed without the consent of the Pastor
Emeritus.*"

Mrs. Eddy is the entire Supreme Church, in her own person, in the matter of powers and authorities.

Although she has provided so many ways of getting rid of unsatisfactory members and officials, she was still afraid she might have left a life-preserver lying around somewhere, therefore she devised a rule to cover that defect. By applying it, she can excommunicate (and *this* is perpetual again) every functionary connected with the Supreme Church, and every one of the twenty-five thousand members of that Church, at an hour's notice—and *do it all by herself without anybody's help.*

By authority of this astonishing By-law, she has only to *say* a person connected with that Church is secretly practising hypnotism or mesmerism; whereupon, immediate excommunication, without a hearing, is his portion! She does not have to order a trial and produce evidence—her *accusation* is all that is necessary.

Where is the Pope? and where the Czar? As the ballad says:

> " Ask of the winds that far away
> With fragments strewed the sea!"

23

The Branch Church's pulpit is occupied by two "Readers." Without them the Branch Church is as dead as if its throat had been cut. To have control, then, of the Readers, is to have control of the Branch Churches. Mrs. Eddy has that control—a control wholly without limit, a control shared with no one.

1. No Reader can be appointed to any Church in the Christian Science world without her *express* approval.

2. She can summarily expel from his or her place any Reader, at home or abroad, by a mere *letter* of dismissal, over her signature, and without furnishing any reason for it, to either the congregation or the Reader.

Thus she has as absolute control over all Branch Churches as she has over the Supreme Church. This power exceeds the Pope's.

In simple truth, *she is the only absolute sovereign in all Christendom.* The authority of the other sovereigns has limits, hers has none. None whatever. And her yoke does not fret, does not offend. Many of the subjects of the other monarchs feel their yoke, and are restive under it; their loyalty is insincere. It is not so with this one's human property; their loyalty is genuine, earnest, sincere, enthusiastic. The sentiment which they feel for her is one which goes out in sheer perfection to no other occupant of a throne; for it is love, pure from doubt, envy, exaction, fault-seeking, a love whose sun has no spot—that form of love, strong, great, uplifting, limitless, whose vast proportions are compassable by no word but one, the prodigious word, *Worship*. And it is not as a human being that her subjects worship her, but as a supernatural one, a divine one, one who has comradeship with God, and speaks by His voice.

Mrs. Eddy has herself created all these personal grandeurs and autocracies—with others which I have not (in this article) mentioned. They place her upon an Alpine solitude and supremacy of power and spectacular show not hitherto attained by any other self-seeking enslaver disguised in the Christian name, and they persuade me that, although she may regard "self-deification as blasphemous," she is as fond of it as I am of pie.

She knows about "Our Mother's Room" in the Supreme Church in Boston—above referred to — for she has been in it. In a recently published *North American Review* article,[1] I quoted a lady as saying Mrs. Eddy's portrait could be seen there in a shrine, lit by always-burning lights, and that C. S. disciples came there and worshipped it. That remark hurt the feelings of more than one Scientist. They said it was not true, and asked me to correct it. I comply with pleasure. Whether the portrait was there four years ago or not, it is not there now, for I have inquired. The only object in the shrine now, and lit by electrics—and worshipped—is an oil-portrait of the horse-hair *chair* Mrs. Eddy used to sit in when she was writing *Science and Health !* It seems to me that adulation has struck bottom, here.

Mrs. Eddy knows about that. She has been there, she has seen it, she has seen the worshippers. She could abolish that sarcasm with a word. She withholds the word. Once more I seem to recognize in her exactly the same appetite for self-deification that I have for pie. We seem to be curiously alike; for the love of self-deification is really only the spiritual form of the material appetite for pie, and nothing could be more strikingly Christian-Scientifically "harmonious."

I note this phrase:

"Christian Science eschews divine rights in human beings."

"Rights" is vague; I do not know what it means there. Mrs. Eddy is not well acquainted with the English language, and she is seldom able to say in it what she is trying to say. She has no ear for the exact word, and does not often get it. "Rights." Does it mean "honors?" "attributes?"

"Eschews." This is another umbrella where there should be a torch; it does not illumine the sentence, it only deepens the shadows. Does she mean "denies?" "refuses?" "forbids?" or something in that line? Does she mean:

"Christian Science denies divine honors to human beings?" Or:

"Christian Science refuses to recognize divine attributes in human beings?" Or:

"Christian Science forbids the worship of human beings?"

The bulk of the succeeding sentence is to me a tunnel, but, when I emerge at this end of it, I seem to come into daylight. Then I seem to understand both sentences—with this result:

"Christian Science recognizes but one God, forbids the worship of human beings, and refuses to recognize the possession of divine attributes by any member of the race."

I am subject to correction, but I think that that is about what Mrs. Eddy was intending to convey. Has her English—which is always difficult to me—beguiled me into misunderstanding the following remark, which she makes (calling herself "we," after an old regal fashion of hers) in her preface to her *Miscellaneous Writings*?[1]

"While we entertain decided views as to the best method for elevating the race physically, morally, and spiritually, and shall express these views as duty demands, we shall claim no especial gift from our divine origin, no supernatural power."

Was she meaning to say:

[1] Page 3.

"Although I am of divine origin and gifted with supernatural power, I shall not draw upon these resources in determining the best method of elevating the race?"

If she had left out the word "our," she might then seem to say:

"I claim no especial or unusual degree of divine origin—"

Which is awkward—most awkward; for one either has *a* divine origin or hasn't; shares in it, degrees of it, are surely impossible. The idea of crossed breeds in cattle is a thing we can entertain, for we are used to it, and it is possible; but the idea of a divine mongrel is unthinkable.

Well, then, what does she mean? I am sure I do not know, for certain. It is the word "our" that makes all the trouble. With the "our" in, she is plainly saying "*my* divine origin." The word "from" seems to be intended to mean "on account of." It has to mean that or nothing, if "our" is allowed to stay. The clause then says:

"I shall claim no especial gift on account of my divine origin."

And I think that the full sentence was intended to mean what I have already suggested:

"Although I am of divine origin, and gifted with supernatural power, I shall not draw upon these resources in determining the best method of elevating the race."

When Mrs. Eddy copyrighted that Preface seven years ago, she had long been used to regarding herself as a divine personage. I quote from Mr. F. W. Peabody's book:[1]

"In the *Christian Science Journal* for April, 1889, when it was her property, and published by her, it was claimed for her, and *with her sanction*, that she was equal with Jesus, and elaborate effort was made to establish the claim."

"Mrs. Eddy has distinctly *authorized* the claim in her behalf, that she herself was the chosen successor to and equal of Jesus."

The following remark in that April number, quoted by Mr. Peabody, indicates that her claim had been previously made, and had excited "horror" among some "good people":

[1] Boston: 15 Court Square.

"Now, a word about the horror many good people have of our making the Author of *Science and Health* 'equal with Jesus.'"

Surely, if it had excited horror in Mrs. Eddy also, she would have published a disclaimer. She owned the paper; she could say what she pleased in its columns. Instead of rebuking her editor, she lets him rebuke those "good people" for objecting to the claim.

These things seem to throw light upon those words, "our [my] divine origin."

It may be that "Christian Science eschews divine rights in human beings," and forbids worship of any but "one God, one Christ"; but, if that is the case, it looks as if Mrs. Eddy is a very unsound Christian Scientist, and needs disciplining. I believe she has a serious malady—"self-deification"; and that it will be well to have one of the experts demonstrate over it.

Meantime, let her go on living—for my sake. Closely examined, painstakingly studied, she is easily the most interesting person on the planet, and, in several ways, as easily the most extraordinary woman that was ever born upon it.

P. S.—Since I wrote the foregoing, Mr. Mc-
Crackan's article appeared (in the March number of the *North American Review*). Before his
article appeared—that is to say, during December, January, and February—I had written
a new book, a character-portrait of Mrs. Eddy,
drawn from her own acts and words, and it was
then—together with the three brief articles previously published in the *North American Review*—ready to be delivered to the printer for
issue in book form. In that book, by accident
and good luck, I have answered the objections
made by Mr. McCrackan to my views, and
therefore do not need to add an answer here.
Also, in it I have corrected certain misstate-
ments of mine which he has noticed, and several others which he has not referred to. There
are one or two important matters of opinion
upon which he and I are not in disagreement;
but there are others upon which we must continue to disagree, I suppose; indeed, I know
we must; for instance, he believes Mrs. Eddy
wrote *Science and Health*, whereas I am quite
sure I can convince a person unhampered by
predilections that she did not.

As concerns one considerable matter I hope to convert him. He believes Mrs. Eddy's word; in his article he cites her as a witness, and takes her testimony at par; but if he will make an excursion through my book when it comes out, and will dispassionately examine her testimonies as there accumulated, I think he will in candor concede that she is by a large percentage the most erratic and contradictory and untrustworthy witness that has occupied the stand since the days of the lamented Ananias.

CONCLUSION

Broadly speaking, the hostiles reject and repudiate all the pretensions of Christian Science Christianity. They affirm that it has added nothing new to Christianity; that it can do nothing that Christianity could not do and was not doing before Christian Science was born.

In that case is there no field for the new Christianity, no opportunity for usefulness, precious usefulness, great and distinguished usefulness? I think there is. I am far from being confident that it can fill it, but I will indicate that unoccupied field—without charge —and if it can conquer it, it will deserve the praise and gratitude of the Christian world, and will get it, I am sure.

The present Christianity makes an excellent private Christian, but its endeavors to make an excellent public one go for nothing, substantially.

This is an honest nation — in private life.

The American Christian is a straight and clean and honest man, and in his private commerce with his fellows can be trusted to stand faithfully by the principles of honor and honesty imposed upon him by his religion. But the moment he comes forward to exercise a public trust he can be confidently counted upon to betray that trust in nine cases out of ten, if "party loyalty" shall require it.

If there are two tickets in the field in his city, one composed of honest men and the other of notorious blatherskites and criminals, he will not hesitate to lay his private Christian honor aside and vote for the blatherskites if his "party honor" shall exact it. His Christianity is of no use to him and has no influence upon him when he is acting in a public capacity. He has sound and sturdy private morals, but he has no public ones. In the last great municipal election in New York, almost a complete one-half of the votes representing 3,500,000 Christians were cast for a ticket that had hardly a man on it whose earned and proper place was outside of a jail. But that vote was present at church next Sunday the same as ever, and as unconscious of its perfidy as if nothing had happened.

Our Congresses consist of Christians. In their private life they are true to every obligation of honor; yet in every session they violate them all, and do it without shame; because honor to party is above honor to themselves. It is an accepted law of public life that in it a man may soil his honor in the interest of party expediency—*must* do it when party expediency requires it. In private life those men would bitterly resent—and justly —any insinuation that it would not be safe to leave unwatched money within their reach; yet you could not wound their feelings by reminding them that every time they vote ten dollars to the pension appropriation nine of it is stolen money and they the marauders. They have filched the money to take care of the party; they believe it was right to do it; they do not see how their private honor is affected; therefore their consciences are clear and at rest. By vote they do wrongful things every day, in the party interest, which they could not be persuaded to do in private life.

In the interest of party expediency they give solemn pledges, they make solemn compacts; in the interest of party expediency they repudiate them without a blush. They would not dream of committing these strange crimes in private life.

Now then, can Christian Science introduce the Congressional Blush? There are Christian Private Morals, but there are no Christian Public Morals, at the polls, or in Congress or anywhere else—except here and there and scattered around like lost comets in the solar system. Can Christian Science persuade the nation and Congress to throw away their public morals and use none but their private ones henceforth in all their activities, both public and private?

I do not think so; but no matter about me: there is the field—a grand one, a splendid one, a sublime one, and absolutely unoccupied. Has Christian Science confidence enough in itself to undertake to enter in and try to possess it?

Make the effort, Christian Science; it is a most noble cause, and it might succeed. It could succeed. Then we should have a new literature, with romances entitled, How To Be an Honest Congressman Though a Christian; How To Be a Creditable Citizen Though a Christian.

THE END

AFTERWORD

Hamlin Hill

Christian Science is undoubtedly the most curious of Mark Twain's full-length works, and quite possibly the one that reveals him most intimately to his audience. Written in several stints over a period of years (like many of his other works), the book offers a variety of tones and moods, suggests the pitfalls of being an author of humor, and reflects a man whose ambivalence to his subject mirrored his own personal anguish.

I

Mark Twain's secretary during most of the final decade of his life, Isabel Lyon, recollected in her old age that her boss nurtured an especially intense dislike for the Frank Warner family of Hartford because "Mrs. Frank Warner was a keen Christian Scientist" and influenced the Clemenses' oldest daughter, Susy; so that when the rest of the family was on the around-the-world tour that produced *Following the Equator*, Susy remained at home, contracted spinal meningitis, but was "so interested in this new religion that in the early stages of her tragic illness she refused to see a doctor, & then it was too late."[1]

Susy may have been the only one whose attraction was perhaps fatal, but all of the distaff side of Clemens' family was variously involved with nonmedical "cures." In this volume, Mark Twain recounts the curing of his mother by a "faith-doctor" (35), and in the footnote on page 36 he refers to the "mind cure" of teenage Olivia Langdon, later his wife, by a "travelling 'quack,'"

Dr. James Rogers Newton. Although Laura Skandera-Trombley has recently disputed Twain's "fictional" romanticizing of Olivia's organic illness, she catalogues the girl's earlier treatments at "Gleason's water cure" in 1860, at a sanatorium in 1863, and with the "Swedish Movement Cure" for two years until 1864.[2] These cures involved various combinations of total rest, kinesthesia, exercise, and gymnastics. And later, in the last years of her life, Olivia was a patient of osteopaths and was diagnosed as having neurasthenia and nervous prostration.

Daughter Clara, who ultimately and ironically became a Christian Scientist, also had recurring ailments of a hysterical nature in the last decade of her father's life, resting in sanatoria and obeying doctors' orders not to see her father. Jean, the youngest child, was diagnosed as epileptic in the 1890s and spent much of the last decade of her life in various cures, spas, and sanatoria. In fact, Mark Twain told his old friend Henry H. Rogers on August 3, 1899, that other methods had been so ineffective with Jean that he was trying a variant of the Swedish Movement Cure, the Kellgren Movement Cure, in Sweden, and would try anything that might help her — "except Christian Science."[3] In short, when Clemens catalogued "the Mind Cure, the Faith Cure, the Prayer Cure, the Mental-Science Cure, and the Christian-Science Cure" (37), he was personally familiar with, and not totally contemptuous of, alternatives to traditional medical practices.

But during the final dozen years of his life, he would have been unable to ignore the notoriety which Christian Science was gaining in the popular press. Between 1899 and 1909, well over a hundred articles appeared in magazines and journals, according to the *Reader's Guide*. Most of them were serious descriptions of or apologies for the religion; but as the following titles suggest, Mark Twain was not the only writer to see comic or satiric possibilities in the faith: "Christian Quackery," "Modern Witchcraft," "The Absurd Paradox of Christian Science."[4] In addition, as Carl Dolmetsch points out, Christian Science's "rapid growth and the publicity given allegedly avoidable deaths among prominent converts like the novelist Harold Frederick in 1898, who refused medical aid, had made the cult a subject of curiosity and controversy among readers in the United States."[5]

Clemens' own ambiguity toward faith healing and his acknowledgment that Christian Science can cure four-fifths of all the pain in the universe (53) put him in the middle of a medical controversy. When the first installment of *Christian Science* appeared in the *North American Review* in 1902, it produced a vehement reaction from physicians. The *Philadelphia Medical Journal* blasted him.

> Mr. Clemens himself comes so near to being a follower of Mrs. Eddy that he has not critical insight enough left to see that her claim to be able to abolish disease is the gist of the whole humbug. He already says that Christian Science can abolish *four-fifths* of the disease that afflicts mankind! Clearly, Mark Twain is already four-fifths Eddyite, and of all the blatherskite he has ever written his latest is a little the most senile.

The journal *American Medicine* agreed.

> When a solemn ignoramus turns philosopher and takes himself seriously we often have the perfection of humor. But when a professional humorist turns into a solemn prophet, we have as a result neither sense nor humor. ... It is a pity that the gay sense of the ludicrous is lost in old age, and sane logic gives place to senile fantasy. In 25 years Eddyism will be as powerless as the Perkins' tractors, and Twain's successor with the cap and bells will make merry over the vaticinations and sociology of Mark himself.[6]

Two medical diagnoses of "senility" should have been enough to stir Mark Twain to response, but he appears not to have known of either review.

He did, however, enter the fray when he received correspondence from W. D. McCrackan, a member of the Christian Science Publication Committee for the state of New York, who submitted a list of Mark Twain's errors in the *North American Review* articles; the humorist responded and even contemplated allowing McCrackan to print his rebuttal along with Twain's own material in a collection scheduled for publication in 1903 but subsequently canceled by Harper and Brothers. He also corresponded with Frederick W. Peabody, a critic of Christian Science, to whom he wrote a half-dozen letters in 1902 and 1903, explaining the target of his ridicule.

Have I given you the impression that I was combating Xn Science? . . . I haven't a thing in the world against it. Making fun of that shameless old swindler, Mother Eddy, is the only thing that I take any interest in. At bottom I suppose I take a private delight in seeing the human race making an ass of itself again — which it has always done whenever it had a chance.[7]

Other reviewers of the articles, on both sides of the controversy, noted ambiguity and inconsistency in both the matter and the manner of the material — its tone, its argument, its coherence. *Harper's Weekly* could not decide "whether Mark Twain approves Christian Science or not" (December 1902); and when the book finally appeared in 1907, the reviewer for the *Spectator* thought readers would be "bewildered by the confused method" of the work (April 6, 1907), while the *Nation* decided that it was neither "a serious nor a humorous contribution to the discussion" (February 14, 1907).

The controversy kept Mark Twain's adrenaline pumping, which he needed to help him combat boredom in his old age, and kept him in the spotlight of debate, which he craved incessantly. He appeared unconcerned with the criticism of his book, although much of it was directed at the haphazard manner of its composition and ultimate construction.

II

Although Mark Twain announced in his 1907 preface to *Christian Science* that book 1 "consists of matter written about four years ago," he began work on the first chapters in 1898 or 1899 in Vienna, and published the first four chapters of the present volume in *Cosmopolitan* magazine in October 1899, under the title "Christian Science and the Book of Mrs. Eddy." To these first four chapters, he added chapters 5 through 8 of book 1 and published them in the English and German editions (Chatto and Windus, Tauchnitz), but not the American edition, of *The Man That Corrupted Hadleyburg* (1900).

In the summer of 1902, Twain returned to the subject of Christian Science, writing chapter 9 of book 1, the fifteen chapters of book 2, six appendixes, "Mrs. Eddy in Error," and the conclusion. After flirting with *Cosmopolitan* and *Harper's Weekly*, he began publishing segments of his manuscript in the *North American Review* in December 1902: in that issue and the one for January 1903, revised versions of chapters 5 to 8 of book 1 appeared; in February, most of chapter 9 of book 1 was published; and the April issue contained "Mrs. Eddy in Error" (331–57 of the present text). The March issue contained a rebuttal of Mark Twain's views by McCrackan, "Mrs. Eddy's Relation to Christian Science."

In early 1903, Clemens' publisher, Frederick A. Duneka of Harper and Brothers, encouraged the humorist to finish his *Christian Science* manuscript so that it could appear that spring as a book, and he repeated his request on February 11. Mark Twain did finish, and *Christian Science* was set in type, proofread, and advertised for sale in the March 21 issue of *Publishers Weekly*. Then, inexplicably, Harper's announced in April that "neither Harper & Brothers nor the *North American Review* will publish in book form Mark Twain's papers on 'Christian Science.'"[8]

Mark Twain reacted with atypical resignation; in an explanation to a potential purchaser, he mused, "The situation is not barren of humor; I had been doing my very best to show in print that the Christian Scientist cult was become a power in the land — well, here was proof: it had scared the biggest publisher in the Union!"[9] Both Albert Brandt and the American Publishing Company offered to undertake the publication, but the volume languished at Harper's until Duneka's interest was rekindled in 1905, apparently because of increasing public hostility to Christian Science. Nevertheless, Twain asked his friend and financial adviser Henry Rogers to retrieve his manuscript on two occasions in 1906 (May 18 and June 13).

Christian Science was published, finally, in February 1907. In spite of his feigned indifference to the success of the book, Twain was obsessed with Christian Science and Mary Baker Eddy. In addition to the present text, additional fragments exist which he discarded from the manuscript. He deleted a "Section IV" from "Christian Science and the Book of Mrs. Eddy"; he proposed and then rejected a piece called "Later Still," a futuristic fantasy allegedly written in the year 2092, which would have been chapter 10 of book 1; he composed an anticipatory response to McCrackan's March 1903 rejoin-

der, which he remembered to include as a postscript to his own February installment; and he penned other fragments for inclusion in his manuscript
somewhere. He even scrawled a few of his typically "primitive" illustrations,
portraits of "Mother" Eddy, which he judiciously refrained from including in
the volume.

More important was a long manuscript fragment Mark Twain composed in
1901 and 1902, although it was not published until 1972: *The Secret History of
Eddypus, the World-Empire* — an expansion of "Later Still," which he published in his February 1903 contribution to the *North American Review* but
deleted from the contents of his book. Elaborately contrived, this version of
what John S. Tuckey has labeled "the nightmare of history" purports to be a
reconstruction of history from the vantage point of the year 2092, with as gar-
bled a version of facts as Huck's description of British history to Jim in chapter 23 of *Adventures of Huckleberry Finn*. As William Macnaughton observes,
"The results of this alternatively speculative, satirical, and playful enterprise
are predictable; nuggets and junk bump together, and the work must be
dipped into rather than read continuously for any length of time."[10]

As an example, in the midst of historical parody to the point of surrealism,
with "his Grace Mark Twain, Bishop of New Jersey" as the prime source,
there is a major element of zany and illogical humor.

> Henry IV was stabbed to death by Coligni on the altar-steps of Canterbury
> Cathedral; Coligni was shot by Charles IX from a window of the Louvre;
> Charles was guillotined by Louis XVI; Louis was assassinated by the Duke
> de Guise; the Duke was beheaded by Marat; Marat was butchered in the
> bath-tub the first time he was ever there, by Charlotte Corday, who was his
> own mother, but was deceived by his resemblance to Mirabeau.

But the frivolity lies on the surface of an apocalyptic vision of history in the
next millennium.

Boston has become known as Eddyflats; the "World-Empire of Holy
Eddypus covers and governs all the globe except the spacious region which
has for countless ages borne the name of China; and which is the only country where an enlightened civilization now exists." The word "religion" is now

"Eddygush." All books and museums have been destroyed. As "Later Still" describes it, the result is "the exalting of the Founder of Divine Science to Second Place in the Holy Family, the extinction of the world's civilizations, and the closing down of the Black Night through whose sombre and melancholy shadows the human race has now been groping hopeless and forlorn these eight hundred years."

Clearly, something about both Christian Science and Mary Baker Eddy obsessed Mark Twain. Although he claimed that he felt no animosity toward the religion, but only its founder, the extent of his writings and vehemence of his rancor suggest that both the premises of the theology and the personality of its founder struck raw nerves too close for calm reaction.

III

Mrs. Eddy, as Macnaughton notes, produced conflicting responses from Mark Twain: "Typically, when speaking of Mrs. Eddy the narrator fluctuates between supercilious contempt on the one hand and awestruck wonder and fear on the other."[11] But even if she was a "shameless old swindler," Mrs. Eddy had traits in common with two women Mark Twain idolized.

As Peter Stoneley astutely recognizes, Joan of Arc "conforms to the same model as Mary Baker Eddy. Without learning or special training of any kind, simply by a divine power of inspiration, Joan was capable of immense tasks, even of the impossible; as Twain tells us, with a metaphor that corresponds with Eddy's feats of healing," Joan "'laid her hand upon this nation, this corpse, and it rose and followed her.'" Stoneley takes the parallel further, noting that Mrs. Eddy was like Joan in "carrying on undaunted in the knowledge that she is right, enacting her own purity of intention in contrast to the politics by which she is surrounded."[12] However susceptible to ridicule Mrs. Eddy's surreal prose might be, her charismatic personality drew forth an "army" of supporters the equivalent of Joan's.

In addition, in 1866 Eddy had slipped and fallen on an icy sidewalk and, after unsuccessful medical treatment, was miraculously and "divinely" cured by a reading of Scripture. The parallel with Olivia Clemens is obvious;

Mark Twain even refers to his wife's "miraculous" cure under similar circumstances in *Christian Science* (36). As he elaborates on the event in his autobiographical dictation of February 13, 1906, the two cases have remarkable elements of similarity. Olivia

> became an invalid at sixteen, through a partial paralysis caused by falling on the ice, and she was never strong again while her life lasted. After that fall she was not able to leave her bed during two years, nor was she able to lie in any position except on her back. All the great physicians were brought to Elmira, one after another, during that time, but there was no helpful result. In those days both worlds [Europe and the United States] were well acquainted with the name of Doctor Newton, a man who was regarded in both worlds as a quack. He moved through the land in state; in magnificence, like a portent; like a circus. Notice of his coming was spread upon the dead walls in vast colored posters, along with his formidable portrait, several weeks beforehand. . . .
>
> Newton came. . . . Newton opened the windows — long darkened — and delivered a short fervent prayer; then he put an arm behind her shoulders and said, "Now we will sit up, my child."
>
> The family were alarmed and tried to stop him, but he was not disturbed and raised her up. She sat several minutes, without nausea or discomfort. Then Newton said, "Now we will walk a few steps, my child." He took her out of bed and supported her while she walked several steps. . . .
>
> His charge was fifteen hundred dollars, and it was easily worth a hundred thousand. For from the day that she was eighteen until she was fifty-six she was always able to walk a couple of hundred yards without stopping to rest.[13]

The comparison ends, however, with Eddy's robust business acumen and Olivia's recurrent ill health and reclusive nature. But both Eddy's doctor and many of Olivia's physicians considered their patients' diseases a result of "hysteria."

Finally, Mark Twain's descriptions of Mrs. Eddy, as John Tuckey suggested in 1972, make it difficult "to escape the impression that Clemens' aversion to [her] had behind it something of the feeling one has toward a successful rival."[14] Possibly the most litigious author in the history of American literature, Mark Twain nevertheless criticized Mrs. Eddy for suing for copyright infringement (139, 221–23). Contemptuous of her thirst for power and authority, Mark Twain himself delighted in his late nickname, "The King." Almost obsessed with money himself, he blamed her for her concern for the Dollar (for example, 201–3). Dependent himself upon the royalties from his books, he ridiculed her for jealously protecting her own writings.

Most poignantly, Mark Twain quotes a man healed by Christian Science: "Nothing is real but Mind; all is Mind"(57). At least part of the time during his old age, Mark Twain's solipsistic universe was identical. Consider Philip Traum's revelation to Theodor in the conclusion of *The Mysterious Stranger*.

> "*Nothing* exists; all is a dream. . . . *Nothing exists save empty space—and you!*" . . .
>
> "And you are not you — you have no body, no blood, no bones, you are but a *thought*. . . .
>
> ". . . In a little while you will be alone in shoreless space, to wander its limitless solitudes without friend or comrade forever — for you will remain a *Thought*, the only existent Thought, and by your nature inextinguishable, indestructible. . . ."

Mrs. Eddy's Mind might turn to nightmare in Mark Twain's hands, but the parallels are compelling. And that may explain the confusing and finally unsuccessful assault which the humorist leveled against the healer.

IV

Everyone agrees that the first few, fictional chapters of *Christian Science* constitute admirable burlesque. Purportedly injured in a fall over a cliff, Mark Twain finds a Christian Science practitioner his only medical help. When "Mrs. Fuller" arrives, she explains that Mark Twain cannot feel pain because "matter has no existence; nothing exists but mind" (9). As she instructs and reads to him, he provides charming skeptical banter about the tenets of

Christian Science. When she explains the "fundamental propositions of Christian Science" (12) — 1. God is All in all. 2. God is good. Good is Mind. 3. God, Spirit, being all, nothing is matter. 4. Life, God, omnipotent Good, deny death, evil, sin, disease" — Mark Twain asks her to repeat this backward and she agrees: "Disease sin evil death deny Good omnipotent God life matter is nothing all being Spirit God mind is Good good is God all in All is God." Mark Twain not only finds the passage more intelligible the second way, but he adapts it himself whenever he confronts a Christian Science tall tale: "All-God, God-good, good-God, Truth, Bones, Liver, one of a series, alone and without equal" (22); "All-Good, Good-Good, Good-Gracious, Liver, Bones, Truth, All down but Nine, Set them up on the Other Alley" (65); "All-Good-Good-Good, Life, Soul, Liver, Bones, one of a series, ante and pass the buck!" (57). He pays Mrs. Fuller's bill with an imaginary check but points out that "now she is suing me for substantial dollars" (38).

Twain's analysis of the value of various mind cures, in the next chapters of book 1, was understandably generous and positive because of his family's history of efficacious results from them. But Mark Twain became tiresome and obsessive when he returned to the subject of Christian Science in book 2. Mrs. Eddy's power, her organizational skills, her complex rules and regulations for the operation of Christian Science — all of these were fit subject for satire. But the humor disappeared in shrill repetition, confused tenors, and dreary tabulation.

Back in 1879, William Dean Howells had asked Mark Twain, who was in Europe attempting to write the book that became *A Tramp Abroad*, if he was reproducing the pungent satire which had marked *The Innocents Abroad*. Twain replied, "I wish I could give those sharp satires on European life which you mention, but of course a man can't write successful satire except he be in a calm judicial good-humor."[15] The dilemma of *Christian Science* is that calm judicial good humor was lost in acerbic bitterness.

NOTES

1. Isabel Lyon, "The Gilded Age. 1873," holograph notes in the Henry W. and Albert A. Berg Collection, New York Public Library, Astor, Lenox, and Tilden Foundations; published by permission.

2. Laura Skandera-Trombley, "Mark Twain's Fictionalizing of Dr. Newton's Miraculous Cure," *American Literary Realism* 26: 82–92 (Winter 1994).

3. *Mark Twain's Correspondence with Henry Huttleston Rogers, 1893–1909,* ed. Lewis Leary (Berkeley: University of California Press, 1969), 403.

4. J. H. Miller, *Blackwood's* 165:658–68 (April 1899); *Independent* 67: 888–90 (October 15, 1909); and J. M. Buckley, *North American Review* 173: 22–34 (July 1901).

5. Carl Dolmetsch, *"Our Famous Guest": Mark Twain in Vienna* (Athens: University of Georgia Press, 1992), 234–35.

6. I am grateful to Stanley S. Blair, James Madison University, for these two medical reviews: *Philadelphia Medical Journal* 11:5 (January 3, 1903), and "Mark Twain on Eddyism," *American Medicine* 5:43 (1903).

7. *What Is Man? and Other Philosophical Writings*, ed. Paul Baender (Berkeley: University of California Press, 1973), 25.

8. *What Is Man?*, 21–28, contains a detailed history of the various publications of Twain's Christian Science materials.

9. Quoted in Hamlin Hill, *Mark Twain: God's Fool* (New York: Harper and Row, 1973), 54.

10. William R. Macnaughton, *Mark Twain's Last Years as a Writer* (Columbia: University of Missouri Press, 1979), 158.

11. Macnaughton, 192.

12. Peter Stoneley, *Mark Twain and the Feminine Aesthetic* (Cambridge: Cambridge University Press, 1992), 92, 121–22.

13. *Mark Twain's Autobiography*, ed. Albert Bigelow Paine (New York: Harper and Brothers, 1924), 2:103–05.

14. *Mark Twain's Fables of Man*, ed. John S. Tuckey (Berkeley: University of California Press, 1972), 22.

15. *Mark Twain-Howells Letters*, ed. Henry Nash Smith and William M. Gibson (Cambridge: Harvard University Press, 1960), 1:248.

FOR FURTHER READING

Hamlin Hill

A critical text of *Christian Science*, together with fragments deleted from the published volume, appeared in *What Is Man? and Other Philosophical Writings*, ed. Paul Baender (Berkeley: University of California Press, 1973). *The Secret History of Eddypus, the World-Empire* was published in *Mark Twain's Fables of Man*, ed. John S. Tuckey (Berkeley: University of California Press, 1972). A popular edition of *Christian Science* with a perceptive introduction by Victor Doyno appeared in 1986 (Buffalo: Prometheus Books).

Carl Dolmetsch provides valuable information on the first stage of the composition of the book in *"Our Famous Guest": Mark Twain in Vienna* (Athens: University of Georgia Press, 1992); and the last decade of Mark Twain's life, including discussions of *Christian Science*, is the subject of Hamlin Hill, *Mark Twain: God's Fool* (New York: Harper and Row, 1973). In *Mark Twain in the Company of Women* (Philadelphia: University of Pennsylvania Press, 1994), Laura E. Skandera-Trombley assesses both the physical and mental health of the distaff side of the Clemens family.

William R. Macnaughton's *Mark Twain's Last Years as a Writer* (Columbia: University of Missouri Press, 1979) contains a critique of *Christian Science*, and Peter Stoneley, *Mark Twain and the Feminine Aesthetic* (Cambridge University Press, 1992), devotes an entire chapter to a complex examination of Mark Twain and Mary Baker Eddy.

A NOTE ON THE TEXT

Robert H. Hirst

This text of *Christian Science, with Notes Containing Corrections to Date* is a photographic facsimile of a copy of the first American edition dated 1907 on the title page. The first edition was published in February 1907; two copies were deposited with the Copyright Office on February 7. Copies printed from the first edition plates, but with no date on the title page, were evidently manufactured as late as 1912. The copy reproduced here has all the points Jacob Blanck mentioned for his "copies first printed" except that the list of illustrations is in six, rather than eight lines (*BAL* 3497). The original volume is in the collection of the Mark Twain House in Hartford, Connecticut (810/C625ch/1907/c. 1).

THE MARK TWAIN HOUSE

The Mark Twain House is a museum and research center dedicated to the study of Mark Twain, his works, and his times. The museum is located in the nineteen-room mansion in Hartford, Connecticut, built for and lived in by Samuel L. Clemens, his wife, and their three children, from 1874 to 1891. The Picturesque Gothic-style residence, with interior design by the firm of Louis Comfort Tiffany and Associated Artists, is one of the premier examples of domestic Victorian architecture in America. Clemens wrote *Adventures of Huckleberry Finn*, *The Adventures of Tom Sawyer*, *A Connecticut Yankee in King Arthur's Court*, *The Prince and the Pauper*, and *Life on the Mississippi* while living in Hartford.

The Mark Twain House is open year-round. In addition to tours of the house, the educational programs of the Mark Twain House include symposia, lectures, and teacher training seminars that focus on the contemporary relevance of Twain's legacy. Past programs have featured discussions of literary censorship with playwright Arthur Miller and writer William Styron; of the power of language with journalist Clarence Page, comedian Dick Gregory, and writer Gloria Naylor; and of the challenges of teaching *Adventures of Huckleberry Finn* amidst charges of racism.

Shelley Fisher Fishkin, professor of American Studies and English at the University of Texas at Austin, is the author of the award-winning books *Was Huck Black? Mark Twain and African-American Voices* (1993) and *From Fact to Fiction: Journalism and Imaginative Writing in America* (1985). Her most recent book is *Lighting Out for the Territory: Reflections on Mark Twain and American Culture* (1996). She holds a Ph.D. in American Studies from Yale University, has lectured on Mark Twain in Belgium, England, France, Israel, Italy, Mexico, the Netherlands, and Turkey, as well as throughout the United States, and is president-elect of the Mark Twain Circle of America.

Hamlin Hill is Distinguished Professor of English and the Ralph R. Thomas Professor of Liberal Arts at Texas A & M University. The recipient of three Fulbright Lectureships and a John Simon Guggenheim Fellowship, he is the author of *Mark Twain and Elisha Bliss* (1964), *Mark Twain: God's Fool* (1973), and (with Walter Blair) *America's Humor From Poor Richard to Doonesbury* (1978). He also edited *Mark Twain's Letters to His Publishers* (1967) and *Essays on American Humor* (1993), and for ten years he wrote the "Mark Twain" chapter for *American Literary Scholarship: An Annual.*

Robert H. Hirst is the General Editor of the Mark Twain Project at The Bancroft Library, University of California in Berkeley. Apart from that, he has no other known eccentricities.

Garry Wills is the author of *Roman Culture* (1966), *Nixon Agonistes* (1970), *Inventing America* (1978), *Explaining America* (1980), *The Kennedy Imprisonment* (1982), *Cincinnatus* (1984), *Reagan's America* (1987), *Under God* (1990), *Lincoln at Gettysburg* (1992), *Certain Trumpets* (1994), and *Witches and Jesuits* (1995). He is adjunct professor of history at Northwestern University in Evanston, Illinois.

ACKNOWLEDGMENTS

There are a number of people without whom The Oxford Mark Twain would not have happened. I am indebted to Laura Brown, senior vice president and trade publisher, Oxford University Press, for suggesting that I edit an "Oxford Mark Twain," and for being so enthusiastic when I proposed that it take the present form. Her guidance and vision have informed the entire undertaking.

Crucial as well, from the earliest to the final stages, was the help of John Boyer, executive director of the Mark Twain House, who recognized the importance of the project and gave it his wholehearted support.

My father, Milton Fisher, believed in this project from the start and helped nurture it every step of the way, as did my stepmother, Carol Plaine Fisher. Their encouragement and support made it all possible. The memory of my mother, Renée B. Fisher, sustained me throughout.

I am enormously grateful to all the contributors to The Oxford Mark Twain for the effort they put into their essays, and for having been such fine, collegial collaborators. Each came through, just as I'd hoped, with fresh insights and lively prose. It was a privilege and a pleasure to work with them, and I value the friendships that we forged in the process.

In addition to writing his fine afterword, Louis J. Budd provided invaluable advice and support, even going so far as to read each of the essays for accuracy. All of us involved in this project are greatly in his debt. Both his knowledge of Mark Twain's work and his generosity as a colleague are legendary and unsurpassed.

Elizabeth Maguire's commitment to The Oxford Mark Twain during her time as senior editor at Oxford was exemplary. When the project proved to be more ambitious and complicated than any of us had expected, Liz helped make it not only manageable, but fun. Assistant editor Elda Rotor's wonderful help in coordinating all aspects of The Oxford Mark Twain, along with literature editor T. Susan Chang's enthusiastic involvement with the project in its final stages, helped bring it all to fruition.

I am extremely grateful to Joy Johannessen for her astute and sensitive copyediting, and for having been such a pleasure to work with. And I appreciate the conscientiousness and good humor with which Kathy Kuhtz Campbell heroically supervised all aspects of the set's production. Oxford president Edward Barry, vice president and editorial director Helen McInnis, marketing director Amy Roberts, publicity director Susan Rotermund, art director David Tran, trade editorial, design and production manager Adam Bohannon, trade advertising and promotion manager Woody Gilmartin, director of manufacturing Benjamin Lee, and the entire staff at Oxford were as supportive a team as any editor could desire.

The staff of the Mark Twain House provided superb assistance as well. I would like to thank Marianne Curling, curator, Debra Petke, education director, Beverly Zell, curator of photography, Britt Gustafson, assistant director of education, Beth Ann McPherson, assistant curator, and Pam Collins, administrative assistant, for all their generous help, and for allowing us to reproduce books and photographs from the Mark Twain House collection. One could not ask for more congenial or helpful partners in publishing.

G. Thomas Tanselle, vice president of the John Simon Guggenheim Memorial Foundation, and an expert on the history of the book, offered essential advice about how to create as responsible a facsimile edition as possible. I appreciate his very knowledgeable counsel.

I am deeply indebted to Robert H. Hirst, general editor of the Mark Twain Project at The Bancroft Library in Berkeley, for bringing his outstanding knowledge of Twain editions to bear on the selection of the books photographed for the facsimiles, for giving generous assistance all along the way, and for providing his meticulous notes on the text. The set is the richer for his advice. I would also like to express my gratitude to the Mark Twain Project, not only for making texts and photographs from their collection available to us, but also for nurturing Mark Twain studies with a steady infusion of matchless, important publications.

I would like to thank Jeffrey Kaimowitz, curator of the Watkinson Library at Trinity College, Hartford (where the Mark Twain House collection is kept), along with his colleagues Peter Knapp and Alesandra M. Schmidt, for having been instrumental in Robert Hirst's search for first editions that could be safely reproduced. Victor Fischer, Harriet Elinor Smith, and especially Kenneth M. Sanderson, associate editors with the Mark Twain Project, reviewed the note on the text in each volume with cheerful vigilance. Thanks are also due to Mark Twain Project associate editor Michael Frank and administrative assistant Brenda J. Bailey for their help at various stages.

I am grateful to Helen K. Copley for granting permission to publish photographs in the Mark Twain Collection of the James S. Copley Library in La Jolla, California, and to Carol Beales and Ron Vanderhye of the Copley Library for making my research trip to their institution so productive and enjoyable.

Several contributors — David Bradley, Louis J. Budd, Beverly R. David, Robert Hirst, Fred Kaplan, James S. Leonard, Toni Morrison, Lillian S. Robinson, Jeffrey Rubin-Dorsky, Ray Sapirstein, and David L. Smith — were particularly helpful in the early stages of the project, brainstorming about the cast of writers and scholars who could make it work. Others who participated in that process were John Boyer, James Cox, Robert Crunden, Joel Dinerstein, William Goetzmann, Calvin and Maria Johnson, Jim Magnuson, Arnold Rampersad, Siva Vaidhyanathan, Steve and Louise Weinberg, and Richard Yarborough.

Kevin Bochynski, famous among Twain scholars as an "angel" who is gifted at finding methods of making their research run more smoothly, was helpful in more ways than I can count. He did an outstanding job in his official capacity as production consultant to The Oxford Mark Twain, supervising the photography of the facsimiles. I am also grateful to him for having put me in touch via e-mail with Kent Rasmussen, author of the magisterial *Mark Twain A to Z*, who was tremendously helpful as the project proceeded, sharing insights on obscure illustrators and other points, and generously being "on call" for all sorts of unforeseen contingencies.

I am indebted to Siva Vaidhyanathan of the American Studies Program of the University of Texas at Austin for having been such a superb research assistant. It would be hard to imagine The Oxford Mark Twain without the benefit of his insights and energy. A fine scholar and writer in his own right, he was crucial to making this project happen.

Georgia Barnhill, the Andrew W. Mellon Curator of Graphic Arts at the American Antiquarian Society in Worcester, Massachusetts, Tom Staley, director of the Harry Ransom Humanities Research Center at the University of Texas at Austin, and Joan Grant, director of collection services at the Elmer Holmes Bobst Library of New York University, granted us access to their collections and assisted us in the reproduction of several volumes of The Oxford Mark Twain. I would also like to thank Kenneth Craven, Sally Leach, and Richard Oram of the Harry Ransom Humanities Research Center for their help in making HRC materials available, and Jay and John Crowley, of Jay's Publishers Services in Rockland, Massachusetts, for their efforts to photograph the books carefully and attentively.

I would like to express my gratitude for the grant I was awarded by the University Research Institute of the University of Texas at Austin to defray some of the costs of researching The Oxford Mark Twain. I am also grateful to American Studies director Robert Abzug and the University of Texas for the computer that facilitated my work on this project (and to UT systems analyst Steve Alemán, who tried his best to repair the damage when it crashed). Thanks also to American Studies administrative assistant Janice Bradley and graduate coordinator Melanie Livingston for their always generous and thoughtful help.

The Oxford Mark Twain would not have happened without the unstinting, wholehearted support of my husband, Jim Fishkin, who went way beyond the proverbial call of duty more times than I'm sure he cares to remember as he shared me unselfishly with that other man in my life, Mark Twain. I am also grateful to my family — to my sons Joey and Bobby, who cheered me on all along the way, as did Fannie Fishkin, David Fishkin, Gennie Gordon, Mildred Hope Witkin, and Leonard, Gillis, and Moss

Plaine — and to honorary family member Margaret Osborne, who did the same.

My greatest debt is to the man who set all this in motion. Only a figure as rich and complicated as Mark Twain could have sustained such energy and interest on the part of so many people for so long. Never boring, never dull, Mark Twain repays our attention again and again and again. It is a privilege to be able to honor his memory with The Oxford Mark Twain.

Shelley Fisher Fishkin
Austin, Texas
April 1996